THE MESSIAH IN THE
OLD AND NEW TESTAMENTS

McMaster New Testament Studies

The McMaster New Testament Studies series, edited by Stanley E. Porter, is designed to address particular themes in the New Testament that are of concern to Christians today. Written in a style easily accessible to ministers, students, and laypeople by contributors who are proven experts in their fields of study, the volumes in this series reflect the best of current biblical scholarship while also speaking directly to the pastoral needs of people in the church today.

The Messiah in the
Old and New Testaments

Edited by

Stanley E. Porter

WILLIAM B. EERDMANS PUBLISHING COMPANY
GRAND RAPIDS, MICHIGAN / CAMBRIDGE, U.K.

Wm. B. Eerdmans Publishing Co.
2140 Oak Industrial Drive N.E., Grand Rapids, Michigan 49505 /
P.O. Box 163, Cambridge CB3 9PU U.K.

Printed in the United States of America

12 11 10 09 08 07   7 6 5 4 3 2

Library of Congress Cataloging-in-Publication Data

The Messiah in the Old and New Testaments /
edited by Stanley E. Porter.
p.   cm. — (McMaster New Testament studies)
Includes indexes.
ISBN: 978-0-8028-0766-3 (pbk.: alk. paper)
1. Messiah — Biblical teaching — Congresses. 2. Bible —
Criticism, interpretation, etc. — Congresses. 3. Jesus Christ —
Messiahship — Congresses. 4. Christianity — Origin — Congresses.
I. Porter, Stanley E., 1956-

BS680.M4M48   2007

232'.1 — dc22

2006034679

www.eerdmans.com

Contents

v

Preface

This collection of papers brings together the thoughts, responses, and revised thoughts of the participants in the 2004 H. H. Bingham Colloquium in New Testament at McMaster Divinity College in Hamilton, Ontario, Canada. The Colloquium, the tenth in a continuing series, was entitled "The Messiah in the Old and New Testaments." This was the most successful colloquium to date, in that we had an excellent set of contributors and a full to overflowing crowd of people who came to hear and interact with the participants. To encourage such interaction, we continued the procedure begun the year before in having a planned respondent built into the program. I believe I speak for both participants and attendees in saying that the responses (there were two sets of responses during the actual conference) added greatly to the quality of the conference itself.

The Bingham Colloquium at McMaster Divinity College provides an opportunity for selected scholars to present their perspectives on a contemporary New Testament theme of relevance to the larger community of both students and laity alike. The 2004 Colloquium expanded that brief in that it included four papers that addressed the Old Testament and writings outside of the New Testament, besides five papers directly on the New Testament itself. In planning the Colloquium, it became obvious that we could not discuss the Messiah in the New Testament without knowing something about what was thought about the Messiah in theological writings that preceded the New Testament. The concern of this volume, like that of its predecessors, is to provide understanding of a topic of relevance for those interested in interpreting the New Testament in today's context.

It was clear that before attempting to understand the notion of Messiah in the New Testament — to say nothing of understanding it as relevant for today's Christian — we had to set the proper foundation. I believe that the contributors who have addressed the Old Testament and other writings have done an excellent job of bringing the major issues to our attention. As a result, I hope that this volume opens up insights into the notion of Messiah that would not otherwise have been possible if the scope of the volume had been more constricted.

The Bingham Colloquium is named after Dr. Herbert Henry Bingham, who was a noted Baptist leader in Ontario. However, his leadership abilities were recognized by Baptists across Canada and around the world. His qualities included his genuine friendship, dedicated leadership, unswerving Christian faith, tireless devotion to duty, insightful service as a preacher and pastor, and visionary direction for congregation and denomination alike. These qualities endeared him both to his own church members and to believers in other denominations. The Colloquium was endowed by his daughter as an act of appreciation for her father. It is with regret, however, that I note that Mrs. Kennedy has now passed on to be with her Lord. I know that she took a great interest in the Bingham Colloquia that she had established in honor of her father, and we wish to continue to remember his work through the conducting of future Colloquia. Future conferences have already been planned and are under way.

I am also very pleased again to be able to thank William B. Eerdmans Publishing of Grand Rapids, Michigan, for undertaking the publication of the McMaster New Testament Studies series, of which this volume is the ninth to appear. Previous colloquia published in this series include *Patterns of Discipleship in the New Testament* (1996), *The Road from Damascus: The Impact of Paul's Conversion on His Life, Thought, and Ministry* (1997), *Life in the Face of Death: The Resurrection Message of the New Testament* (1998), *The Challenge of Jesus' Parables* (2000), *Into God's Presence: Prayer in the New Testament* (2001), *Reading the Gospels Today* (2004), *Contours of Christology in the New Testament* (2005), and *Hearing the Old Testament in the New Testament* (2006). I especially wish to thank Bill Eerdmans, Sam Eerdmans, Michael Thomson, and John Simpson, all of whom have been encouraging of the work that we are doing.

Lastly, I would like to thank the individual contributors for their efforts to deal with their particular area within the larger context of the concept of Messiah. What started as oral presentations have now, with the comments of our respondent firmly in mind, been transformed into these written presentations designed to appeal to a wide variety of readers. The Colloquium, as noted above, was a numerical success certainly, but also, I believe, a successful venue for discussion of a topic of present and continuing importance for scholars, students, and laity alike. The Colloquium would not have been the success that it was were it not for the contribution of the Bingham Trust and the contributors, but also those at McMaster Divinity College who helped to coordinate the day, including Patricia Webb and her conference team, headed by Jenn Bowler. We all hope that this volume will serve as a useful guide to this important topic.

Stanley E. Porter
McMaster Divinity College
Hamilton, Ontario, Canada

Abbreviations

AB	Anchor Bible
ABRL	Anchor Bible Reference Library
AfO	*Archiv für Orientforschung*
AGJU	Arbeiten zur Geschichte des antiken Judentums und des Urchristentums
ANTC	Abingdon New Testament Commentaries
ATD	Das Alte Testament Deutsch
BDB	F. Brown, S. R. Driver, and C. A. Briggs, *Hebrew and English Lexicon of the Old Testament*
BEATAJ	Beiträge zur Erforschung des Alten Testaments und des antiken Judentums
BECNT	Baker Exegetical Commentary on the New Testament
Bib	*Biblica*
BTB	*Biblical Theology Bulletin*
BZAW	Beihefte zur *Zeitschrift für die alttestamentliche Wissenschaft*
BZNW	Beihefte zur *Zeitschrift für die neutestamentliche Wissenschaft*
CBC	Cambridge Bible Commentary
CBQ	*Catholic Biblical Quarterly*
CBR	*Currents in Biblical Research*
ConBOT	Coniectanea biblica, Old Testament
CR:BS	*Currents in Research: Biblical Studies*
DJD	Discoveries in the Judaean Desert
ExpTim	*Expository Times*
FAT	Forschungen zum Alten Testament
HAR	*Hebrew Annual Review*
HBT	*Horizons in Biblical Theology*

Abbreviations

HTR	*Harvard Theological Review*
ICC	International Critical Commentary
ITC	International Theological Commentary
JBL	*Journal of Biblical Literature*
JBQ	*Jewish Biblical Quarterly*
JETS	*Journal of the Evangelical Theological Society*
JHS	*Journal of Hellenic Studies*
JJS	*Journal of Jewish Studies*
JNES	*Journal of Near Eastern Studies*
JNSL	*Journal of Northwest Semitic Languages*
JSJSup	Journal for the Study of Judaism: Supplements
JSNT	*Journal for the Study of the New Testament*
JSNTSup	Journal for the Study of the New Testament — Supplement Series
JSOT	*Journal for the Study of the Old Testament*
JSOTSup	Journal for the Study of the Old Testament — Supplement Series
JSPSup	Journal for the Study of the Pseudepigrapha — Supplement Series
LXX	Septuagint
NASB	New American Standard Bible
NCB	New Century Bible
NIBC	New International Biblical Commentary
NICNT	New International Commentary on the New Testament
NICOT	New International Commentary on the Old Testament
NIGTC	New International Greek Testament Commentary
NIV	New International Version
NIVAC	New International Version Application Commentary
NovTSup	Novum Testamentum — Supplement Series
NSRV	New Revised Standard Version
NT	New Testament
NTS	*New Testament Studies*
NTTS	New Testament Tools and Studies
OBO	Orbis biblicus et orientalis
OT	Old Testament
OTL	Old Testament Library
OTS	Oudtestamentische studiën
RB	*Revue biblique*
RSV	Revised Standard Version
RTR	*Reformed Theological Review*
SBLDS	Society of Biblical Literature Dissertation Series
SBLEJL	Society of Biblical Literature: Early Judaism and Its Literature
SBLMS	Society of Biblical Literature Monograph Series
SBT	Studies in Biblical Theology

SJOT	*Scandinavian Journal of the Old Testament*
SNTSMS	Society for New Testament Studies Monograph Series
SP	Sacra Pagina
SSEJC	Studies in Scripture in Early Judaism and Christianity
STAR	Studies in Theology and Religion
STDJ	Studies on the Texts of the Desert of Judah
TNIV	Today's New International Version
USFISFCJ	University of South Florida International Studies in Formative Christianity and Judaism
VTSup	Supplements to Vetus Testamentum
WBC	Word Biblical Commentary
WMANT	Wissenschaftliche Monographien zum Alten und Neuen Testament
WUNT	Wissenschaftliche Untersuchungen zum Neuen Testament
ZAW	*Zeitschrift für die alttestamentliche Wissenschaft*

Contributors

MARK J. BODA, Professor of Old Testament, McMaster Divinity College, Hamilton, Ontario, Canada

S. A. CUMMINS, Associate Professor of Religious Studies, Trinity Western University, Langley, British Columbia, Canada

CRAIG A. EVANS, Payzant Distinguished Professor of Biblical Studies, Acadia Divinity College, Wolfville, Nova Scotia, Canada

TREMPER LONGMAN III, Robert H. Gundry Professor of Biblical Studies, Westmont College, Santa Barbara, California

I. HOWARD MARSHALL, Honorary Research Professor of New Testament, University of Aberdeen, UK

STANLEY E. PORTER, President, Dean, and Professor of New Testament, McMaster Divinity College, Hamilton, Ontario, Canada

LOREN T. STUCKENBRUCK, B. F. Westcott Professor of Biblical Studies, University of Durham, UK

TOM THATCHER, Associate Professor of Biblical Studies, Cincinnati Christian University, Ohio, USA

CYNTHIA LONG WESTFALL, Assistant Professor of New Testament, McMaster Divinity College, Hamilton, Ontario, Canada

AL WOLTERS, Professor of Religion and Theology/Classical Languages, Redeemer University College, Ancaster, Ontario, Canada

Introduction:
The Messiah in the Old and New Testaments

Stanley E. Porter

When the ancients heard the word "Messiah," what did they understand by this term? Christians have traditionally equated the word "Messiah" with Jesus, but the term has proven to be far more complex than that simple equation. One of the major ongoing disputes is whether and what kind of messianic expectation there is in the Old Testament. No doubt there are a variety of people who are designated or thought of in some way in the Old Testament as God's anointed, such as Cyrus the Persian in Isa 45:1, various prophets, and especially King David and others who were to come in his line.[1] However, the persistent question is whether there was the kind of messianic expectation in the Old Testament as is depicted in the New Testament, that is, the expectation of a single, specific individual designated as God's unique and only Messiah. Scholarly opinion on this point has varied considerably. A scholar such as Sigmund Mowinckel went to great lengths to minimize the sense of messianic expectation to be found in the Old Testament. Instead, he saw the figure of God's anointed as primarily a political figure, that is, the king.[2] By contrast, a scholar such as Helmer Ringgren argued at about the same time that royal psalms and servant passages pointed to a figure beyond the people of Israel.[3] Over the course of time, and especially in recent years, there has been continuing discussion of

---

1. A survey of the evidence is found in R. S. Hess, "The Image of the Messiah in the Old Testament," in *Images of Christ: Ancient and Modern* (ed. S. E. Porter, M. A. Hayes, and D. Tombs; Sheffield: Sheffield Academic Press, 1997) 22-33.

2. S. Mowinckel, *He That Cometh* (New York: Abingdon, 1954).

3. H. Ringgren, *The Messiah in the Old Testament* (SBT 18; London: SCM Press, 1956).

these issues. The result has been a healthy recognition of the need not to over-read the Old Testament and related texts,[4] but there is a residual sense in which a number of passages are indicating something more than simply fulfillment by a figure of the time, or even the people of Israel. As a result, there is discussion of such figures as David, Moses, and the suffering servant, among others, as possibly messianic.[5] Thus, the sense of a legitimate messianic expectation can be found in the documents that preceded and surrounded the New Testament. This would include the Old Testament, as is shown in a recent collection of essays that investigates the potential messianic implications of various parts of the Old Testament.[6] Also to be included would be the range of texts that surrounded the New Testament, such as the Qumran documents and other so-called pseudepigraphal texts.[7]

This variety of understanding extends to the New Testament as well. Some have been highly skeptical about the origins and identification, and

---

4. E.g., K. Pomykala, *The Davidic Dynasty Tradition in Early Judaism: Its History and Significance for Messianism* (SBLEJL 7; Atlanta: Scholars Press, 1995).

5. Some recent studies include A. Laato, *A Star Is Rising: The Historical Development of the Old Testament Royal Ideology and the Rise of the Jewish Messianic Expectations* (Atlanta: Scholars Press, 1997); W. Horbury, *Jewish Messianism and the Cult of Christ* (London: SCM Press, 1998) esp. 5-35.

6. P. E. Satterthwaite, R. S. Hess, and G. J. Wenham, eds., *The Lord's Anointed: Interpretation of Old Testament Messianic Texts* (Grand Rapids: Baker, 1995).

7. See, e.g., A. Chester, "Jewish Messianic Expectations and Mediatorial Figures and Pauline Christology," in *Paulus und das antike Judentum* (ed. M. Hengel and U. Heckel; WUNT 58; Tübingen: Mohr Siebeck, 1991) 17-78; J. H. Charlesworth, ed., *The Messiah: Developments in Earliest Judaism and Christianity* (Minneapolis: Fortress, 1992); J. J. Collins, *The Scepter and the Star: The Messiahs of the Dead Sea Scrolls and Other Ancient Literature* (ABRL; New York: Doubleday, 1995); J. H. Charlesworth, H. Lichtenberger, and G. S. Oegema, eds., *Qumran-Messianism: Studies on the Messianic Expectations in the Dead Sea Scrolls* (Tübingen: Mohr Siebeck, 1998); C. A. Evans, "Qumran's Messiah: How Important Is He?" in *Religion in the Dead Sea Scrolls* (ed. J. J. Collins and R. A. Kugler; Grand Rapids: Eerdmans, 2000) 135-49; Evans, "The Messiah in the Dead Sea Scrolls," in *Israel's Messiah in the Bible and the Dead Sea Scrolls* (ed. R. S. Hess and M. D. Carroll R.; Grand Rapids: Baker, 2003) 85-102 (cf. Evans, "David in the Dead Sea Scrolls," in *The Scrolls and the Scriptures: Qumran Fifty Years After* [ed. S. E. Porter and C. A. Evans; Sheffield: Sheffield Academic Press, 1997] 183-97); and G. S. Oegema, *The Anointed and His People: Messianic Expectations from the Maccabees to Bar Kochba* (Sheffield: Sheffield Academic Press, 1998). Interesting documents regarding Jewish messianic expectations after the New Testament are found in G. W. Buchanan, *Jewish Messianic Movements from AD 70 to AD 1300: Documents from the Fall of Jerusalem to the End of the Crusades* (Eugene, OR: Wipf and Stock, 1978).

certainly the self-consciousness, of Jesus as Messiah.[8] In the New Testament itself, we find various cultural expectations regarding the Messiah, competing definitions of the characteristics of a messianic figure, and differing dimensions of Jesus' life and ministry interpreted in various ways as indicating him as Messiah. As a result, the discussion has tended to concentrate upon Jesus himself, although there is also pertinent discussion of what Paul means when he refers to Jesus Christ, and whether this is a name or retains a titular sense. Concerning Jesus, there are a variety of views among New Testament scholars regarding the messianic claims made by him or about him in the Gospels. Some take what has been called a centrist position (as opposed to the highly skeptical position, mentioned above),[9] while others have been much more positive about the

8. Several of the better-known scholars in this regard are W. Wrede, *The Messianic Secret* (London: James Clarke, 1971 [1901]) (cf. C. Tuckett, ed., *The Messianic Secret* [London: SPCK, 1983]); W. Bousset, *Kyrios Christos: A History of the Belief in Christ from the Beginnings of Christianity to Irenaeus* (Nashville: Abingdon, 1970 [1913]) esp. 70-98; P. Feine, *Theologie des Neuen Testaments* (3rd ed.; Berlin: Evangelische Verlagsanstalt, 1919) 40-44; R. Bultmann, *Theology of the New Testament* (2 vols.; London: SCM Press, 1952, 1955) 1:26-33; R. H. Fuller, *The Foundations of New Testament Christology* (New York: Scribner's, 1965) 23-31, 109-11, 191-92, 230; R. H. Fuller and P. Perkins, *Who Is This Christ? Gospel Christology and Contemporary Faith* (Philadelphia: Fortress, 1983) 41-52; and, more recently, P. M. Casey, *From Jewish Prophet to Gentile God: The Origins and Development of New Testament Christology* (Cambridge: James Clarke, 1991) 41-44.

9. See W. Manson, *Jesus the Messiah: The Synoptic Tradition of the Revelation of God in Christ: With Special Reference to Form-Criticism* (London: Hodder & Stoughton, 1943) esp. 94-98; L. Cerfaux, *Le Christ dans la théologie de saint Paul* (Paris: Cerf, 1943); O. Cullmann, *The Christology of the New Testament* (London: SCM Press, 1959 [1957]) 111-36; W. Kramer, *Christ, Lord, Son of God* (London: SCM Press, 1966); W. G. Kümmel, *The Theology of the New Testament according to Its Major Witnesses: Jesus–Paul–John* (Nashville: Abingdon, 1973) 66-73; L. Goppelt, *Theology of the New Testament* (2 vols.; Grand Rapids: Eerdmans, 1981 [1975]) 1:168-72; J. D. G. Dunn, *Unity and Diversity in the New Testament: An Inquiry into the Character of Earliest Christianity* (Philadelphia: Westminster, 1977) 41-45; Dunn, *Jesus Remembered* (Grand Rapids: Eerdmans, 2003) 615-55; N. A. Dahl, *Jesus the Christ: The Historical Origins of Christological Doctrine* (ed. D. H. Juel; Minneapolis: Fortress, 1991) esp. 15-49; M. De Jonge, "The Earliest Christian Use of *Christos*: Some Suggestions," *NTS* 32 (1986) 321-43; R. E. Brown, *An Introduction to New Testament Christology* (New York: Paulist, 1994) esp. 73-80; R. Schnackenburg, *Jesus in the Gospels: A Biblical Christology* (Louisville: Westminster John Knox, 1995); H. Schwarz, *Christology* (Grand Rapids: Eerdmans, 1998); and E. K. Broadhead, *Naming Jesus: Titular Christology in the Gospel of Mark* (JSNTSup 175; Sheffield: Sheffield Academic Press, 1999) 145-54 (cf. Broadhead, *Prophet, Son, Messiah: Narrative Form and Function in Mark 14–16* [JSNTSup 97; Sheffield: Sheffield Academic Press, 1997]). Cf.

evidence.[10] Recent discussion of the Messiah has tended more and more to endorse the finding of the royal or Davidic Messiah as a pervasive image, while not neglecting the prophetic, priestly, and servant dimensions to various degrees. This collection of essays explores these and related questions regarding the nature and identity of the Messiah in the Old and New Testaments in order to better understand Jesus as Messiah.

The essays in this volume are essentially divided into two parts.[11] The first part is concerned with the Old Testament and those writings that preceded or surrounded the New Testament, and the second part with the writings of the New Testament. The first grouping includes two essays on the Old Testament and two on extrabiblical literature.

In the first essay, Tremper Longman III examines the Law and the Writings in the Old Testament. In keeping with much recent examination of the Messiah in the Old Testament, Longman finds that the contours of a specifically messianic expectation arises only in late and especially post–Old Testament times. The roots of such messianic expectation, however, he sees as much earlier, and as associated with texts that look forward to a future anointed king or priest-figure who brings salvation to the people of

---

C. L. Blomberg, "Messiah in the New Testament," in Hess and Carroll R., eds., *Israel's Messiah,* 111-41, here p. 113, where he refers to the notion of a centrist position.

10. See, e.g., G. Dalman, *The Words of Jesus Considered in the Light of Post-Biblical Jewish Writings and the Aramaic Language* (Edinburgh: T&T Clark, 1909) 289-316; A. E. J. Rawlinson, *The New Testament Doctrine of the Christ* (London: Longmans, Green, 1926) esp. ch. 1; E. Stauffer, *New Testament Theology* (London: SCM Press, 1955) 112-13; O. Betz, *What Do We Know about Jesus?* (London: SCM Press, 1968) 92-93; R. N. Longenecker, *The Christology of Early Jewish Christianity* (London: SCM Press, 1970) esp. 63-70; G. E. Ladd, *A Theology of the New Testament* (Grand Rapids: Eerdmans, 1974) 135-44; C. F. D. Moule, *The Origin of Christology* (Cambridge: Cambridge University Press, 1977) 31-35 (cf. R. T. France, "Development in New Testament Christology," in *Crisis in Christology: Questions in Search of Resolution* [ed. W. R. Farmer; Livonia, MI: Dove, 1995] 63-82); I. H. Marshall, *The Origins of New Testament Christology* (Downers Grove, IL: InterVarsity Press, 1977) 43-62; Marshall, *New Testament Theology: Many Witnesses, One Gospel* (Downers Grove, IL: InterVarsity Press, 2004) *passim;* D. Guthrie, *New Testament Theology* (London: InterVarsity Press, 1981) 236-52; G. B. Caird, *New Testament Theology* (ed. L. D. Hurst; Oxford: Clarendon, 1994) 306-10; M. Hengel, *Studies in Early Christology* (Edinburgh: T&T Clark, 1995) esp. 1-72; N. T. Wright, *Jesus and the Victory of God* (Minneapolis: Fortress, 1996) 486-89; D. Seccombe, *The King of God's Kingdom: A Solution to the Puzzle of Jesus* (Carlisle: Paternoster, 2002) 96-100; Blomberg, "Messiah in the New Testament."

11. I wish to thank the individual contributors for providing abstracts of their essays for the Colloquium, which abstracts I draw freely upon in this summary.

God. Early Jewish and New Testament authors were convinced that many texts had messianic significance, and they read a number of passages in the Law and the Writings in this way. Some of the most important passages include Gen 3:15; 14:17-20; 49:8-12; Num 24:17-19; Deut 18:18-19; Psalms 2 and 110; and Dan 9:24-26, where in the last *māšîaḥ* is actually used.[12] As a result, modern interpreters such as Longman raise the question whether the original authors and audiences of these texts actually understood them as messianic. If they did not, then the question arises of the nature of the New Testament use of this material.

Focusing on another part of the Old Testament canon, Mark J. Boda addresses the issue of the Messiah in the Prophets. He notes that modern Old Testament scholarship has consistently argued that the verbal root *māšaḥ* and the related nominal form *māšîaḥ* are rarely associated with an expected future leader within the Old Testament itself — with the exceptions often noted in Dan 9:24-26 and Isa 61:1.[13] The majority of the passages in the Old Testament describe past or present Hebrew leaders. After examining the terminological evidence in the Old Testament and reviewing expectations regarding a future leader in the Prophets, Boda attempts to show that the employment of the terms "Messiah" and "messianic" is an appropriate way to refer to a variety of future leaders or to functions of a single leader. This provides the foundation for examining the development of such expectations within the Prophets. Boda recognizes some tension within the final sections of the Prophets regarding the character and role of future leaders. This development becomes especially important as one sees the prophetic voice making a transition to a stronger eschatological emphasis.

In his essay on the Messiah in the Qumran documents, Al Wolters treads carefully through the contested claims regarding messianism in the Qumran scrolls. There are questions regarding whether the Qumran community expected one or two messiahs, whether one can speak of a Messiah only when the appropriate Hebrew word is used, and whether other factors must be present to justify speaking of a messianic figure. As a useful guide to his discussion, Wolters analyzes two synthetic treatments of

---

12. By comparison, Gen 3:15; 49:8-12; Psalms 2 and 110; and Dan 9:24-26 are treated in Satterthwaite et al., eds., *The Lord's Anointed*, in significant detail.

13. Again by comparison, these two passages are treated in detail in Satterthwaite et al., eds., *The Lord's Anointed*.

Qumran messianism by leading Qumran scholars. The first is John Collins in his book *The Scepter and the Star: The Messiahs of the Dead Sea Scrolls and Other Ancient Literature*,[14] who tentatively and carefully offers a nuanced differentiation of four different messianic paradigms in the scrolls, relating respectively to king, priest, prophet, and heavenly messiah. The second is by Michael O. Wise, *The First Messiah: Investigating the Savior before Jesus*,[15] who presents a bolder proposal in which a single messianic figure, in many ways foreshadowing Jesus Christ, is the interpretive key to a whole range of Qumran documents. Wolters assesses each treatment in turn before offering his own constructive response to each.

Part I on preceding and surrounding texts concludes with the essay by Loren Stuckenbruck on messianic ideas in the apocalyptic and related literature. His consideration of the notion of the Messiah in the *Psalms of Solomon,* the Similitudes of *1 Enoch, 4 Ezra,* and *2 Baruch* reveals the degree to which messianic speculation varied from author to author, and even within the individual documents themselves. A number of motifs are shared by more than one of these writings, such as the Davidic lineage, preexistence, the effects of messianic disclosure or coming, and other designations that apply from the narrative contexts. However, it remains striking that, while such parallels between traditions exist, none of the motifs is found in all the literature or handled in the same way. These ancient documents, according to Stuckenbruck, ultimately resist any attempt to synthesize their ideas, which are so integral to the particular concerns of the authors and their communities and which depend on the sorts of tradition-historical materials available. Stuckenbruck finds it hard to imagine, for example, that Jewish readers of Daniel 7, *Psalms of Solomon,* or any of the other documents treated in his essay would have understood the text around a basic core tradition about God's eschatological Messiah, since such a notion simply did not exist. What we do have, Stuckenbruck finds, is a series of Jewish documents composed near the turn of the era that were inspired by biblical tradition and subsequent patterns and traditions of interpretation, and that expressed hope in a world in the control of Israel's God.

The essays in Part II deal directly with the various corpora of New Testament writings. We begin with the Gospels, in particular Mark and Matthew. Howard Marshall takes a narrative approach to the Gospel of

14. See footnote 7 above for the full reference.
15. (San Francisco: HarperCollins, 1999).

Mark so that the various christological statements and designations can be appreciated in their several contexts in the teaching, healing, and suffering mission of Jesus. In a passage that has been widely discussed by scholars, Peter's confession,[16] Jesus is recognized by Peter as the Messiah and acknowledged by God as his Son, but Jesus himself, according to Marshall, explains his role more in terms of the Son of Man who must suffer before receiving dominion from God his Father. Marshall finds that, in Mark, the several christological terms bring their individual, distinctive contributions from their Old Testament roots to an understanding of Jesus, but that they take on new significance in the light of the way he lived and died. Thus they to some extent become interchangeable. The Gospel of Matthew tells much the same story as Mark, according to Marshall, but the Christology is enhanced by the addition of fresh material and the Evangelist's way of telling his story. As a result, such aspects of the role and character of Jesus as his filial relation to God, his function as a teacher, and his supreme authority — none of which is absent from Mark — stand out more clearly.

In an essay that treats both the Gospel of Luke and the Book of Acts, rather than developing a number of different ideas, Porter focuses upon two key passages that emphasize Jesus as the anointed prophet and sees how these ideas are developed throughout the two respective works. Luke 4:16-30 is seen as providing a programmatic statement for depicting Jesus as Messiah in Luke's Gospel. Jesus' citation of Isa 61:1-2 and 58:6, and his interpretation in terms of proclaiming forgiveness for captives, set the tone for Jesus' messianic claim as anointed prophet. This theme is also found in Jesus' birth narrative, John the Baptist's anticipation of Jesus, Peter's acclamation of Jesus in Luke 9, Jesus' dealing with the authorities throughout the Gospel, and Jesus' revelation of himself after he is risen. In the Book of Acts, Peter's speech at Pentecost in Acts 2:14-36 provides a similar programmatic statement regarding Jesus as the Messiah. Other pronouncements of Jesus as Messiah are found in Peter's sermon in the temple, Paul's speech in Thessalonica, and Paul's defense before Agrippa. In the Gospel, Luke draws upon a number of Old Testament passages, especially Isaiah but not only prophetic sources narrowly defined, that resonated with cur-

16. Peter's confession is probably the single most widely discussed passage regarding the claims of Jesus regarding being the Messiah. Many of the works cited in footnotes 8, 9, and 10 above devote considerable attention to this passage, especially as found in Mark's Gospel.

rent Jewish thought to depict Jesus as both the messianic prophet, and hence the eschatological prophet coming in the last times, and the fulfillment of Old Testament prophecy concerning the anointed coming one. In both Luke and Acts, the author continues to develop the idea of Jesus as anointed prophet, while also depicting other, and potentially complementary, viewpoints, such as Jesus as royal son of David.

In treating John's Gospel, Tom Thatcher argues that the presentation of Jesus in the Fourth Gospel, though notoriously difficult, is characterized by notable internal tensions and expressed through complex literary motifs such as irony, ambiguity, and misunderstanding. This is the case because John's Christology is largely negative, defining Jesus by what he is not in order to refute the claims of two competing groups, "the Jews" and "the Antichrists." Against the claims of "the Jews," John asserts that Jesus is the Christ, a divine figure. Against the claims of "the Antichrists," John insists that the divine Christ is the historical Jesus. As Christ, Jesus is portrayed as superior to Jewish messianic expectations and, ultimately, superior to Judaism itself. As Jesus, Christ is portrayed as a historical figure that came "in water and blood." As such, according to Thatcher, John evidences both the highest Christology in the New Testament and the greatest interest in Jesus as a historical figure.

Moving from the Gospel material to the rest of the New Testament, we first turn to Paul. Tony Cummins examines the Pauline letters and finds that, for the apostle Paul, what it means for God to disclose himself in Jesus Christ is to incorporate the whole of humanity into Messiah Jesus and thereby into the divine life. The historical and theological dimensions of such a claim are delineated in two interrelated aspects of Paul's Christology. The first is that Jesus' messianic identity encompasses an Israel-specific life and death transposed into a creation-wide glorification. The second is that this pattern and path are replicated in the lives of the messianic and Spirit-empowered eschatological people of God. Cummins focuses this analysis on several representative passages that are central to Paul's major letters — Romans 5–8, 2 Corinthians 3–5, and Galatians 1–2. He shows that Paul's understanding of Jesus as Messiah lies at the heart of his theology, ecclesiology, and eschatology. The Messiah and his faithful followers are agents of a divine life that embraces redemption, reconciliation, and re-creation.

The final essay picks up a number of the works that are often overlooked in discussion of the notion of Messiah in the New Testament, since they are neither records of Jesus and response to him, such as the Gospels, nor writings of Jesus' first major interpreter, Paul. Cynthia Westfall's study of the Messiah in Hebrews and the General Epistles focuses on the early Christian fusing, reframing, and development of the Jewish representations of the Messiah. In Hebrews and the General Epistles, the term "Christ" consistently occurs with words and phrases that can roughly be categorized according to the three royal symbols of enthronement, temple, and victory. The references to believers either sharing in Jesus' messianic position or function or responding to Jesus as king, priest, or victor reflect how the ancient king was bound together with his people and functioned as their representative. Although Hebrews and the General Epistles connect the title of Christ with Jewish messianic associations of enthronement, temple, and victory, the representation of Jesus as Messiah is significantly different from Jewish expectations. Each symbol is reinterpreted. The essential representation of the Christ as the Son of God pervades these epistles, but the extensive development of Jesus' high priesthood and his sanctuary, covenant, and sacrifice in Hebrews is the most significant contribution of this corpus to the early church's representation of the Messiah.

At the Colloquium itself, Craig Evans gave two separate oral responses, one after the first five papers and the other after the next four. Here in the printed volume, he combines these two responses into a single written response. Evans provides useful inroads into the various essays by examining a variety of features. In response to some of the essays, he calls into question some of the assumptions or analyses offered by the papers. In reaction to others, he proposes additional ideas and enhances the presentation. In interpretation of a final group, he calls into question some conclusions and proposes his own analyses and answers to crucial questions regarding depiction of the Messiah. In every case, the response provides an opportunity to see some of the engagement that occurred at the time the papers were originally presented and offers an initial avenue for further exploration. What becomes clear in this discussion is that there is a wealth of material to be discussed from both the Old and New Testaments. Scholarly discussion continues to debate the messianic implications of various books and even individual passages. Even those who clearly endorse Jesus as Messiah find different emphases and themes within the books of the New Testament. These varying pictures provide both a challenge for further understanding of Jesus as the Christ and a complex and multifaceted portrait of the one called by Christians God's anointed one, the Messiah.

PART I
OLD TESTAMENT
AND RELATED PERSPECTIVE

The Messiah:
Explorations in the Law and Writings

Tremper Longman III

To study the idea of the Messiah in the Torah and the Writings is a daunting task indeed. While most Christians today wonder why anyone could miss seeing how Jesus so precisely fulfilled Old Testament prophecy, scholars are apt to wonder how the New Testament authors could presume to use these texts in application to him.

As we will illustrate below in connection with certain selected texts, it is impossible to establish that any passage in its original literary and historical context must or even should be understood as portending a future messianic figure. So in one sense this chapter could be very short. On the other hand, the New Testament as well as intertestamental literature is filled with citations of texts from the Torah and the Writings that are applied with a definite messianic meaning. By what hermeneutical strategy does one get from the Old Testament to these later writings, and should we consider this strategy appropriate?[1]

However, even before getting to those vexed questions we need to define our terms, particularly the term "messiah." When we ask about messianic expectation in the Old Testament, what are we asking?

As many other excellent studies have pointed out, we do not get very

---

1. In this we follow the prescription of P. P. Jenson, "Models of Prophetic Prediction and Matthew's Quotation of Micah 5:2," in *The Lord's Anointed: Interpretation of Old Testament Prophetic Texts* (ed. P. E. Satterthwaite, R. Hess, and G. Wenham; Grand Rapids: Baker, 1995) 190, when he says, "Old Testament specialists attempt to make sense of the phenomenon from back to front; New Testament scholars from front to back." However, in the final analysis, one has to wonder just how different these two starting points really are.

far in our inquiry by pursuing the Hebrew word that can be translated "messiah," though it provides a helpful starting point (see below).[2] The Hebrew word is *māšîaḥ*. With one exception it occurs in reference to contemporary human kings, priests, and (on only two occasions — 1 Kgs 19:16 and Ps 105:15) to prophets (the second reference is enigmatic).[3] The single exception to this is found in Dan 9:25-26, a text that is so difficult that we cannot even be certain whether the *māšîaḥ* in v. 25 is used the same way as in v. 26![4] The verb *māšaḥ* "to anoint" occurs more often than the noun, but never in a way that informs our understanding of a future eschatological figure.

However, the field is well beyond the point of thinking that a concept is limited to a single word. The idea of a messiah may be associated with passages that do not use either *māšîaḥ* or a form of the verb *māšaḥ*.

Yet a further question that arises due to the fact that we do not limit our understanding to the exact word concerns how broadly we understand the concept of messianic expectation, especially as it is applied to Jesus in the New Testament. Some scholars adopt an extremely broad understanding of messianic expectation so that virtually any anticipation of Jesus in the Old Testament is labeled as relevant to the study.[5] On the other hand, it seems more elegant to associate as specifically messianic texts those pas-

---

2. J. Oswalt, "msh," in *New International Dictionary of Old Testament Theology and Exegesis* (ed. W. A. Van Gemeren; Grand Rapids: Zondervan, 1997-) 2:1123-26, provides an excellent discussion.

3. The issues revolve around the identity of the referent as well as the nature of parallelism. In regard to the referent, we must first of all keep in mind that this part of the psalm describes the period of the patriarchs. It is true that Abraham is called a prophet in Gen 20:7, but Psalm 105 does not refer to him alone but to the family of God. Probably the best understanding of the term is that the poet is using honorific terms ("anointed ones" and "prophets") from a later time and applying them to the people of God in the patriarchal period. However, this understanding of the verse might still allow for the equation of "anointed" and "prophet" if one insists on an A=B approach to the relationship between the first and second cola. However, following James Kugel (*The Idea of Biblical Parallelism* [New Haven: Yale University Press, 1979]), it is better to see an "A, what's more B" relationship at work here. That is, the people of Israel are here described metaphorically as God's "anointed" and then as "prophets" in the second colon. We should take note of the parallel between Ps 105:15 and 1 Chron 16:22.

4. And of course there is a debate over whether the reference is authentically future-oriented or *ex eventu*.

5. A particularly clear example of this is found in G. van Groningen, *Messianic Revelation in the Old Testament* (Grand Rapids: Baker, 1990).

sages that anticipate a future leader of God's people who is connected to a role in which the ritual of "anointing" is found. We will begin by discovering just how broad or narrow the category is in the Old Testament.

I should also point out that Mark Boda and I have split the study of the Old Testament between us. So he has the Prophets while I have the Torah and Writings. Unfortunately, it turns out that in order to understand the later recognition of the messianic import of certain passages in the Torah and the Writings we have to understand them in the light of the Prophets. Therefore with apologies to Dr. Boda and the promise to keep such references to a minimum, I find myself forced to at least introduce some general ideas from the Prophets, in particular 2 Samuel 7.

Yet another issue that complicates the study has to do with varying ideas about the composition of biblical books. I would hazard to guess that few Old Testament scholars would agree in detail about how and when the books of the Torah and the Writings came into existence. Of course, the following presentation assumes certain conclusions about these matters, and only rarely will I have the luxury of time to argue for these views or to present alternatives.

The Use of the Term *MŠḤ* in the Torah and the Writings

In the Pentateuch, anointing (and the root *mšḥ*) is connected to consecration rituals for the most part, and, when it comes to people, it is the priests who are anointed for special service to God. The root does not occur in Genesis in connection with people and only once otherwise in a ritual in which Jacob anointed a pillar (Gen 31:13). The book of Exodus describes anointing oil kept on hand at the tabernacle, presumably for use in consecration rituals (Exod 25:6). While the tabernacle and its furniture are anointed (Exod 30:26; 40:9, 10, 11), the only people anointed are the priests (Exod 28:41; 29:7; 30:30; 40:15), and this latter usage continues in Leviticus (4:3, 5, 16; 6:20, 22; 8:12) and Numbers (3:3; 35:25), while there is no use of the root in the book of Deuteronomy. From the Torah, we come to the conclusion that one who is anointed is set apart for special service to God. We also note that it is only the priest who is described as anointed, and this rather frequently.

As we turn our attention to the Writings, we find ourselves in a different sphere when it comes to the root *mšḥ*. No longer is "to anoint" applied to priests. We move from the realm of the cult to the realm of the court.[6] The virtually exclusive use of words formed from *mšḥ* has to do with the king. This is particularly true of the Psalms (2:2; 18:50 [51]; 20:6 [7]; 28:8; 45:7 [8]; 84:9 [10]; 89:20 [21], 38 [39]; 132:10, 17). The root is also used in Chronicles (1 Chron 16:22[7]; 2 Chron 6:42) and Lamentations (4:20) to refer to the king. Daniel 9:25, 26 associates the root *mšḥ* (here *māšiaḥ*) with another term from the court, *nāgîd* "prince." Of additional interest is the fact that nearly all of these references to the anointed king highlight the king's role as protector and vanquisher of Israel's enemies. Even Lam 4:20, which speaks of the demise of the LORD's anointed at the hands of the enemy, may be using this title with irony.

If we restrict our focus to passages in the Torah and the Writings, we come to the following observations. In the Torah the word is almost exclusively used of an anointed priest and in the Writings of an anointed king. However, in both cases, with the exception of Dan 9:25 and 26 to be discussed below, the word is used to refer to a present, not a future, priest or king. The terms' occurrences do not in and of themselves justify the expectation of an eschatological figure, either priestly or royal, and certainly not prophetic.

Background to the Psalms' Use of *MŠḤ* in the Former Prophets

The Torah uses *māšaḥ* for priests, and the Writings uses it for kings. We can explain the origin of the connection between kings and anointing only by means of appeal to the Former Prophets, in particular the books of Samuel.

While the Torah anticipated kingship (note especially predictive texts like Gen 49:8-12 and Num 24:17, to be discussed below), there were of course no kings during this time period. However, when Saul becomes the first king, he is known as God's anointed (1 Sam 10:1; 12:3, 5; 15:17; over all he is called anointed some fifteen times). Of even more significance for

---

6. Dan 9:24 provides an exception in that this verse anticipates the anointing of a sacred place, but even here the next two verses speak of an "anointed prince," thus moving back into the court.

7. For the use in 2 Chron 16:22, a parallel with Ps 105:15, see footnote 3.

our topic, as we will see, David's anointing is mentioned a number of times, sixteen in all, and the ritual of his anointing is narrated in 1 Samuel 16. Solomon, Jehu, and a number of other kings are also specifically connected with anointing.

Thus, the practice of anointing kings in the historical books provides a historical background to the anointed king in the Psalms. Even so, these references in and of themselves still do not encourage readers to understand the anointed king in the Psalms to be anything but references to contemporary kings rather than a future eschatological ruler. It is, of course, in the latter sense that the term is applied to Jesus in the New Testament. In the next section, we will choose one of the royal psalms that mention the anointed king and interpret it within its Old Testament setting.

Psalm 2 as a Coronation Psalm

Psalm 2 draws our attention for three reasons. First, it is a royal psalm that refers to the king as the LORD's anointed (2:2). Second, it is frequently cited in the New Testament in reference to Christ's identification as the Messiah (Mk 1:11 [and parallels]; 9:7 [and parallels]; Acts 4:23-31; 13:33; Rom 1:4; Heb 1:5; 5:5; 2 Pet 1:17; Rev 11:18; 19:19; to name a selection). Third, it appears likely that Psalm 2 was intentionally placed at the beginning of the Psalter to serve as a kind of introduction to the whole book. Thus, as Gerald Wilson points out, its presence at this point may serve as a key to the interpretation of the royal psalms that follow.[8]

Psalm 2 is a significant poem for us to study considering its relationship with the Davidic covenant, even alluding to the crucial section where God describes the father-like relationship he has with the king (Ps 2:7 echoes 2 Sam 7:14).

As we read the psalm in its Old Testament context, we have no reason to insist that the human composer consciously intended the referent of the anointed to reach beyond the human ruler. Those many scholars who argue that the psalm is a coronation psalm may well be correct, though it is

---

8. G. Wilson, *Psalms, Volume 1* (NIVAC; Grand Rapids: Zondervan, 2002) 107-8. Wilson also notes that some early Greek texts of Acts 13:33 refer to Psalm 2 as the "first psalm" and may indicate that in some editions of the psalms it stood as the introduction to the whole book.

certainly not the only possible understanding of the contemporary use of this text.

The first stanza expresses bewilderment at the attempt of the nations to throw off the bondage of the LORD and his anointed king. We are somewhat at a loss to understand exactly what kind of historical background generated such a thought. There were few time periods when Israel or Judah under the Davidides had vassals who would contemplate throwing off their shackles. Even those times — like that of David himself, when Israel did exercise sovereignty over nearby states — do not exactly fit the rather grandiose claims implied by this first stanza. In its ancient setting, however, this may simply be the type of hyperbole generated by the beginning of a new reign.

Perhaps one of the strongest arguments in favor of a setting of this psalm at the time of the coronation may be seen in the words God speaks in stanza two, which underline the futility of the nations: "I have set my king on Zion, my holy hill" (2:6). However, God does not say this is happening at the time of the recital of the psalm. Indeed, I can think of an alternate setting for the psalm, namely at the initiation of holy war. The divine words then become a reminder of the divine establishment of the monarch on the eve of a military engagement. But whether this psalm has a setting at the coronation or before a holy war makes no difference to the point relevant to our present study, which is that the contents of the psalm can be explained in terms of its contemporary setting.

In the third stanza, God turns his attention away from the rebellious nations and on to the anointed king. It is here that he reminds him of their special relationship as father and son in language reminiscent of 2 Samuel 7. He then offers the king the power necessary to dominate all nations to the ends of the earth. Finally, in the fourth stanza, God speaks a last time to the kings of the nations, warning them to avoid destruction at the hands of his anointed by submitting to his power.

Before contemplating later uses of Psalm 2, I do want to make one more reflection on its original setting. Psalm 2 has no authorship attribution, though Acts 4:25-26 cites the psalm and attributes it to David.

As I contemplate the history of Israel and then later of Judah, I am hard pressed to think of a period other than David's that would be better suited for the composition and first use of this poem. Not that this is crucial to the purpose of this paper, but it allows me to be more concrete in my understanding of how this poem came to be used.

So let's assume for the sake of argument that Psalm 2 was composed during the reign of David. If it is a coronation poem,[9] or for that matter if it is a pre–holy war song, it would be available for use in later reigns. What strikes me as I survey the history of the monarchy from Solomon through Zedekiah is just how hollow this poem would sound — that is, if it was actually used — during later reigns of the kings of Judah. I say this in the light of the fact that apostasy, syncretistic worship, and the like were rampant among later Davidic rulers. The Deuteronomic historian, at least, does not display later kings as exemplars of Yahwistic faith. It is true that Kings gives us a picture of the kings in monochrome as its historian-theologians provide an answer to the question of the exile. If we take Chronicles seriously,[10] perhaps many kings started out like Abijah, pious, but ended up apostate. And in any case, even with apostate or syncretistic kings, they must have been aware that their kingship was contingent on their descent from David, whose dynasty was established by the God Yahweh. Even Manasseh may have had the choir sing Psalm 2 at his inauguration even as he was shipping idols into the Holy of Holies.[11]

But to the pious, Psalm 2 must have sounded hollow. It may have been the dissonance between the content and tone of Psalm 2 and the reality of Judah's kings and their political subordination to other great world powers that set their minds wondering whether Psalm 2 had repercussions beyond that which may be read from a minimal reading of the poem.

This dissonance, of course, would have reached its ultimate crisis point at the time Zedekiah was removed from the throne by Nebuchadnezzar and a relatively weak Babylonian appointed governor came to manage Judah in his place.

In the light of these political realities, what should be done with Psalm 2? The pious would have wrestled with this in the light of the Davidic covenant, which after all claimed that, though rebellion would be punished, God would not "take my steadfast love from him as I took it

9. Though of course, if it is David, it could not be a coronation song per se, since it presupposed the Davidic covenant of 2 Samuel 7, though one might imagine a celebration of a confirmation ritual of the dynastic succession secured in that covenant.

10. For this and other historical issues in this paper, consult I. Provan, V. P. Long, and T. Longman III, *A Biblical History of Israel* (Louisville: Westminster John Knox, 2003).

11. Even today non-religious political leaders in America surround their inaugurations with religious trappings.

from Saul, whom I put away from before you. Your house and your kingdom shall be made sure forever before me; your throne shall be established forever" (2 Sam 7:15-16).

For those who were utterly convinced that God would not lie or deceive, they would come to believe that the psalm did more than describe present realities.[12] They would look to the future for a king who would fit the picture of Psalm 2.[13] The fact was, as is often pointed out, that even David and other faithful kings never really fit the picture of the world-dominating feared king of Psalm 2. This would allow for the understanding that Psalm 2 was not being understood in a completely new way, but rather that the later audience was now discerning the deeper meaning of the poem. Later we will contemplate the hermeneutics of such a change in reading.

Messianism and the Shape of the Psalter

Now again, let me say that I am looking at Psalm 2 as a single example of a genre of royal psalms that I am suggesting would be understood by some at least in a different way toward the end of the Old Testament time period. Gerald Wilson and others want to go even further and suggest that this later messianic reading of the psalms shaped the very structure and order of the Psalms. Before continuing, I want to pause to comment on this approach to the book.

In the 1980s Brevard Childs suggested that there might be some rationale to the arrangement of the Psalms;[14] and, in a brilliant analysis, his student Gerald Wilson carried through the program of his mentor in his

---

12. This seems to be what W. Horbury, *Jewish Messianism and the Cult of Christ* (London: SCM Press, 1998), is getting at when he says, "'Messianism' owes its own continuing influence throughout the Second Temple period in large part to the convergence between its thematic importance in the Hebrew Scriptures and the pressures of contemporary Jewish life" (5).

13. K. Heim, "The Perfect King of Psalm 72: An 'Intertextual' Inquiry," in Satterthwaite et al., eds., *The Lord's Anointed*, 224, identifies this as C. Westermann's view as expressed in *The Living Psalms* (Edinburgh: T&T Clark, 1989) 56-57, in R. E. Clements, "The Messianic Hope in the Old Testament," *JSOT* 43 (1989) 3-19, and in M. J. Selman, "Messianic Mysteries," in Satterthwaite et al., eds., *The Lord's Anointed*, 281-302.

14. B. S. Childs, *Introduction to the Old Testament as Scripture* (Philadelphia: Fortress, 1979) 511-13.

published dissertation *The Editing of the Hebrew Psalter*[15] and numerous studies that followed.

Elsewhere I provide an extensive description and critique of Wilson's views,[16] but for our purposes I will be relatively brief. Pivotal to his understanding of the structure and its meaning is his belief that certain key psalms are placed at what he calls the seams of the Psalter. The seams are the opening and closing psalms of the five "Books" of the Psalms, or at least selective examples of such. What strikes Wilson is the occurrence of psalms that seem to have to do with the Davidic covenant. Psalm 2 is the first such; while not mentioning David even in the title nor mentioning the covenant, it is connected to the covenant because of the language we have already noted that alludes to 2 Samuel 7. Wilson believes that this psalm announces the Davidic covenant. Psalm 41, which closes Book 1, is taken as a statement of confidence in the Davidic covenant — this in spite of the fact that the covenant is not mentioned or alluded to in the body of the psalm.

While Wilson does not comment on the opening composition of Book 2 as relevant, he does believe the closing psalm, 72, is. This psalm is a psalm of Solomon according to the title, but he treats it as a psalm of David and a prayer for Solomon. He believes that this psalm provides for the passing on of the covenant promises from David to his son.

When we come to the end of Book 3, for the first time the concern with the Davidic covenant becomes explicit. According to Wilson, Psalm 89 is about "a covenant remembered but a covenant failed. The Davidic covenant introduced in Ps 2 has come to nothing and the combination of three books concludes with the anguished cry of the Davidic descendants."[17]

Here I will introduce my first critical remark about this project. If the redactors of the Psalter wanted us to think this is a cry of Davidic descendants at the time they sensed the failure of the covenant, presumably later in history, why would they attribute the book to Ethan the Ezrahite who is mentioned in 1 Kings 4 as a renowned wise man at the time of Solomon, perhaps implying that he established his fame during David's reign? Also, it seems too harsh to say that this psalm is about the failure of the Davidic

15. G. H. Wilson, *The Editing of the Hebrew Psalter* (Chico, CA: Scholars Press, 1985).

16. In "Narrative Impulses in the Interpretation of the Psalms, Proverbs, and Song of Songs: A Reappraisal," the 2002 Brownlee lecture, sponsored by the Institute for Antiquity and Christianity, held at Claremont Graduate University, April 18, 2002.

17. Wilson, *Editing of the Hebrew Psalter*, 213.

covenant. The hope implied in the appeal to God makes it clear that the psalmist does not think the covenant has failed; God just needs to be goaded into action by this extreme language. Further, reaching back now to his comments about Psalms 2 and 41, I am somewhat troubled that neither of these psalms is explicitly Davidic nor concerned with the covenant.

With these criticisms in mind, let's continue with Wilson's theory. We pick up the account with Book 4, which is taken by Wilson as the answer to the dilemma expressed by Psalm 89 at the end of Book 3. It asserts Yahweh as king and particularly our refuge (a theme picked up and developed by Jerome Creach).[18] So it is a call to trust Yahweh now that the monarchy is gone.

As for Book 5, Wilson does not believe that this section could be as ingeniously edited as the other books since a number of psalms came into the collection via preexistent groups. In conclusion he states that this fifth book is an answer to the "plea of the exiles to be gathered from the diaspora."[19] The answer is to trust and depend on Yahweh.

Thus, Wilson sees a development within the structure of the Psalter from a confident assertion of Davidic covenant to its failure and then a reassertion of hope in Yahweh's kingship in the absence of the monarchy. In other words, the shape of the Psalter takes on messianic proportions, since Wilson also describes a connection with David here.

> Following the lead of Psalm 107 it seems that in some sense the fifth book was intended to stand as an answer to the plea of the exiles to be gathered from the diaspora. The answer given in that deliverance and life thereafter is dependent on that attitude of dependence and trust on YHWH alone. David is seen modeling his attitude of reliance and dependence in Pss 108–110 and 138–145 and is rewarded with YHWH's protection. Throughout, emphasis falls on YHWH's power and former acts of mercy as evidence of trustworthiness. This attitude of dependence on YHWH will issue in obedience to his Law as set forth in Ps 119 which is to serve as man's guide on the way of righteousness and life.[20]

18. J. Creach, *Yahweh as Refuge and the Editing of the Hebrew Psalter* (Sheffield: Sheffield Academic Press, 1996).

19. Wilson, *Editing of the Hebrew Psalter,* 227.

20. Wilson, *Editing of the Hebrew Psalter,* 227. Indeed, Wilson's concept of the editorial shaping of the Psalter has moved toward a more explicit statement of its messianic intentions. In one of his most recent articulations of his views, he recognizes a two-stage process. Accepting the view of C. Rösel (*Die messianische Redaktion des Psalters: Studien zu*

I have already raised some of the many questions we may have about this proposed macrostructure to the book of Psalms. For instance, his interpretation of certain key psalms (41 and 89, for instance) is questionable and raises suspicion of an attempt to make them fit his theory. Further, to make this scheme work, Wilson must be selective in the psalms he chooses to include in his analysis. A number of the "seam" psalms work against his ideas, so he simply ignores them (42 and 73, for example). In addition, there are psalms that explicitly speak of the Davidic covenant that are ignored in his work. For instance, Psalm 132 is not discussed, but it is a Davidic psalm that is positive about the relationship between the Davidic king and Yahweh in a way that Wilson's theory would not lead us to suspect.

One final and, in my opinion, devastating difficulty with his approach to Psalter structure is that there is no explicit statement or guidance of editorial grouping. Wilson makes a lot of use of what he recognizes as implicit, subtle indicators. He, of course, is aware that there are no explicit indicators of editorial organization except for Ps 72:20.

My question is: If the arrangement were so important to the meaning of the book as a whole, wouldn't it be more likely that explicit indicators would be built into the text? Moreover, if his idea of structure were implicitly understood among the early redactors and the early receptors of the material so that an explicit comment was not necessary, the case would be supported if we had some early rabbinic statements that showed awareness of this. I am unaware of such comments, though not an expert on this material, but I would expect that Wilson and other supporters would make much of such a comment if they were aware of it.

Furthermore, when we take a close look at the one explicit indicator of editorial arrangement, namely Ps 72:20, if anything it indicates a nonchalant attitude toward organization. This verse announces the conclusion to the psalms of David, even though there are a number of Davidic psalms

---

Enstehung und Theologie der Sammlung Psalm 2–89 [Stuttgart: Dalwer Verlag, 1999]), he believes that there was a stage of the Psalter that included Psalms 2–89. The presence of Psalm 2 at the head of this collection would already have given it a messianic feel. However, it would lead to an expectation of the restoration of the human monarchy. But the addition of Books 4 and 5 moves this expectation toward a divine messianic kingship. See G. Wilson, "Psalms and Psalter: Paradigm for Biblical Theology," in *Biblical Theology: Retrospect and Prospect* (ed. Scott Hafemann; Downers Grove, IL: InterVarsity Press, 2002) 100–110. Psalm 132 plays a more significant role in his most recent analysis than in his original work.

to follow. It is an explicit organizational feature that does not work any longer, but is nonetheless retained.

In a later article Wilson criticizes John H. Walton[21] for letting a hypothesis drive his conclusions as he tries to determine his own version of what the arrangement of psalms signifies. Wilson rightly responds that it is too easy to make it work. I respectfully suggest, however, that Wilson himself is guilty of the same charge. Granted, his hypothesis is not as specific as others. His hypothesis is simply that there is an arrangement. However, this general hypothesis is actually much easier to make work than the specific ones offered by Walton, Arens, and Goulder. Once that hypothesis is made there is no question but an answer will be found. The fact that this arrangement was not noticed before 1985 should make us pause and suggest that it was imposed rather than described from what is there.

Back to the Pentateuch

To summarize our argument thus far, we have recognized that the concept of "anointed priest" in the Pentateuch and "anointed king" in the Psalms always refers to the contemporary human king. This seems to be an accurate reading of the intention of the author and its first reception. However, with the failure of the monarchy and in the light of the promise to David of an eternal dynasty, the thoughts of some would have turned to the possibility of a future anointed king.

As such thoughts arose in the mind of later readers of the text, this would color their understanding of other texts concerning kingship, even in those places where "anointed" is not explicit. In particular, texts in the Pentateuch that anticipate a future king would be read in a new way. I believe that this explains how later audiences understood texts like Gen 49:10 and Num 24:17:

> The scepter shall not depart from Judah,
>   nor the ruler's staff from between his feet,
> until tribute comes to him;
>   and the obedience of the peoples is his.

(Gen 49:10)

21. See G. Wilson, "Psalms and Psalter," citing J. H. Walton, "Psalms: A Cantata about the Davidic Covenant," *JETS* 34 (1991) 21-31.

From the historical context of Jacob's last will and testament for his sons, it is hard not to think that this oracle anticipates the rise of the Davidic dynasty. It is not anticipating a future eschatological figure beyond David and his dynasty.[22] The same may be said for the Numbers passage:

> I see him, but not now;
>> I behold him, but not near —
> a star shall come out of Jacob,
>> and a scepter shall rise out of Israel;
> it shall crush the borderlands of Moab,
>> and the territory of all the Shethites.
>
> (Num 24:17)

Balaam's oracle again anticipates the rise of the monarchy in Israel, but after the failure of the monarchy the idea that it anticipated a greater king who would derive from the Davidic line might have captured the imagination of the people.

Warrior King and Priest?
Rereading Genesis 14 and Psalm 110

Psalm 110 is certainly the most enigmatic song in the collection and, perhaps for the same reason, also the most cited in the New Testament (Matt 22:41-45 [and parallels]; 1 Cor 15:25; Heb 1:3; 5:6; 7:17, 21). One of the main reasons why this psalm is so difficult has to do with the divine declaration that the king is a "priest forever according to the order of Melchizedek" (v. 4). With this we have a difficult psalm citing an obscure event from Genesis 14.

The psalm begins with a divine oracle directed to the king who is the psalmist's lord to the effect that he will subdue the king's enemies. This or-

---

22. T. D. Alexander, "Messianic Ideology in the Book of Genesis," in Satterthwaite et al., eds., *The Lord's Anointed*, 19-39, suggests that, when understood within the broader narrative of Genesis with its emphasis on the preservation of the seed of Judah, Gen 49:8-12 refers beyond David and Solomon to a messianic figure. He also believes that the language of the subjugation of the "peoples" (v. 10b) refers to something beyond David's accomplishments. However, I believe he reads too much into the text, at least as understood within the context of the original author and audience of Genesis.

acle also reveals that the king is one who has assumed a position of power and honor at God's right hand.

The proclamation of the king as a priest according to the order of Melchizedek comes after the psalmist assures the king of Yahweh's commission that he should lead his people in battle. The poem ends with the assurance that God is with the king and his army with the result that he will successfully render violent judgment on the nations.

But why is the king associated with priesthood, and why specifically the priesthood of Melchizedek? Other texts express concern that kings not assume priestly prerogatives (1 Sam 13:8-15). However, Melchizedek does provide a precedent for a priest-king, and one who greets Abraham after successful holy war and receives a portion of the plunder. Melchizedek provides a pretext for attributing to the king priestly functions without blurring the distinction between the kingship and Aaronic priesthood.

Understood in this way, Psalm 110, like Psalm 2, may be understood either as a coronation psalm or as a pre–holy war song. The title attributes the psalm to David; and, though the historical narrative never declares that David was a priest, he sometimes acted like a priest (2 Samuel 6) and his sons are called priests in an admittedly enigmatic verse (2 Sam 8:18).

The point is that Psalm 110 is not an obvious exception to the rule established above or to my understanding of the rereading of the psalms in the light of the demise of the monarchy. Here, though, we learn that God promised David not only an eternal dynasty but also a priesthood that will last forever. Furthermore, this priest-king is a warrior.

The Coming Warrior

So far we have looked at texts in the Torah and Writings that are not explicitly eschatological.[23] I want to turn our attention now to Daniel, also of course in the Writings. The second part of the book (chapters 7–12) is ostensibly eschatological,[24] and included in its vision of the future is the in-

---

23. I am using the term "eschatological" in the narrow sense here. Genesis 49:8-12 and Num 24:7 are explicitly eschatological in the sense that they looked to the future establishment of the Davidic monarchy.

24. Of course, there are differences even among evangelical scholars on this. Compare J. Goldingay, *Daniel* (WBC; Waco: Nelson, 1989), and T. Longman III, *Daniel* (NIVAC; Grand Rapids: Zondervan, 1999).

trusion of a warrior king who will liberate his people from bondage to evil human kingdoms. Most memorable is the description of the one like the son of man appearing on the clouds of heaven:

> I saw one like a human being
>> coming with the clouds of heaven.
> And he came to the Ancient One
>> and was presented before him.
> To him was given dominion
>> and glory and kingship,
> that all peoples, nations, and languages
>> should serve him.
> His dominion is an everlasting dominion
>> that shall not pass away,
> and his kingship is one
>> that shall never be destroyed.
>
> (Dan 7:13-14)

This fascinating text shares a similar eschatological hope of future deliverance with other late biblical prophetic voices (Zechariah 14; Malachi 4). It is clear that in the future a warring king would appear, commissioned by God (the Ancient of Days) to battle the evil human kingdoms represented by the hybrid beasts in the first part of the vision. What is particularly intriguing about the description of this figure is that there are hints that this king himself is divine. What I am referring to is the description of the figure riding the cloud. This image has an ancient pedigree, of course, extending back into ancient Near Eastern mythological texts that describe the war god, typically a storm god, riding a cloud into battle. One thinks immediately of the cloud-rider Baal. In a number of poetic and prophetic texts, Yahweh is described as riding the cloud into battle (Pss 18:10-13; 68:33; 104:3; Isa 19:1; Nah 1:3). Thus, the human appearance of the chariot rider is especially deserving of note.

A Prophetic Messiah?

Though the textual evidence is even subtler than that concerning a messianic warrior-king and priest, the New Testament's use of Deuteronomy 18 raises a question about whether we should talk about the rise of a messianic prophetic figure. The dynamic appears to me to be much the same.

Deuteronomy 18:15-22 announces that God will raise up a prophet like Moses for the people of Israel. While the expectation is expressed in terms of a singular prophet, this singular is rightly understood as a collective singular since the people's request for a mediating spokesperson that leads to this promise is a constant need. In other words, Deuteronomy 18 understood within its ancient context may be perfectly explainable in terms of the rise of the prophetic movement and prophets like Samuel, Elijah, Elisha, Isaiah, and so on.

However, even the post-Mosaic redactor of Deuteronomy 34 states that "there has never been another prophet like Moses" (Deut 34:10). As we look at the rest of the Old Testament, in other words, we see that there are prophets like Moses in the sense of sharing the characteristics of Moses as prophet,[25] but none that are "like Moses" in the sense of his preeminence. Numbers 12:3-8 also seems to indicate this when it says that, while God speaks to Moses face to face, he speaks to the prophets by "visions and dreams."

In any case, Acts 3:17-23 and 7:37 allude to Deuteronomy 18 and cite Jesus as the (singular) Prophet that that passage anticipated. What seems to be happening here is an exploitation of the fact that the expectation was expressed by means of a singular, collective though it may be.[26]

We may grant all this and still question whether it is a specifically messianic idea. The grounds for believing so are simply based on the occasional evidence that prophets, like priests and kings, were anointed for their task (1 Kgs 19:16; Isa 61:1-2; Ps 105:15).

Expectation at the Close of the Old Testament Time Period

What then was the expectation of a Messiah at the close of the Old Testament time period? What should it have been?

Intertestamental and New Testament literature suggests that expec-

---

25. Notice that the call of Jer 1:4-10 has an echo of the call of Moses in order to make that connection.

26. Of course, the way Galatians 3 applies the Abrahamic promise of a seed to Jesus is analogous.

tation was all over the map.[27] Some Jewish people did not expect a Messiah. Others thought that the Messiah would be a priestly figure, still others a royal deliverer. Some scholars interpret the evidence to suggest that at least one group of Jewish thinkers believed there would be two messiahs, one priestly and one royal.

From what we know we can be certain that the New Testament did not create the idea of the Messiah. But we can also be sure that there was nothing like a commonly agreed delineation of what the Messiah would be like. The latter point means that modern-day Christians who shake their heads about why the Jewish people did not universally recognize the Messiah, considering all the fulfilled prophecy, really do not understand Old Testament literature.

Indeed, we can illustrate the lack of clarity of expectation by appeal to John the Baptist. What was he expecting?

> Even now the ax is lying at the root of the trees; every tree therefore that does not bear good fruit is cut down and thrown into the fire. . . . I baptize you with water for repentance, but one who is more powerful than I is coming after me; I am not worthy to carry his sandals. He will baptize you with the Holy Spirit and fire. His winnowing fork is in his hand, and he will clear his threshing floor and will gather his wheat into the granary; but the chaff he will burn with unquenchable fire. (Matt 3:10-12)

John expects the Messiah to be a warrior in the tradition of Daniel 7, Zechariah 14, and Malachi 4. We can understand his later doubts about Jesus when he hears that he is healing the sick, exorcising demons, and preach-

---

27. At least this seems to be the dominant view of the matter, which as I will argue makes sense of the reaction of people like John the Baptist and the two disciples on the road to Emmaus. This view that there was no unified messianic expectation at the time of Jesus is well represented by the work of J. Neusner, *Messiah in Context: Israel's History and Destiny in Formative Judaism* (Philadelphia: Fortress, 1984) ix-xxiii, 1-16; and J. H. Charlesworth, "From Jewish Messianology to Christian Christology: Some Caveats and Perspectives," in *Judaisms and Their Messiahs at the Turn of the Christian Era* (ed. J. Neusner et al.; Cambridge: Cambridge University Press, 1987) 225-64. Also note the other contributions in *Judaisms and Their Messiahs* as well as the book edited by Charlesworth, *The Messiah: Developments in Earliest Judaism and Christianity* (Minneapolis: Fortress, 1992). For the view that there is a basic coherence in the royal aspect of messianic expectation, see W. Horbury, *Jewish Messianism and the Cult of Christ* (London: SCM Press, 1998).

ing the good news. "Are you the one who is to come, or are we to wait for another?" (Matt 11:3).[28]

Thus, we must acknowledge that the Old Testament did not provide the first century CE with a clear blueprint for the Messiah. If even the forerunner, Jesus' own cousin, feels some cognitive dissonance concerning the relationship between Old Testament expectation and the person and earthly ministry of Jesus, we can understand why others of that generation struggled.

The Surprising Fulfillment

Again, while there was no *agreed upon* specific description of the expected Messiah in the first century CE,[29] there was an expectation and there were common themes to the expectation. Based on what we have seen in the Torah and Writings, those common themes would include kingship, priesthood, and warfare.

Jesus himself provided the focal point that crystallized messiahship in the minds of his followers. His fulfillment may have been surprising, but once they saw him in the light of the resurrection, they knew him. They may not have anticipated him, but after the resurrection the Scriptures fell into place for them. Luke 24 describes two post-resurrection appearances of Christ that illuminate this point.

In the first, Jesus walks with two of his disciples who are utterly confused and dismayed at his recent crucifixion. They do not recognize him;[30] and as they express their consternation, they reveal their previous expectation when they say, "we had hoped that he was the one to redeem Israel" (Luke 24:21). Jesus replies: "Oh, how foolish you are, and how slow of heart

---

28. In his response to my paper delivered at the conference, Craig Evans made the insightful suggestion that John's doubts were not triggered by Jesus' healings and exorcisms, but rather by the fact that since, according to Isaiah 61, the Messiah was going to set the prisoners free, Jesus may not be the Messiah since John is still in prison. Even though this may be a better explanation of John's doubts, it still supports my central idea that John does not understand the meaning of his own prophetic words. In other words there is still a transition from physical to spiritual warfare.

29. A point made by J. H. Charlesworth, "Preface," in Charlesworth, ed., *The Messiah*, xv.

30. "Their eyes were kept from recognizing him" (Luke 24:16).

to believe all that the prophets have declared! Was it not necessary that the Messiah should suffer these things and then enter into his glory?" These words are backed by his appeal to Scripture, when the narrator reports that "beginning with Moses and all the prophets, he interpreted to them the things about himself in all the scriptures" (24:25-26).

Soon thereafter, he appears to a broader group of disciples, and Luke reports the event as follows:

> Then he said to them, "These are my words that I spoke to you while I was still with you — that everything written about me in the law of Moses, the prophets, and the psalms must be fulfilled." Then he opened their minds to understand the scriptures, and he said to them, "Thus it is written, that the Messiah is to suffer and to rise from the dead on the third day, and that repentance and forgiveness of sins is to be proclaimed in his name to all nations, beginning from Jerusalem. You are witnesses of these things. And see, I am sending upon you what my Father promised; so stay here in the city until you have been clothed with power from on high." (Luke 24:44-49)

There is much about this passage that we can debate; however, there are certain things that are clearly delineated here. First, the disciples had an expectation, though it was apparently not clearly formed or accurate. The imperfection of their expectation is implied by their confusion at the time of the crucifixion and also about reports of the empty tomb. Second, Jesus is angry or at least disappointed that they did not know what to expect. After all, he taught them during his earthly ministry. I hope this isn't disrespectful, but he sounds like a peeved professor who has labored to teach his students something that they just haven't understood. Third, he gives them another lesson, a lesson in hermeneutics, that we are to assume they finally understood in the light of the resurrection. From this point on, the disciples cannot read the Old Testament except in the light of the resurrected Jesus.

Hermeneutical Implications

On the basis of this text, I would like to take the opportunity to issue a plea concerning our own Christian reading of the Old Testament. I say this in the light of the reticence among Old Testament scholars, even evangelical Old Testament scholars, to read the Old Testament in the light of the resurrection. From Walter Kaiser to John Walton to John Goldingay, but for different reasons, we hear that it is wrong to "impose" the New Testament onto the Old Testament.[31] I agree that it is necessary for serious study of the Old Testament to begin with the question, difficult enough in itself: How did the Old Testament author(s) and first hearers understand the text? In our study of the concept of the Messiah in the Torah and Writings, we have done just that, concluding that it is highly unlikely that composer(s) and first audience had an inkling of the messianic significance of what they were saying.[32]

However, even before the Christ event, due to the unfolding drama of the history of redemption and the progress of revelation, the reading of this material changed.[33] This climaxes in the crucifixion and resurrection of Christ. Christ himself urges his disciples to understand the Old Testament Scriptures in the light of his person and work.[34]

31. W. Kaiser, *Toward an Exegetical Theology* (Grand Rapids: Baker, 1998); J. Goldingay, *Old Testament Theology: Israel's Gospel* (Downers Grove: InterVarsity Press, 2003). For J. Walton, see how he handles (or doesn't) New Testament allusions to Genesis in his *Genesis* (NIVAC; Grand Rapids: Zondervan, 2002).

32. I am admittedly simplifying the picture here by talking only about the Divine and human author. Actually, the picture is more complicated since many of the biblical books have a history of composition, which means that we should also reflect on the intention of editors. This was pointed out to me by C. Evans in his response to the oral presentation of this paper. However, though not directly addressed in the paper, I would say that later editors would have an increasing sense of the deeper meaning of the text in the light of the unfolding events of redemptive history.

33. Note J. G. McConville's insightful comment in regard to a developing messianic understanding of certain Old Testament texts: "The interpretation of the Old Testament is not a one-way, but a two-way flow, in which contemporary situations were compared with the Scriptures, and the Scriptures were then brought to bear, sometimes in (to us) unexpected ways, on the situations. The Old Testament, indeed, underwent a good deal of reinterpretation even as hopes of deliverance were being worked out." See McConville, "Messianic Interpretation of the Old Testament in Modern Context," in Satterthwaite et al., eds., *The Lord's Anointed*, 13.

34. The comments of P. Jenson ("Models of Prophetic Prediction," 211) on Matthew's quotation of Mic 5:2 are relevant here: "The adaptation of the quotation thus displays a creativity and a faithfulness that is impressive. The verse is not regarded as an apologetic joker that will merely prove the messiahship of Jesus. Rather, it is a flexible entity that can be adapted in order to draw out the significance of Micah's prophecy and link it with other texts that speak of the person and work of the promised king."

This perspective, of course, raises the much vexed and recently discussed question of the locus of meaning of a text. It may sound as if I am moving from an authorial-based interpretation to a reader-based approach, but I am not. Rather, I am suggesting that, though the human authors "spoke better than they knew" (cf. 1 Pet 1:10-12), there is another Author whose intentions come to perfect fulfillment. If one wants to call this *sensus plenior*, I have no objection.[35]

But let me conclude by reflecting on the words of John the Baptist, which I commented upon earlier. He spoke of the coming of a violent Messiah, but what he was thinking as he "authored" these words was thrown into question when Jesus began his ministry of healing and preaching the Good News. Rather than slaying sinners and Gentiles, he was perceived as their "friend" (Matt 11:19).

Does that mean that the words of John were incorrect because they did not conform to his conscious understanding (intention)? Not at all. In the first place, Jesus' actions during his earthly ministry can be seen as an act of violence in the spiritual realm. As Susan Garrett has pointed out, the exorcisms are a form of holy war.[36] Paul understands Jesus' death and resurrection (Col 2:13-15) and his ascension (Eph 4:7-10, citing the holy war psalm, 68) as a military victory. Indeed, it inaugurates a period of spiritual

---

35. W. Kaiser and J. Sailhamer, both defenders of lodging the meaning of a text in the conscious intention of the human author, must labor mightily or simply ignore more obvious interpretations as they exegete these texts in a way that suggests that the original authors actually were thinking of a future messianic figure like Jesus. For instance, Kaiser does not even interact with the most obvious possibility that Genesis 49 and Numbers 24 refer to the future Davidic monarchy coming from the tribe of Judah; rather, he simply presumes that the Messiah was in mind (Kaiser, *The Messiah in the Old Testament* [Grand Rapids: Zondervan, 1995] 50-57). Note Kaiser's comment about Old Testament messianic texts that a "straightforward understanding and application of the text leads one straight to the Messiah and to Jesus of Nazareth, who has fulfilled everything these texts said about his first coming" (232).

J. Sailhamer argues that the narrative of the Pentateuch is set within a poetic framework and that the narrative needs to be interpreted through the lens of these intentionally placed poems. These poems are each marked with the phrase "in the last days," thus giving the Pentateuch an eschatological significance. He argues this way to posit a connection between Jesus and the Pentateuch's promise of a future king in texts like Genesis 49 and Numbers 24. See Sailhamer, *Old Testament Theology: A Canonical Approach* (Grand Rapids: Zondervan, 1995).

36. S. R. Garrett, *The Demise of the Devil: Magic and the Demoniac in Luke's Writings* (Minneapolis: Augsburg Fortress, 1989).

holy war in which the church participates (Eph 6:10-20). But even more significantly, Jesus' own words (Matthew 24; Mark 13; Luke 21), the epistles, and Revelation indicate that Jesus' earthly ministry was phase one of a two-phase redemptive work. Indeed, the divine warrior will return and bring final judgment against God's human and spiritual enemies (Rev 19:11-21 being a particularly salient example).

Conclusion

This paper has examined the theme of the Messiah in the Torah and the Writings. The study has been necessarily selective, though I think illustrative.[37] If I had restricted my study to the intention of the human authors or the reception of its first readers, this would have been a short paper indeed. However, redemptive events and later fuller revelation reveal a more profound intention at work, one recognized by the New Testament authors and applied to Jesus of Nazareth. Read in the light of that fuller meaning, this paper is shorter than it could be, choosing just a handful of examples to illustrate the point. Indeed, in final analysis, I believe that we should understand the entire Old Testament in the light of Jesus Christ.

37. If this were an exhaustive study, we would have included an analysis of recent attempts to discern the messianism of Chronicles (e.g., H. G. M. Williamson, "The Dynastic Oracle in the Books of Chronicles," in *Isac Leo Seeligmann,* vol. 3 [ed. A. Rofe and Y. Zakovitch; Jerusalem: Magnes, 1983] 305-18) and also explored the potential connection between wisdom and messiah. Though the sage is never described as anointed with oil, wisdom is connected with an endowment of the Holy Spirit and in that sense may be described as anointed. A recent interesting attempt to see the themes of wisdom and messiah played out in Ecclesiastes may be seen in R. Perrin, "Messianism in the Narrative Frame of Ecclesiastes?" *RB* 108 (2001) 37-60.

Figuring the Future:
The Prophets and Messiah

Mark J. Boda

Defining Messiah, Defining Our Study

For an Old Testament scholar to venture into a study of Messiah is a daring act indeed, especially in light of the following comment by Ron Clements: "virtually all of the major books on Old Testament theology say very little at all about such messianic hope and, even when they do, do so in a very guarded and circumscribed way."[1] The reason for its absence in Old Testament theologies is obvious if one accepts the dominant view of the Old Testament evidence, expressed for example by Roland Murphy long ago:

> It is a fact that the term "messiah," as a *terminus technicus* designating the ideal king who was to come, does not occur in the Old Testament. It received this connotation only towards the beginning of the Christian era, whereas in itself it means merely the "anointed," referring to kings and priests.[2]

With such a strong consensus evident within Old Testament scholarship in the twentieth century, is there any use in proceeding further?

Part of the challenge that faces us revolves around this issue of "ter-

---

1. R. E. Clements, "The Messianic Hope in the Old Testament," *JSOT* 43 (1989) 3-19, here 4, noting exceptions in Childs and Schmidt.

2. R. E. Murphy, "Notes on Old Testament Messianism and Apologetics," *CBQ* 19 (1957) 5-15, here 5. In footnote 3 he adds: "It is not likely that Ps 2,2 and Dn 9,25 are exceptions to this statement."

minus technicus," cited by Murphy. This was highlighted by Magne Sæbø, who, when addressing the issue of messianism and eschatology, noted: the "problem of terminology is, moreover, a problem of the right *point of departure,* for the final result depends very much on where the starting point lies which determines the way ahead."[3] Thus, before we can consider the topic of the Messiah in Hebrew prophecy, it is essential that we carefully define the study and its attendant terms. What then do we mean by "Messiah"?

On the one hand, John J. Collins defines "Messiah" as "a future figure who will play an authoritative role in the end time, usually the eschatological king," while James H. Charlesworth (on behalf of his colloquium), on the other, concludes that this term refers "to a present, political and religious leader who is appointed by God, applied predominantly to a king, but also to a priest and occasionally a prophet."[4] Slipping somewhere between these two is Walter H. Rose, who defines it as "a future royal figure sent by God who will bring salvation to God's people and the world and establish a kingdom characterized by features like peace and justice."[5]

---

3. M. Sæbø, "Zum Verhältnis von 'Messianismus' und 'Eschatologie' im Alten Testament: Ein Versuch terminologischer und sachlicher Klärung," in *Der Messias* (ed. I. Baldermann, E. Dassmann, O. Fuchs, and B. Hamm; Jahrbuch für biblische Theologie; Neukirchen-Vluyn: Neukirchener Verlag, 1993) 25-55; translated as M. Sæbø, "On the Relationship between 'Messianism' and 'Eschatology' in the Old Testament: An Attempt at a Terminological and Factual Clarification," in *On the Way to Canon: Creative Tradition History in the Old Testament* (ed. M. Sæbø; JSOTSup; Sheffield: Sheffield Academic Press, 1998) 197-231; see similarly John Bright: "A clear definition of terms is always desirable, and that is especially the case here, for the word 'eschatology' as it relates to the Old Testament has been used in more than one way, and this has not infrequently created confusion in the minds of students"; J. Bright, *Covenant and Promise: The Prophetic Understanding of the Future in Pre-exilic Israel* (Philadelphia: Westminster, 1976) 18.

4. J. J. Collins, *The Scepter and the Star: The Messiahs of the Dead Sea Scrolls and Other Ancient Literature* (AB Reference Library; New York: Doubleday, 1995) 11; J. H. Charlesworth, ed., *The Messiah: Developments in Earliest Judaism and Christianity* (Minneapolis: Fortress, 1987) xv. Charlesworth was citing the endorsement of the members of the colloquium on the use of the term "Messiah" in the Old Testament; see J. J. M. Roberts, "The Old Testament's Contribution to Messianic Expectations," in the same volume, 31-51. I am thankful to Thomas Thompson for drawing my attention to this work: T. L. Thompson, "The Messiah Epithet in the Hebrew Bible," *SJOT* 15 (2001) 57-92, here 57.

5. W. H. Rose, *Zemah and Zerubbabel: Messianic Expectations in the Early Postexilic Period* (JSOTSup; Sheffield: Sheffield Academic Press, 2000) 23; I am indebted to Dan Block for drawing my attention to the definitions of Collins and Rose: D. I. Block, "My Servant

These three definitions highlight the difficulty of finding a definitive starting point for this study. Points of divergence are obvious: Is this a present, future, or eschatological figure? Is this a royal, priestly, or prophetic figure? These questions reveal the multidimensional character of any definition of a figure called "Messiah."

First of all, this figure is defined according to a particular sociological role. For Collins and Rose this figure is royal, while for J. J. M. Roberts this figure is predominantly royal but could also be priestly or prophetic. Second, this figure is defined according to a temporal reference. For Roberts the figure is present, while for Rose and Collins the figure is future. Third, even the temporal future can be nuanced further: for while both Rose and Collins speak of a future figure, the latter characterizes this future as qualitatively "eschatological" and "end time."

The reason for this divide within scholarship is related, at least partially, to the historical and literary evidence that is under purview. The focus of Roberts's study was the Hebrew Bible; for Rose it was the late prophetic books; while for Collins it was Second Temple Judaism and Christianity. Nevertheless, it is important that we at least identify what we mean by our terms even if we are focusing on different textual and temporal evidence. In order to do that, a closer look at both the sociological role and temporal reference is in order; and there is no better place to start than with the Hebrew semantic range that gave messianic expectation its terminology.

Sociological Role

Semantic Range of māšah

The verbal root *māšah*, the adjectival form *māšîah*, and the nominal forms *mašhāh* and *mishāh* occur 130 times in the Old Testament.[6] Of these words *mašhāh* is the most obscure, occurring only once in Num 18:8 to refer to "consecrated portion," a gloss also found for *mishāh* on two occasions

---

David: Ancient Israel's Vision of the Messiah," in *Israel's Messiah in the Bible and the Dead Sea Scrolls* (ed. R. S. Hess and M. Daniel Carroll R.; Grand Rapids: Baker Academic, 2003) 17-56, here 23.

    6. *māšah* (37x), *māšîah* (68x), *mašhāh* (1x), and *mishāh* (24x); notice also the related term *mimšah* in Ezek 28:14 in reference to an angelic being.

(both in Lev 7:35). Usually *mišḥāh* is found in a collocation with *šemen* (oil) to signify the "ointment" used to consecrate the priests (e.g., Exod 25:6; Lev 8:2, 10, 12, 30). The verbal root *māšaḥ* is used in a more generic way to refer to the act of smearing a substance (usually oil) on something else. Thus, it is used for applying oil to a weapon (Isa 21:5; 2 Sam 1:21) or cakes (Exod 29:2; Lev 2:5; 7:12; Num 6:15), but also for applying perfumes/ointments to one's body (Amos 6:6) or paint to a house (Jer 22:14). Nevertheless, it is used most commonly in ceremonial rituals connected with consecrating sacred objects (altar, vessel), buildings (tabernacle, temple), and especially people to an office or role within Israel. The semantic range of the adjective *māšîaḥ* is nearly restricted to this final gloss: that is, to describe people who are consecrated to an office or role within Israel.

King, Priest, and Prophets

It is interesting that the verbal and adjectival forms are both connected with three key sociological functionaries within Israel's texts: king, priest, and prophet.[7] As noted by Collins, Rose, and Roberts above, the most common use of these two forms is in reference to the royal stream. The monarch is anointed as well as called the anointed one.

> *māšaḥ:* Jdg 9:8; 9:15; 1 Sam 9:16; 10:1; 15:1, 17; 16:3, 12, 13; 2 Sam 2:4, 7; 3:39; 5:3 (= 1 Chron 11:3); 5:17; 12:7; 2 Sam 19:11; 1 Kgs 1:34, 39, 45; 5:15; 19:15, 16; 2 Kgs 9:3, 6, 12; 11:12; 23:30; 2 Chron 22:7; 23:11; 29:22; Ps 89:21 [Eng 20]; 45:8 [Eng 7] (Niphal: 1 Chron 14:8).
>
> *māšîaḥ:* 1 Sam 2:10, 35; 12:3, 5; 16:6; 24:7[2x], 11; 26:9, 11, 16, 23; 2 Sam 1:14, 16; 19:22; 23:1; Pss 2:2; 18:51 (= 2 Sam 22:51); 20:7; 28:8; 84:10; 89:39, 52; 132:10 (= 2 Chron 6:42), 17; Isa 45:1; Lam 4:20; Dan 9:25-26.[8]

However, Roberts was correct to note the priestly connection because references to priests and anointing are the second most abundant, with spe-

---

7. Uncertain is the evidence of two passages: Hab 3:13 and Ps 28:8. In the first *'am* (people) is paralleled with *māšîaḥ*, but one cannot assume that these are to be equated, for the two lines may be referring to two different entities that were saved: (1) the people as a whole, and (2) an anointed leader. In the second, people and anointed one are in a couplet, and most likely it refers to the people as a separate entity from the anointed.

8. For this evidence see BDB.

cial focus on the high priest as the one anointed and called the anointed one.

> *māšaḥ*: Exod 28:41; 29:7, 29; 30:30; 40:13, 15^{3x}; Lev 7:36; 8:12; 16:32; Num 3:3; 35:25; 1 Chron 29:22 (Niphal: Lev 6:13)[9]
> *māšîaḥ*: Lev 4:3, 5, 16; 6:15

Finally, although rare, there are texts that indicate that prophets are also anointed and considered anointed ones. In particular, alongside a reference to the anointing of a royal figure (Jehu), 1 Kgs 19:16 refers to Elijah anointing Elisha "as prophet in your place." Many have suggested that the figure in Isa 61:1 who is "anointed" is a prophetic figure because of his role of proclamation. Furthermore, Ps 105:15 (//1 Chron 16:22) parallels the plural of *māšîaḥ* with "my prophets."[10] This evidence then reveals that the terminology associated with the Hebrew root *māšaḥ* was connected with the three major socio-religious functionary streams in Israel: king, priest, prophet.[11]

Timing

The evidence on sociological role confirms Roberts's broader definition of the Messiah in the Old Testament, but it remains to be seen whether his temporal reference can also be accepted. He, along with many Old Testament scholars, has suggested that a close look at the temporal reference when this terminology appears in the Old Testament reveals that the vast majority of the texts are focused on a present figure, with only a couple looking to a future figure (Isa 45:1; 61:1) and possibly only one looking to a figure inaugurating an eschatological era (Dan 9:24-26).

However, there are reasons to question this conclusion. First of all,

---

9. Or things sacred, tabernacle, vessels: Gen 31:13; Num 7:1; Exod 29:36; 30:26; 40:9, 10, 11; Lev 8:10, 11; Dan 9:24 (Niphal: altar Num 7:10, 84, 88).

10. This is, indeed, odd as the psalmist is speaking about the patriarchs, but no matter how you understand the connection between the patriarchs and prophets, the fact still remains that the psalmist is linking *māšîaḥ* with prophecy.

11. Even though A. Laato recognizes this, he limits "Messiah" to the royal stream. See Laato, *A Star Is Rising: The Historical Development of the Old Testament Royal Ideology and the Rise of the Jewish Messianic Expectations* (USFISFCJ; Atlanta: Scholars, 1997) 3.

this approach is based on a historicist stance that views the texts of the Old Testament merely as annals of the past. That is, it is assumed that when a text in, for example, the Deuteronomic History employs messianic terminology it is merely recording a past event in which a reference was made to a then present figure (e.g., 2 Sam 22:51). However, although I am confident that the texts of the Deuteronomic History are rooted in the pre-exilic period, many of them were brought into their final form in the exilic period and, as the end of 2 Kings 25 reveals, in a time when there was need for an enduring hope for the reinstitution of at least royal leadership. Or, further, when Psalm 2 makes reference to the "messiah" it is often noted that this psalm finds its *Sitz im Leben* in the coronation ceremony of ancient Judahite kings and thus is referring to a contemporary figure.[12] However, it has long been noted that Psalm 2 joins Psalm 1 as an introduction to the Psalter as a whole and has been placed in this position at a late date after the monarchy was no longer a political reality.[13] It appears that the intention of the editors who drew the Psalter together was to signal a future messianic hope.[14] These two examples show us that, although references to "messianic" figures may have referred to "present" figures in their "original" historical settings, they have been taken up to encourage future hope in a later era. Furthermore, when these texts establish the validity of "anointed" figures in the past and note their enduring quality (especially references to *'ōlām*), they are establishing something that has serious implications for future hope.

Second, if a future orientation can be discerned in references to Messiah in the Old Testament, one may legitimately challenge the distinction that has often been made between simple future and eschatological future. Such a distinction is based on a certain view of time that may have more to do with later temporal conceptions than with ancient Hebrew views of "es-

12. W. H. Brownlee, "Psalms 1-2 as a Coronation Liturgy," *Bib* 52 (1971) 321-36; S. E. Gillingham, "The Messiah in the Psalms: History and the Psalter," in *King and Messiah in Israel and the Ancient Near East* (ed. J. Day; JSOTSup; Sheffield: Sheffield Academic Press, 1998) 209-237.

13. E.g., G. H. Wilson, *The Editing of the Hebrew Psalter* (Chico, CA: Scholars, 1985); G. H. Wilson, "The Use of Royal Psalms at the 'Seams' of the Hebrew Psalter," *JSOT* 35 (1986) 85-94; J. C. McCann, *The Shape and Shaping of the Psalter* (JSOTSup; Sheffield: JSOT, 1993).

14. See also the use of *māšîaḥ* in Pss 89:39 and 132:10, two passages that appear to be offering hope of an enduring and future role for a royal figure by leveraging the Davidic tradition.

chatology." This issue has been long debated among Old Testament scholars, with lines drawn between those who denied that "eschatology" in the sense of the final days was a component in anything but the late proto-apocalyptic texts and others who saw the eschatological as central to prophecy.

Walther Eichrodt clearly differentiated between the priestly and the prophetic, between the official and the charismatic.[15] In his view, the priestly worldview was founded securely on "the concept of permanent order," while the prophetic represented a "radical critique of the status quo." Such a critique led Eichrodt to argue for eschatology as part of the prophetic worldview from the outset: "they look to the break up of the old world, to bring about the beginnings of a new development, the nucleus of a new world-order, and to perfect this into a second creation."[16] Thus, for Eichrodt, there is no use in contrasting the prophetic (or simple future) and the eschatological (eschatological future): "to try to see in eschatology an indifferent or inferior appendix to the prophetic system of thought is a fundamental misunderstanding of prophetism."[17]

Although Eichrodt's distinction between the status quo and the eschatological reflects the general trend within scholarship, this is not true of his fusion of the prophetic and the eschatological. Whereas Eichrodt sees the eschatological at the heart of prophetic religion, Sigmund Mowinckel limits the eschatological to texts that express a clear break between two eras: the "present state of things and the present world order will suddenly come to an end and be superseded by another of an essentially different kind."[18] Although Mowinckel would agree that there is a relationship between the eschatological and the prophetic, he sees this relationship through a traditio-historical lens as he traces the development of prophetism from historically oriented prophecy of the pre-exilic period to the futurism of Deutero-Isaiah. Although Deutero-Isaiah indicates the way that

---

15. W. Eichrodt, *Theology of the Old Testament* (OTL; Philadelphia: Westminster, 1961) 1:385.

16. Eichrodt, *Theology*, 1:385.

17. Eichrodt, *Theology*, 1:385. Eichrodt's distinction between the "status quo" and the "eschatological" reflects the general trend within the scholarly guild. This has been expressed most cogently by O. Plöger and P. D. Hanson, who have argued for distinct sociological groups on the basis of these two categories: theocratic/hierocratic and apocalyptic/eschatological; see p. 51 n. 58, below.

18. S. Mowinckel, *He That Cometh* (Oxford: Oxford University Press, 1958) 125.

ultimately leads from "a purely this-worldly futurism" to eschatology, it is not eschatological because of its national and political character. So also J. P. M. van der Ploeg calls for a stricter definition of eschatology as "the knowledge of the end": "a sudden and definitive end of this era of the world, or even of the world itself, and the ushering in of a new era and a new world."[19] Although many texts, such as Deutero-Isaiah, speak of a "happy future, quite different from the present state of affairs," it is not eschatology in the strict sense. Only Daniel gives us this sense and represents the end of an evolution that was "eschatology in the making."[20]

This appeal to distinct eras as the key to defining eschatology is, however, used by many scholars to support Eichrodt's approach. Johannes Lindblom discerns the eschatological in prophetic material by noting the implication of two eras in the phrases "the days are coming," "on that day," and "at the end of days."[21] John Bright argues that it is appropriate to use the term "eschatology" when speaking of the prophets, for there he finds "an orientation toward the future, a future hope, that was characteristic and unique. . . . [T]here had already emerged the anticipation of a definitive divine intervention through which God would first bring judgment on this people and then, in the farther future, would deliver them and restore them, and bring his purpose for them to a triumphant conclusion."[22] Although Sæbø sees a distinction between futurism and eschatology, he finds eschatology in the prophets from Amos and Isaiah onward.[23] So also Donald E. Gowan finds eschatology in the Hebrew Bible in "those promises that speak of a future with significant discontinuities from the present."[24]

Gerhard von Rad challenges those who do not find eschatology in the Hebrew Bible because "they say the prophetic predictions do not embrace the idea of an absolute end of time and history."[25] He continues: "To do this, however, is tantamount to applying a concept of time to the prophets'

---

19. J. P. M. van der Ploeg, "Eschatology," in *The Witness of Tradition: Papers Read at the Joint British-Dutch Old Testament Conference Held at Woudschoten, 1970* (ed. A. S. van der Woude; OTS; Leiden: Brill, 1972) 89-99, here 89.

20. Van der Ploeg, "Eschatology," 97.

21. J. Lindblom, *Prophecy in Ancient Israel* (Philadelphia: Fortress, 1962) 360-62.

22. Bright, *Covenant and Promise*, 19.

23. M. Sæbø, "Messianism in Chronicles: Old Testament Background of the New Testament Christology," *HBT* 2 (1980) 85-109, here 96.

24. D. E. Gowan, *Eschatology in the Old Testament* (Philadelphia: Fortress, 1986) 1-2.

25. G. von Rad, *Old Testament Theology* (Edinburgh: Oliver and Boyd, 1962) 2:99-125.

teaching of which they themselves were quite unaware. If, as I have already suggested, this concept of time simply did not exist for the prophets, it is perfectly possible to say that the event which they foretell is a final one even if we, with our different presuppositions, would describe it as still 'within history.'"[26] Thus von Rad is reticent to create sharp distinctions between "Jahweh's action within history and his action at the end of it."[27]

This debate reveals that once one has observed a future orientation within at least some of the "messianic" texts of the Old Testament, the challenge remains as to how one treats this future in the Old Testament and in particular how one defines "eschatology." Those who define "eschatology" in ahistorical, cosmic, cataclysmic, final ways restrict eschatology to late apocalyptic writings in the Hebrew Bible, and even then, as von Rad has noted, "not with absolute precision." However, those who understand eschatology as a future hope that envisions the breaking in of a new era have a greater openness to the presence of this phenomenon in the Old Testament. This latter approach appears more consistent with the evidence of Old Testament expectation.

Beyond Terminology, Defining the Study

Investigations of Messiah within the Old Testament have often been limited to those passages in which either *māšah* or *māšîah* appears. Such a lexically circumscribed agenda has been provided, for example, in the recent articles of Thomas Thompson and Richard S. Hess, both of which contribute greatly to the study of the "messianic" within the Old Testament.[28] These kinds of studies identify passages that use the language associated

26. Von Rad, *Old Testament Theology*, 2:115.

27. Von Rad, *Old Testament Theology*, 2:115; so also G. E. Ladd, "Eschatology," in *The International Standard Bible Encyclopedia* (ed. G. W. Bromiley; Grand Rapids: Eerdmans, 1979) 2:130-43, here 132: "The biblical perspective does not allow for the sharp disjunction between 'history' and 'beyond history' that is often found in contemporary theology. The cleavage between history and eschatology in the Old Testament is never radical, for the God who will reveal Himself by a grandiose theophany in the eschatological consummation has already manifested Himself and does not cease manifesting Himself in the course of history."

28. R. S. Hess, "The Image of the Messiah in the Old Testament," in *Images of Christ: Ancient and Modern* (ed. S. E. Porter, M. A. Hayes, and D. Tombs; Roehampton Institute London Papers; Sheffield: Sheffield Academic Press, 1997) 22-33; Thompson, "Messiah Epithet," 57-82.

with the roots identified above and mine these for attributes or functions attached to these figures either past, present, or future. However, what is often missed in this lexical approach is that the qualities and functions may merely be features of the various (and separate) functionaries with whom they are associated and as a result may tell us nothing about the qualities of *māšîaḥ*.

To explain this, let me use a neutral (but related) example: the "servant of YHWH." It is well known that this "epithet" is used regularly throughout the Old Testament to denote special status for certain religious and civil functionaries within Israel. This term is attached to such luminaries in Israel's history as Abraham, Isaac, Jacob, Moses, Joshua, David, Hezekiah, Eliakim, Zerubbabel, the Suffering figure in Isaiah 40–66, as well as the key groups of prophets (e.g., 2 Kgs 17:13, 23) and Levitical singers (e.g., Pss 113:1; 134:1; 135:1). If we mined these various passages and tried to construct a composite sketch of the "servant," we would find that this figure is one who combined a vast array of functions and qualities. However, most of these functions and qualities really have little to do with the role of "servant"; rather, they have to do with the respective function of these figures as leader, priest, king, or prophet. In the same way, our study above has demonstrated that the terms *māšaḥ* and *māšîaḥ* normally function in the Old Testament as terms denoting the special character of an individual as one consecrated by God for a particular function among God's people; thus, to study the "messiah" or the "messianic" cannot be reduced to an investigation of these lexemes and their attendant texts.[29]

Furthermore, the use of *māšaḥ*/*māšîaḥ* for various functionaries suggests that such terms provided generic language in Hebrew for different kinds of special leadership figures. In light of the role of this word in Hebrew, it is then not surprising that, as Hebrew speakers and writers sought to ex-

---

29. So similarly: J. D. Hays, "If He Looks like a Prophet and Talks like a Prophet, Then He Must Be . . . : A Response to Daniel I. Block," in Hess and Carroll R., eds., *Israel's Messiah in the Bible and the Dead Sea Scrolls*, 57-69: "The image of the messiah and the idea of messianism comprise a broad concept that far outreaches the few instances where the term 'anointed' is used. It is the concept that we are seeking to define, not merely one particular Hebrew word" (60); and, in a much earlier era, H. H. Rowley, "The Suffering Servant and the Davidic Messiah," in *The Servant of the Lord and Other Essays on the Old Testament* (ed. H. H. Rowley; Oxford: Basil Blackwell, 1965) 63-93, here 63: "While the term Messiah, or Christ, does not appear to be actually used of the Davidic descendant in the Old Testament, the concept of the Davidic Messiah is familiar enough."

press future expectations, these terms were employed for describing future ideal leadership figures. Rather than an abuse of Hebrew language and literature, reference to *māšaḥ/māšiaḥ* within Second Temple Judaism and nascent Christianity was actually a natural outgrowth of the Hebrew tradition.[30]

Thus, studying Messiah in the Old Testament need not be so daring an act as expressed at the outset of this section, since the term "Messiah" appears to have been used generically for religious functionaries operative in Hebrew society and tradition, functionaries for whom there was hope of an enduring role. Adopting such an approach to Messiah in the Old Testament does justice to the use of this term, not only on the literary level of the final form of the text, but also within the social context from which these texts have arisen. It also opens the way for greater dialogue with scholars studying the phenomena of Messiah and messianic within Second Temple Judaism and Christianity, as the present volume provides.

Prophets and Messiah

No Old Testament tradition is more closely associated with messianic expectation in popular Jewish and Christian consciousness than the prophets. Such a consciousness is the result of a long history of reflection on the large corpus of prophetic literature. To deal adequately with this literature would require (and has required!) a monograph of its own, and so this article will be more focused. In light of my definition of "Messiah" above, I will investigate the broader phenomenon of "messianism," that is, present description and future expectation of socio-religious functionaries,[31] but will limit this exploration to the final phase of the prophetic corpus, that is, to Haggai-Malachi.

The reason I have chosen this focus is not only due to the limited space of this paper, my own expertise, and the appearance of recent sur-

---

30. Laato, *Star Is Rising*, 3-4, although noting that the Hebrew terminology related to Messiah can be used of king, high priests, and prophets, then explicitly states that the goal of his monograph is to show how this terminology moved from denoting the king chosen by YHWH to "*terminus technicus*, 'Messiah,' for a coming eschatological figure." The broader view of the figure is already seen in the Old Testament; the key is the move to the future and eschatological.

31. I use this terminology to avoid the problem of denoting prophets as filling an "office"; cf. D. L. Petersen, *The Roles of Israel's Prophets* (JSOTSup; Sheffield: JSOT, 1981).

veys on the Messiah in the Old Testament and the Prophets,[32] but more so because of the role that the Haggai-Malachi corpus plays within Hebrew and Christian tradition.

First of all, in historical perspective these books provide records of those who prophesied after the exile to a Jewish community in the midst of the reformulation of faith, religion, and society without the advantage of independent nationhood. These books then offer us a window into the ways the Jewish community's view of leadership was being shaped after the exile. Key trajectories are set in this era that would have a great impact on the faith of Second Temple Judaism, which would in turn provide a context for Christianity. It is well known that these books played a major role in shaping messianic expectation within Second Temple Judaism, nascent Christianity, and beyond, and so it is appropriate to investigate the perspective of these books.[33]

Second, in redactional perspective, recent research on the Book of the Twelve as well as Haggai, Zechariah, and Malachi has advocated that these three books at one time formed an independent corpus that was incorporated into the Book of the Twelve in the final stages of its development.[34] Thus, there is some justification for dealing with this sub-group within prophetism.

---

32. See especially J. J. M. Roberts, "The Old Testament's Contribution to Messianic Expectations," in Charlesworth, ed., *The Messiah*, 31-51; P. E. Satterthwaite, R. S. Hess, and G. J. Wenham, eds., *The Lord's Anointed: Interpretation of Old Testament Messianic Texts* (Tyndale House Studies; Carlisle, UK: Paternoster/Grand Rapids: Baker, 1995); Day, ed., *King and Messiah in Israel;* and Block, "My Servant David," 17-56.

33. For the impact on Judaism and Christianity see M. J. Boda, *Haggai-Zechariah Research: A Bibliographic Survey* (Tools for Biblical Studies; Leiden: DEO Publishing, 2003); M. J. Boda, *Haggai/Zechariah* (NIVAC; Grand Rapids: Zondervan, 2004).

34. Some include Zechariah 9–14 in this Haggai-Malachi corpus (e.g., A. Schart, "Putting the Eschatological Visions of Zechariah in Their Place: Malachi as a Hermeneutical Guide for the Last Section of the Book of the Twelve," in *Bringing out the Treasure: Inner Biblical Allusion and Zechariah 9–14* [ed. M. J. Boda and M. H. Floyd; JSOTSup; Sheffield: Sheffield Academic Press, 2003] 333-43); others do not (e.g., P. L. Redditt, "Zechariah 9–14: The Capstone of the Book of the Twelve," in Boda and Floyd, eds., *Bringing out the Treasure*, 305-32), treating it as the final insertion after the number of books had reached twelve. For a full review of this stream of research, see P. L. Redditt, "Recent Research on the Book of the Twelve as One Book," *CR:BS* 9 (2001) 47-80; P. L. Redditt, "The Work of the Book of the Twelve Seminar," in *Thematic Threads in the Book of the Twelve* (ed. A. Schart and P. Redditt; BZAW; Berlin: de Gruyter, 2003) 1-26; M. J. Boda, "Majoring on the Minors: Recent Research on Haggai and Zechariah," *CBR* 2 (2003) 33-68.

Third, in tradition perspective, these books portray self-awareness of their place in the history of prophetism in particular and revelation in general.[35] Haggai draws on earlier traditions and language from the former and latter prophets as well as the Torah, not only to summon the people to rebuild the temple, but also to paint a picture of a glorious future.[36] Zechariah sums up this Persian period phase well when he introduces his summary of the message of prophetism by referring to the "earlier prophets" (1:4; 7:7) and describes the Torah as the authoritative covenant document (Zech 5:1-4).[37] Zechariah 9–14 is universally recognized as a pastiche of quotations, allusions, and echoes drawn from the Torah and the Former and Latter Prophets.[38] Malachi mines earlier Torah and Prophetic tradition to confront dysfunction and announce a new age, concluding with a call to remember the Torah and to expect Elijah.[39]

Finally, while many Christian scholars assume that the longer prophetic books of Jeremiah, Ezekiel, and especially Isaiah were formative for New Testament Christology, there is an odd absence of influence from these books on the key Gospel passion accounts. For instance, one would expect to see the influence of Isaiah 52–53, one of the key "Suffering Servant" passages (cf. Acts 8:33), but it appears that Luke is the only Gospel that cites Isaiah 52–53 in connection with the crucifixion (Luke 22:37//Isa 53:12). Instead, formative for the suffering of the Messiah are passages from the Psalms (Ps 22//Matt 27:46; Mark 15:34; John 19:24; Ps 41:9//John 13:18; Ps 118//Matt 21:42; Mark 12:10-11) and Zechariah (Zech 11//Matt 27:10; Zech 12//John 19:37; Zech 13//Matt 26:31; Mark 14:27), a fact that encourages a closer study of Zechariah within the prophetic corpus.

Our focus, then, will be on the way in which Haggai, Zechariah, and

35. See a similar approach to this issue of messianism in J. H. Sailhamer, "The Messiah and the Hebrew Bible," *JETS* 44 (2001) 5-23, who mines the later stages of the formation of the Hebrew Bible for messianic hope.

36. J. Kessler, *The Book of Haggai: Prophecy in Early Persian Yehud* (VTSup; Leiden: Brill, 2002).

37. J. E. Tollington, *Tradition and Innovation in Haggai and Zechariah 1–8* (JSOTSup; Sheffield: JSOT, 1993).

38. See Boda and Floyd, eds., *Bringing out the Treasure*.

39. E. M. Meyers, "Priestly Language in the Book of Malachi," *HAR* 10 (1986) 225-37; R. Kugler, *From Patriarch to Priest: The Levi-Priestly Tradition from Aramaic Levi to Testament of Levi* (SBLEJL; Atlanta: Scholars, 1996) 18-21; J. M. O'Brien, *Priest and Levite in Malachi* (SBLDS; Atlanta: Scholars, 1990) 87-106.

Malachi treat socio-religious figures in their own day and then create expectation for such figures in the future.[40]

Haggai-Malachi

Recent Research

Alberto Ferreiro's recent publication of the Ancient Christian Commentary on the Twelve Prophets reveals the fixation of the early church on the books of Haggai, Zechariah, and Malachi as a source for their understanding of Jesus Christ.[41] Such an interest in these books within the Christian community is not surprising, considering the attention afforded these books within the New Testament witness.[42] This in turn is also not exceptional, for one can discern an equal fascination with the eschatological and messianic in Haggai, Zechariah, and Malachi within Second Temple Judaism. Such fascination, however, demands careful assessment. What relationship is there between the later Jewish and Christian appropriation of these books and the original message of the books themselves? In what way can they be sources for messianic and/or eschatological theology?

Reflection over the past decade on these books has offered a range of viewpoints on this issue.[43] For example, in treating Haggai and Zechariah 1–8, Janet Tollington concluded that these prophets affirmed Zerubbabel as the inheritor and representative of the enduring Davidic legacy, even if the latter prophet equally affirmed a diarchic rule of sacral and secular leadership until the reinstitution of independent rule.[44] In contrast, Kenneth Pomykala denies any Davidic royalist or messianic expectation to Haggai or Zechariah (1–8), whether connected to Zerubbabel or the mysterious *ṣemaḥ*,[45] even if these prophets provided the foundation for later messianic

---

40. For a full review of research, see Boda, *Haggai-Zechariah Research*; Boda, *Haggai/Zechariah*.

41. A. Ferreiro, ed., *The Twelve Prophets* (Ancient Christian Commentary: Old Testament; Downers Grove, IL: InterVarsity Press, 2003) 219-313.

42. Cf. Boda, *Haggai-Zechariah Research*, 31-34, 124, 174-78, 241-47; and the introduction to Boda, *Haggai/Zechariah*.

43. See fuller review in Boda, *Haggai-Zechariah Research*, 20-31.

44. Tollington, *Tradition and Innovation*.

45. This term (which is transliterated by some scholars as *Zemah*) will be used

reflection.[46] Antti Laato intertwines evidence from ancient Near Eastern temple rebuilding ceremonies with the Davidic royal traditions to show that Zerubbabel was considered a royal messianic figure in both Haggai and Zechariah. In the latter, however, there is a closer relationship between priestly and royal figures, as can be seen in the "Branch" prophecies (Zech 3; 6) and the two olive trees in Zechariah 4, and in its final form there is "a distinction between the ideal figures of the future (the Branch and the Priest) and the figures of the historical present (Zerubbabel and Joshua)."[47] R. A. Mason, while cautiously affirming evidence of a hope for a Davidic royal renewal in Haggai, suggests that Zechariah's original vision of a priestly-royal diarchy was modified to embrace the emerging theocracy under the priests.[48] Rose rejects a royalist/messianic reading of Hag 2:20-23, but does affirm such for Zechariah 1–8, but only in connection with the "Zemah" figure, who is not equated with Zerubbabel.[49] Thomas Pola interprets Zechariah 1–6 as a document that highlights how the cult, temple, and priesthood are given responsibility for preserving the messianic and eschatological hope.[50] Zerubbabel symbolically affirms this by his involvement in the temple building, and Zechariah trumpets it with his declaration that the priesthood was a sign that a future Messiah would one day emerge (Zech 3:8), a hope preserved by the memorial crown in the temple (Zech 6:14). John Kessler restricts his focus to the book of Haggai, but emphasizes that this book affirms the prophetic stream by highlighting the role and success of the prophetic institution in the early Persian period.[51] In terms of all three

---

throughout this paper to transliterate the Hebrew term that has traditionally been translated as "Branch" in Jer 23:5; 33:15; Zech 3:9; 6:12. The term denotes vegetation or growth, rather than the branch of a tree; cf. Rose, *Zemah and Zerubbabel.*

46. K. E. Pomykala, *The Davidic Dynasty Tradition in Early Judaism: Its History and Significance for Messianism* (SBLEJL; Atlanta: Scholars, 1995) 45-60.

47. Laato, *Star Is Rising,* 202.

48. R. A. Mason, "The Messiah in the Postexilic Old Testament Literature," in Day, ed., *King and Messiah in Israel,* 338-64.

49. Rose, *Zemah and Zerubbabel;* W. Rose, "Messianic Expectations," in *Yahwism After the Exile: Perspectives on Israelite Religion in the Persian Era* (ed. B. Becking and R. Albertz; STAR; Assen: Royal Van Gorcum, 2003) 168-85.

50. T. Pola, *Das Priestertum bei Sacharja: Historische und traditionsgeschichtliche Untersuchungen zur frühnachexilischen Herrschererwartung* (FAT; Tübingen: J. C. B. Mohr [Paul Siebeck], 2002); T. Pola, "Form and Meaning in Zechariah 3," in Becking and Albertz, eds., *Yahwism After the Exile,* 156-67.

51. Kessler, *Book of Haggai.*

functionary streams, Kessler demonstrates that Haggai affirms the enduring validity of all three streams in the Persian period, even if this involved a "hermeneutic of equivalents" that achieved continuity with pre-exilic patterns through "functional equivalents often involving theological compromises."[52] He finds some space between an outright rejection of a royalist reading of Hag 2:20-23 and the opposite messianic reading of the same passage. Thus the royal stream is affirmed, even if for now this would involve a provisional partnership with Persian imperialism.

Similar diversity of opinion is evidenced in the study of royal/messianic tradition in Zechariah 9–14. Some argue for an enduring Davidic royal tradition centered on leadership figures;[53] others see a trend of democratization in which this same tradition is now connected to the entire community;[54] while still others see an abandonment of such traditions in favor of hope in a Divine Warrior enacting salvation alone.[55] In relation to the enduring role of the prophet in Zechariah 9–14, some scholars have concluded that this corpus hails the end of prophecy.[56] In response, others have highlighted the fact that Zechariah 9–14 contains a polemic against false prophecy attached to idolatrous leadership.[57] While there appears to be little explicit focus on the

---

52. Kessler, *Book of Haggai*, 27.

53. E.g., S. L. Cook, "The Metamorphosis of a Shepherd: The Tradition History of Zechariah 11:17 + 13:7-9," *CBQ* 55 (1993) 453-66; C. L. Meyers and E. M. Meyers, "The Future Fortunes of the House of David: The Evidence of Second Zechariah," in *Fortunate the Eyes That See: Essays in Honor of David Noel Freedman in Celebration of His Seventieth Birthday* (ed. A. Beck; Grand Rapids: Eerdmans, 1995) 207-22; I. Duguid, "Messianic Themes in Zechariah 9–14," in Satterthwaite et al., eds., *The Lord's Anointed*, 265-80; W. H. Schmidt, "Hoffnung auf einen armen König. Sach 9,9f. als letzte messianische Weissagung des Alten Testaments," in *Jesus Christus als die Mitte der Schrift. Studien zur Hermeneutik des Evangeliums* (ed. C. Landmesser, H.-J. Eckstein, and H. Lichtenberger; BZNW; Berlin: de Gruyter, 1997) 689-709; Laato, *Star Is Rising*, 208-18.

54. E.g., A. Leske, "Context and Meaning of Zechariah 9:9," *CBQ* 62 (2000) 663-68; cf. Mason, "Messiah," 351-57, who retains a role for the Davidides but with far greater communal emphasis.

55. E.g., Pomykala, *Davidic Dynasty*, 112-26.

56. E.g., D. L. Petersen, *Late Israelite Prophecy: Studies in Deutero-Prophetic Literature and in Chronicles* (SBLMS; Missoula: Scholars, 1977).

57. E.g., E. M. Meyers, "The Crisis of the Mid-Fifth Century BCE: Second Zechariah and the 'End' of Prophecy," in *Pomegranates and Golden Bells: Studies in Biblical, Jewish, and Near Eastern Ritual, Law, and Literature in Honor of Jacob Milgrom* (ed. D. P. Wright, D. N. Freedman, and A. Hurvitz; Winona Lake: Eisenbrauns, 1995) 713-23; E. M. Meyers, "Messianism in First and Second Zechariah and the End of Biblical Prophecy," in *"Go to the*

priestly stream in Zechariah 9–14, in an earlier age this was linked to the fact that this was a polemic against the hierocratic hegemony in Jerusalem by apocalyptic visionaries.[58] This view has been challenged of late with the suggestion that Zechariah 9–14 arose from the priestly stream as well.[59]

Malachi has also been a key contributor to the messianic debate over the past decade, especially in relationship to exegesis on 3:1 and 3:23-24 [Eng. 4:4-5]. The debate has centered on the identity of the messengers and "lord" in 3:1, and suggestions have ranged from royal to priestly to prophetic figures (see further below).

In the context of this extensive debate, we embark on an auspicious mission: to identify messianic (whether royal, priestly, or prophetic) themes within Haggai-Malachi. This will involve an evaluation of the stance of the writers toward these various streams in the present as well as any expectations for their future.

Haggai

Treatment of the Present

Unquestionably, the focus of the book of Haggai is the construction of the Second Temple. The prophet challenges a lethargic community to begin restoration anew (1:1-11) and then encourages them at three key junctures: at the start of the work (1:12-15), after a month of preparation (2:1-9), and finally in two phases on the day of the foundation laying (2:10-19, 20-23). Although all themes in this book are subservient to the larger concern of structural renewal, the prophet does affirm sociological rejuvenation in these prophetic messages. Three key socio-religious functionaries, familiar to the reader from depictions of pre-exilic Israel and Judah, are affirmed in each of the prophetic speeches. The royal stream is represented by Zerubbabel, son of Shealtiel and grandson of the Davidic royal Jehoiachin,

---

Land I Will Show You": Studies in Honor of Dwight W. Young (ed. J. E. Coleson and V. H. Matthews; Altertumskunde des Vorderen Orients; Winona Lake: Eisenbrauns, 1996) 127-42.

58. O. Plöger, *Theocratie und Eschatologie* (3rd ed.; WMANT; Neukirchen-Vluyn: Neukirchener Verlag, 1968); P. D. Hanson, *The Dawn of Apocalyptic: The Historical and Sociological Roots of Jewish Apocalyptic Eschatology* (rev. ed.; Philadelphia: Fortress, 1979).

59. S. L. Cook, *Prophecy and Apocalypticism: The Postexilic Social Setting* (Minneapolis: Fortress, 1995).

the second-to-last king of Judah. The priestly stream is evident in Joshua, son of Jehozadak and grandson of Seraiah, the last Zadokite priest, who served in the first temple (2 Kgs 25:18; cf. 1 Chron 5:40 [Eng. 6:14]). The prophetic message is directed to these two figures in terminology intended to echo the Davidic first temple building tradition. The responsive "remnant" gathers around these figures and embraces this building project. The prophetic stream is represented by Haggai himself, whose message is equated with the voice of the Lord, even as the prophet is identified as the *mal'āk YHWH* (messenger of the Lord; 1:12-13). Haggai thus legitimates the three key pre-exilic covenant figures for the present restoration era.

Expectation for the Future

At two points in the book, however, a future orientation takes shape. In both cases, present faithfulness forms the foundation for future promises. First, after encouraging the people in the early stages of the rubble clearing, the prophet promises a future shaking of the cosmos that will result in the filling of the temple with material glory from foreign nations (2:6-9). Although the early church did find in this pericope a reference to a future messianic figure ("the Desired One"), identified as Jesus, this view has no foundation in the original text.[60] Second, after affirming the people for their faithfulness in laying the foundation of the temple (2:10-19), the prophet promises again a future shaking of the cosmos, but this time the speech is addressed exclusively to Zerubbabel ("governor of Judah") and the result is the catastrophic shattering of the political and military hegemony of foreign nations and the installation of Zerubbabel ("son of Shealtiel") as Davidic vice regent of YHWH on earth (2:20-23).[61] Some interpreters have challenged the argument that the words used in this oracle

---

60. The Vulgate reads: *et veniet desideratus cunctis gentibus*, echoed in the famous hymn: "Come thou long-expected Jesus, dear desire of every nation." For a proponent of this view (slightly modified), cf. H. Wolf, "'The Desire of All Nations' in Haggai 2:7: Messianic or Not?" *JETS* 19 (1976) 97-102.

61. Some have wrongly seen in this Haggai (and also Zechariah) fomenting rebellion against Persia in light of present upheavals in Mesopotamia; so L. Waterman, "The Camouflaged Purge of Three Messianic Conspirators," *JNES* 13 (1954) 73-78; cf. critique in P. R. Ackroyd, "Two Old Testament Historical Problems of the Early Persian Period," *JNES* 17 (1958) 13-27; J. Kessler, "The Second Year of Darius and the Prophet Haggai," *Transeuphratène* 5 (1992) 63-84; Kessler, *Book of Haggai*, based on chronological data.

are drawn from vocabulary of Davidic royal appointment[62] because the various lexemes are used in other contexts as well.[63] However, the only context in which all of this vocabulary intersects is that associated with Davidic appointment; and, furthermore, it is difficult to deny the echo of Jeremiah's prophetic judgment of Jehoiachin's line in Jeremiah 22.

While Haggai's two descriptions (2:6-9, 20-23) share similar lexical stock in describing cosmic upheaval,[64] they possess slightly different temporal markers. Haggai 2:6-9 expects this upheaval "in a little while" (2:6), while 2:20-23 expects it "on that day" (2:23).[65] The day that is spoken of here is the period of activity referred to in vv. 21b-22, that is, the day of God's overthrowing of the world.[66] The close connection in terms of vocabulary between vv. 6-9 and vv. 20-23 suggests that these events are coterminous. Here, in contrast to the other prophetic literature, "on that day" appears to refer to "in a little while," a conclusion supported by the naming of the historically present Zerubbabel in v. 23.[67]

62. E.g., "take" *(lāqaḥ):* 2 Sam 7:8; 2 Kgs 14:21; 23:30; "my servant": 2 Sam 3:18; 7:5, 8; 1 Kgs 11:32, 34, 36; 1 Chron 17:4; 2 Chron 32:16; Pss 78:70; 89:3; 132:10; "chosen" *(baḥar):* 1 Sam 16:8-10; 2 Sam 6:21; Ps 78:70.

63. See especially Rose, *Zemah and Zerubbabel;* Rose, "Messianic Expectations," 168-85; but also Pomykala, *Davidic Dynasty,* 45-53; contrast Meyers, "Messianism," 128.

64. Nogalski's comments that 2:21-22 cannot be connected to 2:6-9 because 2:21-22 envisions the nations' annihilation in contrast to the nations' contribution to the temple in 2:6-9 represent a misunderstanding of the imagery; J. D. Nogalski, *Literary Precursors to the Book of the Twelve* (BZAW; Berlin: de Gruyter, 1993) 231. Haggai 2:21-22 is not speaking of the annihilation of the nations, but rather of the subjugation of their military power; cf. H. W. Wolff, *Haggai: A Commentary* (Continental Commentaries; Minneapolis: Augsburg, 1988) 103: "What Yahweh is going to annihilate is not the nations themselves but their militant nature."

65. Some scholars treat v. 23 separately from vv. 20-22, either on form critical or on thematic grounds, suggesting that the phrase "on that day" is a "typical redactional device" to unite originally disparate oracles; Wolff, *Haggai,* 102; Nogalski, *Literary Precursors,* 229-31; S. J. De Vries, *From Old Revelation to New: A Tradition-historical and Redaction-critical Study of Temporal Transitions in Prophetic Prediction* (Grand Rapids: Eerdmans, 1995). Although it is possible that we have here a redactional seam, I follow Petersen who identifies it as a transition from general to specific events; D. L. Petersen, *Haggai and Zechariah 1–8: A Commentary* (OTL; London: SCM Press, 1984) 102; cf. M. J. Boda, "Haggai: Master Rhetorician," *Tyndale Bulletin* 51 (2000) 295-304.

66. Contra Bauer who sees here the final day of the Feast of Tabernacles; L. Bauer, *Zeit des zweiten Tempels-Zeit der Gerechtigkeit. Zur sozio-ökonomischen Konzeption im Haggai-Sacharja-Maleachi-Korpus* (BEATAJ; Frankfurt: Lang, 1992).

67. So C. L. Meyers and E. M. Meyers, *Haggai, Zechariah 1–8: A New Translation with Introduction and Commentary* (AB; Garden City: Doubleday, 1987) 69: "Haggai's expectations

Summary

Haggai's treatment of leadership figures is firmly rooted in the historic realities of the early Persian period. He affirms the traditional prophetic, royal, and priestly streams and identifies each of them with figures active within his community. There is, however, a slight orientation to the future with the hope of cosmic upheaval that results in material glory for the temple and material prosperity for the community, but also in a renewal of national independence and international rule. He centers this hope on the figure of Zerubbabel, and, although it is possible that this could be referring to Zerubbabel as the founder of a new dynasty, in light of the close association between 2:6-9 and 2:20-23 it appears that the original expectation was focused on his lifetime.

Zechariah 1–8

Vision-Oracle Complex (Zechariah 1:7–6:15)

At the core of Zechariah 1–8 lies the vision-oracle complex in 1:7–6:15.[68] Most of the pericopes offer promises of renewal for the community as a whole. In the main, these hopes are placed in the presently unfolding circumstances, verified by the fact that they are the response of God to the impassioned cry of the Angel of the Lord who voices the pain of the seventy-year wait for divine mercy (1:12).[69] However, at one point, in one of the oracle expansions to the night visions (2:14-17 [Eng. 10-13]), there is a more remote temporal perspective. This is in connection with the expan-

---

emerged from the historical present, which involved the building of the temple and the immediate potential for a monarchic state under the rule of a Davidide who in all likelihood would be Zerubbabel." Similarly, Kessler, *Book of Haggai*, 270: "Zerubbabel is therefore the guarantor for that which had not yet been fulfilled, but which soon will be"; contra B. Uffenheimer, "Zerubbabel: The Messianic Hope of the Returnees," *JBQ* 24 (1996) 221-28, here 224.

68. For fuller argumentation on the issues dealt with here, see M. J. Boda, "Oil, Crowns and Thrones: Prophet, Priest and King in Zechariah 1:7–6:15," *JHS* 3 (2001) Art. 10 = M. J. Boda, "Oil, Crowns and Thrones: Prophet, Priest and King in Zechariah 1:7–6:15," in *Currents in Biblical and Theological Dialogue* (ed. J. K. Stafford; Winnipeg: St. John's College, University of Manitoba, 2002) 89-106.

69. M. J. Boda, "Terrifying the Horns: Persia and Babylon in Zechariah 1:7–6:15," *CBQ* 67 (2005) 22-41.

sion of Jerusalem to include "many nations" who will enter into covenant with YHWH when he takes up residence "in that day."

While the communal vision is dominant in Zech 1:7–6:15, at a few points the prophetic message focuses on socio-religious figures in the restoration community. Most interpreters turn immediately to the two central visions in the night vision series for this focus, and probably the most common point of discussion is the enigmatic fifth vision, with its scene of a lamp stand fueled by two olive trees (4:1-6a, 10b-14). These olive trees are identified in the final phase of the interpretation as *šᵉnê bᵉnê-hayyiṣhār* ("the two sons of fresh oil") who are "standing beside the Lord of all the earth" (4:14). Often this phrase is translated as "the two anointed ones" and linked to the two key leadership figures associated with the early Persian period: Joshua, the Zadokite high priest, and, of course, Zerubbabel, the Davidic governor of Yehud. For most interpreters this vision is expressing the political realities of Yehud in the Persian period, highlighting the elevated role of the priest in this new era and preparing the way for hierocratic hegemony in later centuries.[70] However, as I have argued elsewhere in detail, these olive trees are not the recipients of oil, but rather the sources, suggesting that, if anything, these oil trees signify the source of anointing in Israel, which was often the prophet, sometimes the priest, but never the king.[71] This helps us understand the presence of the two prophetic speeches in the center of Zechariah 4 (vv. 6b-10a), which offer encouragement and credibility to Zerubbabel, truly a source of oil for the project. It is not by might or power, but by God's Spirit through his prophets that this project will be accomplished.

These two short prophetic speeches in the center of Zechariah 4 assuredly find their *Sitz im Leben* in ceremonies connected with clearing and founding activity at the temple site. As is typical of such refounding ceremonies in the ancient Near East, the participation of the monarch was essential, and it appears that Zerubbabel is acting the royal part, officially on behalf of the Persian emperor, but unofficially as Davidic scion. In this

70. Tollington, *Tradition and Innovation,* modifies this by seeing here indications that Zechariah championed diarchic rule, which would sustain the community until the arrival of a Davidic royal.

71. Boda, "Oil, Crowns and Thrones"; cf. D. W. Rooke, "Kingship as Priesthood: The Relationship between the High Priesthood and the Monarchy," in Day, ed., *King and Messiah in Israel*; Rose, *Zemah and Zerubbabel.*

way, then, the prophetic voice affirms the enduring role of the royal house in the life of the community.[72]

Whereas Zechariah 4 highlights the present role of royal and prophetic figures, two other passages focus (at least initially) on the priestly figure of Joshua. In Zechariah 3 and 6:9-15 both Joshua and his attendants are affirmed as legitimate priestly functionaries. In each case, however, the text alludes to the imminent appearance of one called ṣemaḥ.[73] This intertwining of priestly and royal figures is drawn assuredly from the description of the restoration in Jeremiah 33 (cf. ch. 23), where the futures of the royal and priestly lines are intertwined and assured by the rhythms of the cosmos.[74] In both Zechariah 3 and 6, the realization of priestly hope is centered on the present figure of Joshua. However, the royal ṣemaḥ figure belongs to the imminent future when he will come and usher in a new day of cleansing and prosperity (3:9-10) as well as rebuilding the temple (6:12-13, 15).[75] Although he is never identified by name in the immediate prophetic pericopes, the two prophetic speeches inserted into the center of Zechariah 4 (vv. 6b-10a) make it clear that Zerubbabel was the one who not only prepared the temple site for construction (vv. 6b-7) but also laid the foundation (v. 9a) and would bring the construction to completion (v. 9b). Furthermore, the phrase "you will know that the Lord Almighty has sent me to you" appears after the rebuilding prophecy of both ṣemaḥ (6:15) and Zerubbabel (4:9). This

72. A. Laato, "Zechariah 4,6b-10a and the Akkadian Royal Building Inscriptions," *ZAW* 106 (1994) 53-69; Laato, *Star Is Rising*, 197-200; and M. J. Boda, "From Dystopia to Myopia: Utopian (Re)visions in Haggai and Zechariah 1-8," in *Utopia and Dystopia in Prophetic Literature* (ed. E. Ben Zvi; Helsinki: Finnish Exegetical Society; Göttingen: Vandenhoeck & Ruprecht, 2006) 210-48.

73. Often inappropriately translated as "Branch"; cf. Rose, *Zemah and Zerubbabel*.

74. As with his denial of Davidic connections to Zerubbabel in Hag 2:20-23, so in his denial of connections to Zechariah's ṣemaḥ, Pomykala, *Davidic Dynasty*, 53-56, cannot be followed.

75. Rose, *Zemah and Zerubbabel*, has argued that this is an allusion to a messianic future figure, but not to Zerubbabel. L. Tiemeyer, "The Guilty Priesthood (Zech. 3)," in *The Book of Zechariah and Its Influence* (ed. C. M. Tuckett; Aldershot: Ashgate, 2003) 1-20, is not willing to accept that Joshua was present in Judah before Zerubbabel nor that Zechariah could have received this vision/oracle prior to the arrival of either, so she has recently argued that the reference to ṣemaḥ in 3:8b must be an addition to the text, which places her in company with W. Rudolph (*Haggai, Sacharja 1-8, Sacharja 9-14, Maleachi* [Gütersloh: Mohr, 1976]), who says this gives the removal of sin from the land an "eschatological character and turns it into a description of the general removal of all sin in the day when the Messiah comes" (p. 2).

showcases Zerubbabel as the figure who did indeed appear with others from "far away" to help build the temple.[76]

Prose Sermon Inclusio (Zechariah 1:1-6; 7:1–8:23)

The hope of this vision-oracle core, however, is ultimately tempered by the prose sermon inclusio that now brackets the entire complex.[77] While 1:1-6 engenders hope through the sensitive response of the people to the penitential cry of Zechariah, 7:1–8:23 reveals that the conditions are not yet ripe for the realization of the restoration in its fullness. The prophet highlights rebellious patterns in the present that echo pre-exilic patterns. This leads to the verdict of enduring exilic conditions for this community coupled with the call to a repentance, which will transform their mournful fasts into joyous feasts that evidence the realization of the hopes for the community in Zech 2:14-17 [Eng. 10-13]: the presence of God and the expansion of Jerusalem "in those days" with people from "all languages and nations" (8:20-23). Strikingly absent, however, from 7:1–8:23 is reference to a future hope for socio-religious functionaries, as Uffenheimer has ably summarized: "Significantly, he omits the political aspects of the prophetic 'days to come'; neither does he mention, by word or even allusion, the Shoot, or the re-establishment of the Davidic kingdom. Redemption now is entirely disconnected from political implementation. This, then, is the last step taken in the process of 'sobering' the dangerous aspirations awakened with the appearance of Zerubbabel."[78]

---

76. Four sections in Zech 1:7–6:15 share various commonalities in vocabulary and style: Zech 2:10-17 [Eng 6-10]; 3:1-10; 4:6b-10a; and 6:9-15: (1) 4:6b-10a and 6:9-15 both contain the formula, "the word of the Lord to" (*dᵉbar-YHWH 'el:* 4:6, 8; 6:9); (2) 2:10-17; 4:6b-10a; and 6:9-15 all contain the prophetic formula, "then you will know that the Lord Almighty has sent me" (*wîda'tem kî-YHWH ṣᵉbā'ôt šᵉlāḥānî:* 2:13, 15 [Eng. 9, 11]; 4:9; 6:15); (3) 3:1-10 and 6:9-15 both refer to the *ṣemaḥ* figure in connection with an address to the priestly figure Joshua; (4) 4:6b-10a and 6:9-15 both refer to the building of the temple. These commonalities suggest that they all belong to a common redactional level within this corpus, forging an even closer relationship between Zerubbabel and the *ṣemaḥ* figure.

77. Cf. M. J. Boda, "Zechariah: Master Mason or Penitential Prophet?" in Becking and Albertz, eds., *Yahwism After the Exile,* 49-69; M. J. Boda, "From Fasts to Feasts: The Literary Function of Zechariah 7–8," *CBQ* 65 (2003) 390-407.

78. Uffenheimer, "Zerubbabel," 227.

Summary

The core vision-oracle complex in 1:7–6:15 has a similar sociological and temporal perspective on the renewal to that evidenced in Haggai. Sociologically, there is great focus on the revitalization of the community as a whole, but not at the expense of a renewal of the traditional socio-religious functionaries of pre-exilic Judah, that is, royal, priestly, and prophetic figures.[79] These three functionaries are presented in ways that establish their interconnectedness. Priest and king are linked in Zechariah 3 and 6, prophet and priest in Zechariah 3, and prophet and king in Zechariah 4. Each is essential to the other; the appearance and function of one secures hope for the appearance of another. This tripartite balance, however, does highlight a slight shift from the book of Haggai and the pre-exilic situation. First, the priestly role is on the ascendancy, evidenced by exclusive control over temple affairs and the granting of both crown and throne to the next future royal in court. In Haggai the focus is clearly on the royal stream. Second, the role of the royal stream is distanced from military or political control and focused on the rebuilding project, as is evident in the declaration "not by might, nor by power" in 4:6b-10a, a contrast to the close association with military power in Haggai.[80]

Temporally, the hopes expressed in 1:7–6:15 are considered realized in the present age, something that is true for both community and leadership. However, there are hints of a more remote future, signaled by the use of the phrase "in that day," one linked to the appearance of God and the other with the appearance of the royal ṣemaḥ figure. The prophetic oracles in Zech 4:6b-10a, however, identify Zerubbabel as the fulfillment of the prophecy of this royal figure and thus, as with Haggai, suggest a fulfillment in the near future. However, this expectation that future hope has been realized in the present restoration community is tempered in the prose ser-

79. The evidence above clearly contradicts the denial of Pomykala, *Davidic Dynasty*, 60, that "Zechariah 1–8 sets forth hope for a davidic messiah," even though when he does entertain the possibility of the royal stream of thought, his conclusions are similar to mine, especially in the contrast between Zechariah 1–8 and Haggai. This evidence also contradicts A. S. van der Woude, "Serubbabel und die messianischen Erwartungen des Propheten Sacharja," *ZAW* 100 Supplement (1988) 138-56, who denies that the ṣemaḥ figure and the figures in 4:14 relate to present figures, asserting that they belong only to the future high priest and prince.

80. Meyers and Meyers, "Future Fortunes," 209.

mon inclusio which transfers hopes of restoration to a later era (1:1-6; 7:1–8:23) and makes no mention of socio-religious functionaries. This temporal perspective, at least, will only be accentuated in the sections that follow in Zechariah 9–14 and Malachi.

Zechariah 9–14

The latter half of the book of Zechariah is clearly distinguished from the first half by the presence of the superscription *maśśā' dᵉbar YHWH* (oracle, the word of YHWH; 9:1; 12:1) and the vastly different prophetic genre that is employed.[81] As has been the trend in Haggai and Zechariah 1–8, the focus of the prophetic voice is on the community as a whole, but one cannot ignore key texts that reflect on the past, present, and future of leadership figures.

Structure

Zechariah 9–14 can be divided into two sections, separated not only by the superscription *maśśā'* in 9:1 and 12:1, but also by the form, style, and mood of the prophecies contained therein. The two oracles in chs. 9–10 are focused on both Israel and Judah, exhibit a positive mood, and convey hope of return from exile, triumph over enemies, and renewal of prosperity in what appears to be the near future. The two oracles in chs. 12–14 do not mention Israel, focusing rather on Jerusalem and Judah, exhibit a much darker mood, and envision a future attack on and cleansing of God's people as well as a victory through God in a more remote future (on that day: 12:3, 4, 6, 8, 9, 11; 13:1, 4; 14:4, 6, 8, 9, 13, 20, 21).

Leadership Figures

This transformation in form, style, and mood is showcased by highlighting a key contrast between chs. 9–10 and 12–14 over the issue of kingship, a contrast that reveals a change in treatment of the traditional pre-exilic

---

81. For details on the structure of Zechariah 9–14 and its relationship to Zechariah 1–8, see M. J. Boda, "Reading Between the Lines: Zechariah 11:4-16 in Its Literary Contexts," in Boda and Floyd, eds., *Bringing Out the Treasure*, 277-91; Boda, "Fasts to Feasts," 390-407.

leadership functionaries. After describing the march of the divine warrior YHWH in 9:1-7 and his taking up residence in 9:8, the prophet announces the arrival of a royal figure in Zion (9:9-10) who will proclaim peace and exercise global rule. Reference to kingship also appears in chap. 14, the concluding chapter of this literary complex. However, in this case that king is clearly identified as YHWH alone, with no reference to the Davidic line (14:9). This contrast identifies for us an important development that takes place in the course of Zechariah 9–14, which represents a considerable departure from the approach to community and leadership functionaries evidenced in Haggai and Zech 1:7–6:15.

Indications of this development are foreshadowed in the opening section of Zechariah 9–14. The focus is clearly on YHWH as divine warrior in 9:1-8 as he marches down the Levant and takes up residence on his throne in Zion. It is only then that he presents Zion with her king.[82] This sequence is essential to the proper definition of kingship in Judah. In Hebrew tradition the human king was considered a vice-regent of YHWH on earth, not the sovereign king himself (Psalm 2). The key to the identification of the sovereign king appears to be linked to the exercise of military power, a connection that is made explicit in the Song of the Sea, which begins by lauding YHWH as a great warrior (Exod 15:1-3) and ends by declaring his sovereign authority over Israel and the nations (15:18).[83] Similarly, the crisis over kingship in the early part of the book of Samuel is linked to Israel's request for a human ruler in the midst of a military crisis (1 Sam 8:20; 12:12), a request that ends with a king of military stature (9:2). In the former prophets it is the insignificant boy named David who comes in the name of YHWH of hosts to take on the giant and is qualified for kingship in Israel (1 Samuel 17). Therefore, the human king encountered in Zech 9:9-10 meets YHWH's requirements for kingship. He is ṣadîq, that is, one who judges righteously; nôšāʿ, one who is saved, referring to his dependency on YHWH for deliverance; ʿānî, humble or afflicted, as he rides on a

---

82. Some have suggested that this king is YHWH himself or the remnant of Judah (cf. Leske, "Context and Meaning," 663-78), but these options cannot be accepted because (1) this is a speech of YHWH to the personified city of Zion about a "king"; (2) YHWH calls him "your king" (your = Zion); and (3) the speech contains significant allusions to Psalm 72. Cf. Meyers, "Messianism," 127-42; Meyers and Meyers, "Future Fortunes," 207-22; F. Laubscher, "The King's Humbleness in Zechariah 9:9: A Paradox?" *JNSL* 18 (1992) 125-34.

83. This interlacing of royal and military imagery is recognized also by Meyers and Meyers, "Future Fortunes," 220.

lowly donkey. Iain Duguid has noted the close connection between Zech 9:10 and the traditions from which it draws. In contrast to Ps 72:13, where the king "saves" the needy, this king is saved and is afflicted (the latter often paralleled with "needy" and found in Psalm 72).[84] This description of a royal figure is carefully nuanced to avoid triumphalism, a rhetorical tactic that not only draws on the tradition of kingship in Israel but also is essential in the wake of the failure of the royal house that precipitated the exile.

This opening revelation of the relationship between divine and human kingship thus prepares the way for the exclusive focus on the divine in ch. 14, but it does not explain the absence of human kingship in ch. 14. Key to this development is the complex sign-act depicted in the core passage that lies at the seam in Zechariah 9–14 between chs. 9–10 and 12–14 — that is, Zech 11:4-16. As I have argued elsewhere in detail, these sign-acts depicting the failure of a good shepherd and the appointment of a bad one play off of two prophecies within Ezekiel (chs. 34 and 37) that are concerned with the state of present leadership and the hope for future faithful Davidic leadership.[85] Underlying the sign-act in Zechariah 11, however, is a crisis in Davidic leadership that most likely occurred at the end of Zerubbabel's rule and led to the appointment of his son-in-law to the governorship and, following him, non-Davidides. Any hope of a unified province under Davidic rule appears to have died with the demise of Zerubbabel's leadership. This helps us to understand the transition from a focus in chs. 9–10 on Israel and Judah to the focus in chs. 12–14 on Judah and Jerusalem.

Further evidence of leadership crisis can be discerned in what are often identified as the Shepherd seams in Zechariah 9–14; 10:1-3a; 11:1-3; 11:17; 13:7-9.[86] These all lie at transitions between major oracular units in Zecha-

---

84. Duguid, "Messianic Themes," 265-80. Duguid also notes a contrast to the military triumphalism of Gen 49:8-11, the imagery of which has been transferred to YHWH himself. T. Collins, "The Literary Contexts of Zechariah 9:9," in Tuckett, ed., *The Book of Zechariah and Its Influence*, 29-40, shows how 9:9-10 uses the genre of the proclamation of the arrival of a king and also is closely allied with Psalm 72.

85. Boda, "Reading Between the Lines," 277-91.

86. Both K. Elliger, *Das Buch der zwölf kleinen Propheten. II. Die Propheten Nahum, Habakuk, Zephanja, Haggai, Sacharja, Maleachi* (7th ed.; ATD; Göttingen: Vandenhoeck & Ruprecht, 1975) 143-44, and P. L. Redditt, "Israel's Shepherds: Hope and Pessimism in Zechariah 9–14," *CBQ* 51 (1989) 631-42, do a superb job of identifying these redactional seams in Zechariah 9–14. J. Tromp, "Bad Divination in Zechariah 10:1-2," in Tuckett, ed., *The Book of Zechariah and Its Influence*, 41-52, has recently encouraged us to read at least 10:1-2 apart from chs. 9-10.

riah 9–14 and share in common shepherd imagery and prophetic condemnation. Reading them from beginning to end reveals an increasing severity in the situation parallel to an increasing severity in the punishment of the shepherds. This series reaches a climax in 13:7 as YHWH awakens his sword against the irresponsible shepherd he had appointed over the people in punishment for their rebellion against his good shepherd.[87] The death of this shepherd actually represents a crucial turning point in the drama created by the shepherd pieces, for after the resultant scattering a refined remnant returns in covenant fidelity to YHWH. The precise identity of these shepherds is difficult to determine, but in light of the identification of the bad shepherd in 11:4-16 as one who followed the demise of a Davidic shepherd, that is, Zerubbabel, it is possible that these shepherds are images of provincial leadership that followed Zerubbabel, possibly including even his own son-in-law.[88] Whether it also involved members of the Zadokite leadership is difficult to tell, even though one can discern a development in the Zecharian tradition from early affirmation to later careful delimitation to even outright criticism of priests within Judah (cf. Zech 3; 6:9-15; 7:5), and it appears from the book of Malachi that even the Zadokites could be tempted into idolatrous relationships (cf. Mal 2:10-16; 3:5).[89] As for the prophets, it appears that at least some of the problems can be linked to false prophetic activity that is in turn connected to idolatrous practices (Zech 10:2; 13:2-6).

But what does this then say about the stance of those responsible for Zechariah 9–14 toward the traditional socio-religious figures? While some have suggested that the strong criticism against prophecy in 13:2-6 indicates that the end of prophecy is near, this is hardly likely in light of the fact that Zechariah 9–14 identifies itself as a prophetic writing and draws heavily on the prophetic tradition for its imagery and message (9:1; 12:1). Rather, what is attacked here is false prophecy, a fact that is

---

87. Cook, "Metamorphosis," 453-66, notes that although the shepherd at the end of ch. 11 and the shepherd in 13:7 are connected, a cleansing has occurred in 12:10–13:1.

88. See Meyers, "Messianism," 131, who does note that there were two Davidic sons who could have succeeded Zerubbabel (Meshullam and Hananiah), but that their brother-in-law and sister were chosen instead: "in all probability to keep the Davidic name in the public eye but at the same time making it quite clear that in the Persian Empire there was no turning back to the old monarchist pattern and that royalty played a more symbolic role than anything else."

89. Boda, "Fasts to Feasts," 405.

made clear by the consistent linkage between prophecy and idolatry.[90] The contrast between the vision of the Davidic king in 9:9 and that of YHWH in 14:9 has suggested to others that hope of a renewed Davidic kingship is no longer operative. However, this does not take into account consistent echoes of key Davidic prophecies from Jeremiah and Ezekiel throughout the Shepherd units and sign-acts, echoes that remind the people of God's enduring hope for the Davidic line while at the same time reminding them of God's willingness to discipline the line.[91] It especially does not take account of explicit references to the Davidic clan in chs. 12 and 13.

These chapters clearly identify the Davidic clan as in need of renewal, along with Jerusalem and the rest of Judah. The "house of David" will mourn for their treatment of God (12:10, 12)[92] and receive cleansing from God's fountain (13:1). There is concern on the part of the prophet that the "honor of the house of David and of Jerusalem's inhabitants" not exceed that of Judah, but such honor is still available to David (12:7). Similarly, in a shocking comparative, the weakest of Judah will be "like David" and the house of David "like God, like the *mal'āk YHWH* [angel of the Lord] going before them" (12:8).[93] Although carefully nuancing David's role within Judah, the prophet does not appear to be sidelining the Davidic house. Does this then mean that this prophet is merely maintaining the orientation toward the Davidic house that was discerned in Haggai and Zech 1:7–6:15? Maybe so, but there is a fascinating line of evidence that may reveal that the prophet in Zechariah 9–14 is suggesting a new way forward that does

---

90. T. W. Overholt, "The End of Prophecy: No Players without a Program," *JSOT* 42 (1988) 103-15.

91. M. J. Boda and S. E. Porter, "Literature to the Third Degree: Prophecy in Zechariah 9–14 and the Passion of Christ," in *Translating the Hebrew Bible* (ed. R. David and M. Jinbachian; Montreal: Médiaspaul, 2005) 215-54.

92. Zech 12:10 is often treated as a messianic prophecy (since it is cited in the New Testament at John 19:37), but Zech 12:10 appears to be speaking about the metaphorical piercing of God, rather than an allusion to Josiah (it is not surprising that Zech 12:10 appears only in John 19:37, considering one focus in John is to intertwine Jesus and YHWH); see Boda, *Haggai/Zechariah*; contra R. A. Rosenberg, "The Slain Messiah in the Old Testament," *ZAW* 99 (1987) 259-61; Duguid, "Messianic Themes," 276; A. Laato, *Josiah and David Redivivus: The Historical Josiah and the Messianic Expectations of Exilic and Postexilic Times* (ConBOT; Stockholm: Almqvist & Wiksell, 1992) 290-91; cf. Laato, *Star Is Rising*.

93. The second part of this phrase appears to be an addition that seeks to soften the original connection to divinity, as also the ancient versions do; cf. Mason, "Messiah," 357.

offer continuity with past prophetic hopes for leadership and yet, simultaneously, considerable discontinuity.

The renewal among God's people that follows God's triumph over the nations begins with thorough corporate mourning for their treatment of YHWH. It is the description of this mourning that may offer the prophet's way forward. Zechariah 12:12 begins with the summary statement that the entire land will mourn within their clans, separated by gender. This summary statement is then broken down into its constituent parts with reference to the clans of David, Nathan, Levi, and Shimei, ending with a general reference to the remaining clans. The singling out of these four clans is striking and begs the question of its significance. Some have seen this list as a summary of the entire leadership caste of the community (royal: David; prophetic: Nathan; priestly: Levi; sapiential: Shimei),[94] but one could also take this list as identifying clans within clans — that is, the clans of David are to mourn, but in particular the clan of Nathan achieves special status within the Davidic house.[95] So also the clans of Levi are to mourn, but in particular the clan of Shimei achieves special status within the Levitical house. Biblical tradition identifies Nathan as one of David's many sons (2 Sam 5:14), even though Solomon's line is the one that is chosen to lead the nation both for good and ill. Biblical tradition also indicates that there was a Shimei in the Levitical line, the son of Levi's son Gershom (1 Chron 6:17; cf. Exod 6:16-17; Num 3:17-18), even though the leading family of the Levites was usually identified as that of Levi's other son Kohath, whose descendants included not only Aaron, but also the great Zadokite line that served the Davidic kings and were represented in Haggai and Zechariah 1–8 by the high priest Joshua (1 Chron 6:1-15; cf. Hag 1:1-12; Zechariah 3). A further twist to this priestly genealogy must be mentioned. Zechariah, the prophet, is linked to a descendant named Iddo (Zech 1:1, 7), and, interestingly, a man named Zechariah was a leader in the

---

94. R. L. Smith, *Micah-Malachi* (WBC; Waco: Word Books, 1984) 277; C. Stuhlmueller, *Rebuilding with Hope: A Commentary on the Books of Haggai and Zechariah* (ITC; Grand Rapids: Eerdmans, 1988) 149.

95. So also Meyers, "Messianism," 138; for other proponents see Pomykala, *Davidic Dynasty*, 122n.232. Cf. R. E. Brown, *The Birth of the Messiah: A Commentary on the Infancy Narratives in the Gospels of Matthew and Luke* (new updated ed.; AB Reference Library; New York: Doubleday, 1993), with M. D. Johnson, *The Purpose of the Biblical Genealogies with Special Reference to the Setting of the Genealogies of Jesus* (Cambridge: Cambridge University Press, 1969) 59n.3, 240-42, on the significance of Nathan in Luke's genealogy of Jesus.

priestly family of Iddo according to Neh 12:16. This name Iddo is associated with a family of Levites that also is linked to the line of Gershom (1 Chron 6:21), the same family as that of Shimei in Zech 12:13. In light of the crisis in leadership identified in the Shepherd seams of Zechariah 9–14, this evidence may suggest that Zechariah 9–14 offers enduring hope for the royal and priestly lines, retaining affirmation of the Davidic and Levitical lines while looking to different clans within those traditional lines to carry the agenda forward.

Summary

No matter what we do with this evidence for a modification of royal and priestly hopes, it is certain that Zechariah 9–14 seriously tempers the idyllic portrait offered in Haggai and Zech. 1:7–6:15, furthering the trend seen already in Zechariah 7–8. There is enduring hope for socio-religious functionaries within Israel, but in the wake of the leadership crisis in late-sixth-century Yehud greater weight has been shifted onto YHWH. The priestly house is largely ignored; the prophetic stream is suspect, though not disqualified.[96] The royal stream is carefully nuanced at the outset: YHWH is the sovereign, and the king is dependent upon him. As the text progresses there is clearly a crisis in the royal stream, and even if it is not sidelined, there are suggestions of its secondary character.[97] Accompanying this has been an increasing transfer of hope to the remote future: "on that day." Thus, in the face of a tightening Persian stranglehold on Yehud, Zechariah 9–14 reflects "the collapse of any hope for political independence," which transferred "Israel's dreams of a restored and independent kingdom . . . increasingly to the eschatological realm."[98]

96. Contra Petersen, *Late Israelite Prophecy,* 45: "classical Israelite prophecy was a thing of the past and claims for contemporary manifestations of prophecy were to be denied."

97. As W. J. Dumbrell, "Kingship and Temple in the Post-Exilic Period," *RTR* 37 (1978) 33-42, here 40, says, agreeing with Hanson: there is "a greatly diminished Davidic interest in these chapters"; and Pomykala, *Davidic Dynasty,* 125, asserts, probably too strongly, yet in agreement with Mason: "there is no evidence of a hope for a davidic king or messiah"; cf. R. A. Mason, "The Relation of Zech 9–14 to Proto-Zechariah," *ZAW* 88 (1976) 227-39, here 237.

98. Meyers and Meyers, "Future Fortunes," 210; for the impact of dissonance between early Persian expectations and reality, especially as related to Zerubbabel, see (guardedly) R. P. Carroll, *When Prophecy Failed: Cognitive Dissonance in the Prophetic Traditions of the Old Testament* (New York: Seabury, 1979) 157-68.

Malachi

Following Zechariah 8, the two "oracle" *(maśśā')* superscriptions in 9:1 and 12:1 signal key seams in what appears to be a unified corpus stretching from chs. 9 to 14 (especially seen in the Shepherd units that draw the entire corpus together). However, a third *maśśā' (oracle)* superscription appears immediately following Zech 14:21, introducing what we know today as the book of Malachi. What follows, however, does not display literary links with the previous *maśśā' (oracle)* material and thus should be distinguished from it on one level, even if it is related by its shared identity in the Book of the Twelve (Hosea-Malachi) and possibly in an original Haggai-Malachi corpus.[99]

One significant contrast between Zechariah 9–14 and the book of Malachi is that the latter is far more rooted in the historical circumstances of a community operating in what appears to be Persian-period Yehud. As Smith writes: "Malachi was not primarily concerned with the future. His primary interest was the 'here and now.'"[100] The prophet confronts dysfunctional patterns within this community, ranging from inappropriate sacrifices to insufficient tithes and offerings, from idolatry to injustice. In addition, the prophet employs the vocative voice, confronting his audience in personal and direct ways (1:6; 2:1; 3:6).

Clearly this prophet views the life of the community through the lens of the temple and its services, as Robert Kugler has so aptly written: "the book was mainly concerned with the cult and the priestly abuse of it."[101]

---

99. See M. H. Floyd, "The *Maśśā'* as a Type of Prophetic Book," *JBL* 121 (2002) 401-22; for the redaction of this book, see P. L. Redditt, "The Book of Malachi in Its Social Setting," *CBQ* 56 (1994) 240-55.

100. R. Smith, "The Shape of Theology in the Book of Malachi," *Southwestern Journal of Theology* 30 (1987) 26.

101. R. Kugler, "The Levi-Priestly Tradition: From Malachi to 'Testament of Levi'" (Ph.D. diss., University of Notre Dame, 1994) 49. (Unfortunately Kugler's excellent and extensive chapter on Malachi was excised when the dissertation was published as *From Patriarch to Priest: The Levi-Priestly Tradition from Aramaic Levi to Testament of Levi* [SBLEJL 9; Atlanta: Society of Biblical Literature, 1996]). On the social background to this book and various views, see J. W. Rogerson, "The Social Background of the Book of Malachi," in *New Heaven and New Earth — Prophecy and the Millennium* (ed. R. Hayward and P. J. Harland; VTSup; Leiden: Brill, 1999) 171-79; Redditt, "Book of Malachi," 240-55; J. L. Berquist, "The Social Setting of Malachi," *BTB* 19 (1989) 121-26. This book appears to express concern over the present group functioning as priests in the temple and looks to a future that includes purification of the Levites for service in the temple.

This is obvious in the prophet's attack on defiled sacrifices (1:6-14), unrighteous priests (3:2-5), and insufficient tithes and offerings (3:6-12), but it is also evident in attacks on foreign marriages (2:10-12) that have "desecrated the sanctuary" and attacks on divorces (2:13-16) for which God rejects their offerings so that they must "flood the Lord's altar with tears." This prophetic voice is positive and passionate for the temple and its services and concerned with the present state of the community and its sacral leadership.

What is interesting is that Malachi makes no mention of the royal stream of leadership that has been so important in the prophetic corpora we have considered so far.[102] Reference is made to a "governor" (Mal 1:8), but there is not even an implicit link to the Davidic or royal tradition in the book. Rather, Malachi is fixated on the priestly and prophetic streams.

Malachi 2:1-9

Malachi's concern over the priesthood comes to the fore in 2:1-9, a passage addressed directly to the "priests" (2:1). In this attack the prophet calls down a curse on those who were to bring blessing to the community and threatens to spread defiled matter on their faces and thus disqualify them from their office. The concern of the prophet is clearly for what he calls the "covenant with Levi," which is presently under threat by the priestly administration in the temple (2:8).[103] The core concern seems to be related to the integrity of both priestly instruction and practice. In this passage we are told that the priest was nothing less than *mal'āk YHWH* ("the messenger of the Lord"; 2:7). While some have seen this as indicative of an agenda for priestly replacement of prophetic functions, Andrew E. Hill has rightly

---

102. Even if A. Bentzen, "Priesterschaft und Laien in der jüdischen Gemeinde des fünften Jahrhunderts," *AfO* 6 (1930-31) 280-86, did try to link the messenger in 3:1 to a royal figure, albeit with emendation; cf. Dumbrell, "Kingship and Temple," 33-42; and esp. Mason, "Messiah," 338-64.

103. On this covenant with Levi and the Levi tradition in Malachi and the Old Testament, see R. Fuller, "The Blessing of Levi in Dtn 33, Mal 2, and Qumran," in *Konsequente Traditionsgeschichte* (ed. R. Bartelmus, T. Krüger, and H. Utzschneider; OBO; Fribourg, Switzerland: Universitätsverlag Freiburg Schweiz; Göttingen: Vandenhoeck & Ruprecht, 1993) 31-44; O'Brien, *Priest and Levite in Malachi*; Meyers, "Priestly Language," 225-37; Kugler, "Levi-Priestly Tradition," 41-70; B. Glazier-McDonald, "Mal'ak habberit: The Messenger of the Covenant in Mal 3:1," *HAR* 11 (1987) 93-104.

treated this as merely a "clarification of the ideal of priest as teacher of Yahweh's law."[104] The term "messenger" cannot be seen as the exclusive possession of the prophets in Israel, considering that it is used outside of Malachi only five other times (Isa 42:19; 44:26; 2 Chron 36:15-16; Hag 1:13). The vast majority of uses of this term are connected to a heavenly being, that is, an angel. While there does not appear to be a denigration of the prophetic function, neither is there a rejection of the priestly office, even though Malachi vehemently attacks the priestly administration of his day. The covenant with Levi is secure, even if the present representatives must be disciplined and even removed.[105]

Malachi 3:1-2

The bulk of the book of Malachi is focused on the present, but at a couple of points a future orientation breaks in, signaled by such vocabulary as "the day of his coming" (3:2), the "coming day" (3:19 [Eng. 4:1]) or "that coming great and dreadful day of the Lord" (3:23 [Eng. 4:5]). The first of these occurs in the much-debated verse 3:1, where in answer to the people's disillusionment with divine justice the prophet promises the sudden appearance of one called "lord," whose appearance will be prepared for by one called "my messenger" and whose appearance is either equated with or

---

104. A. E. Hill, *Malachi* (AB; New York: Doubleday, 1998) 212; cf. P. A. Verhoef, *The Books of Haggai and Malachi* (NICOT; Grand Rapids: Eerdmans, 1987) 258; Fuller, "Blessing of Levi," 31-44. The replacement view was espoused in an earlier era by J. M. P. Smith, "Malachi," in *A Critical and Exegetical Commentary on Haggai, Zechariah, Malachi and Jonah* (ed. H. G. T. Mitchell, J. M. P. Smith, and J. A. Brewer; ICC; Edinburgh: T&T Clark, 1912) 40, and more recently by Meyers, "Priestly Language," 231. D. L. Petersen, *Zechariah 9–14 and Malachi: A Commentary* (OTL; Louisville: Westminster John Knox, 1995) 192n.52, likens this aspect of Malachi to the Chronicler who sought to "invest Levites with prophet-like authority." On the priestly role in Torah ruling see Hag 2:10-14; cf. J. Begrich, "Die priestliche Thora," in *Weiden und Wesen des Alten Testament* (ed. P. Volz, F. Stummels, and J. Hempel; BZAW; Berlin: Töpelmann, 1936) 63-88; H. Huffmon, "Priestly Divination in Israel," in *The Word of the Lord Shall Go Forth* (ed. C. L. Meyers and M. O'Connor; Winona Lake: Eisenbrauns/ASOR, 1983) 355-59; E. M. Meyers, "The Use of Tôrâ in Haggai 2:11 and the Role of the Prophet in the Restoration Community," in Meyers and O'Connor, eds., *The Word of the Lord Shall Go Forth*, 69-76.

105. There is a long history of research on the social context lying behind the book of Malachi. See recently, Berquist, "Social Setting of Malachi," 121-26; O'Brien, *Priest and Levite in Malachi*; Redditt, "Book of Malachi," 240-55; Kugler, "Levi-Priestly Tradition," 41-70; Rogerson, "Social Background," 171-79.

parallel to one called "the messenger of the covenant."[106] The key issue under debate is the identity of these three individuals in 3:1.[107]

Clearly the text defines one of the three as a figure who prepares the way. That is, the one called "my messenger" prepares the way for the appearance of at least the "lord" (*'ādôn*). Commentators universally agree that this *'ādôn* is a reference to YHWH because (1) this one "whom they seek" appears to be responding to their question: "Where is the God of justice?" (2:17); (2) YHWH has just said that the messenger will prepare the way before him (3:1); and (3) it is claimed that this one has ownership over the temple.[108] David L. Petersen, among others, has suggested that "my messenger" is the same as the "messenger of the covenant" who appears with the "lord."[109] Beth Glazier-McDonald, however, deems this unlikely because it fuses a figure who prepares the way with one who accompanies the *'ādôn* who emerges "suddenly." In this view the arrangement of the language, the use of "suddenly," and the parallel language between the line with "lord" and that with "messenger of the covenant" disqualify any

---

106. Conrad studies the various "messengers" in the Twelve and sees the shift from the designation "prophet" to that of "messenger" as significant, suggesting that this indicates a replacement of prophecy with a restored messenger or angelic presence. See E. W. Conrad, "Messengers in Isaiah and the Twelve: Implications for Reading Prophetic Books," *JSOT* 91 (2000) 83-97. It appears that the term "messenger" does carry with it considerable weight rhetorically; it is used to bolster the prophetic figures in Haggai and Malachi, as can be seen in Hag 1:12 in which the "voice of YHWH their God" is equated with the "message of the prophet Haggai," a phrase that is then linked to Haggai's status as "messenger of YHWH" in 1:13. There is clearly a crisis in prophetic credibility in Haggai-Malachi (cf. Boda, "Haggai: Master Rhetorician," 295-304), and the "messenger" nomenclature is one of many strategies to bolster the credibility of this new era of prophecy.

107. Some have tried to avoid the issue by excising vv. 1b-4 as a later expansion due to its use of third-person speech, e.g., Petersen, *Zechariah 9–14*, 207; R. A. Mason, *The Books of Haggai, Zechariah and Malachi* (CBC; Cambridge: Cambridge University Press, 1977) 152. But even if this argument could be sustained, it still does not explain why the one responsible for this expansion would place the lord and the messenger of the covenant alongside each other. The switch to third-person speech is common in prophetic speech, making this redactional solution unnecessary; cf. B. Glazier-McDonald, *Malachi, the Divine Messenger* (SBLDS 98; Atlanta: Scholars, 1987) 129n.16.

108. See Hill, *Malachi*, although it is possible that *'ādôn* here is merely a reference to a human lord/master, and thus a priest, or that the "temple" here is a reference to a king coming to his palace (as in 1 Kgs 21:1; 2 Kgs 20:18//Isa 39:7//2 Chron 36:7; Dan 1:4; Isa 13:22; Nah 2:7; Ps 45:9, 16; Hos 8:14; Amos 8:3; Joel 4:5; Prov 30:28; Ps 144:12).

109. Petersen, *Late Israelite Prophecy*, 42-43; cf. E. H. Merrill, *Haggai, Zechariah, Malachi: An Exegetical Commentary* (Chicago: Moody, 1994) 429-30.

equation between the "messenger of the covenant" and "my messenger." In light of this, however, how does Glazier-McDonald explain the relationship between YHWH and this "messenger of the covenant"?

Glazier-McDonald contends that the language of messenger in 3:1 is drawn from the book of Exodus, in particular Exod 23:20, which speaks of YHWH sending a "messenger" who would go before God's people to guard them on the journey.[110] This she links to the first messenger in Mal 3:1, that is, "my messenger." However, she then returns to this same passage to explain the parallel relationship between YHWH and the "messenger of the covenant" in 3:1: "This corresponds well with the Exodus passage where the roles of Yahweh and his messenger seem to merge (22:21f) [sic],"[111] concluding that "the messenger . . . is Yahweh's mode of self revelation."[112] Through this line of argumentation Glazier-McDonald is seeking to undermine Petersen's claim for an equation of "my messenger" and the "messenger of the covenant" and in the process has actually bolstered his case.[113]

First Petersen and later O'Brien have emphasized the role of the messenger in Exod. 23:20-22 as "covenant enforcer."[114] As covenant enforcer the "messenger" is called upon to deliver prophetic covenant lawsuits against the people. Such a role is filled in the Old Testament by both heavenly (Judg 2:1-5)[115] and human beings (1 Sam 2:27-36; 2 Sam 12:7-12; 1 Kgs 21:17-24).

If this messenger figure then both prepares for and accompanies YHWH in Mal 3:1, what kind of figure is this? Bruce Malchow has argued that the messenger here is a priestly figure, in particular because of the identification of Levi as the "messenger of YHWH" in Mal 2:7.[116] The evi-

---

110. Glazier-McDonald, *Malachi*, 129-32; so also D. K. Berry, "Malachi's Dual Design: The Close of the Canon and What Comes Afterward," in *Forming Prophetic Literature: Essays on Isaiah and the Twelve in Honor of John D. W. Watts* (ed. J. W. Watts and P. R. House; JSOTSup; Sheffield: Sheffield Academic Press, 1996) 269-302, here 281.

111. This should read 23:21f.

112. Glazier-McDonald, *Malachi*, 131.

113. O'Brien notes this fusion of figures and links it to the fact that messengers in the Old Testament (whether angelic or human) function as "the 'alter-ego' of the sovereign"; O'Brien, *Priest and Levite in Malachi*, 75.

114. Petersen, *Late Israelite Prophecy*, 43-44; O'Brien, *Priest and Levite in Malachi*, 74-75.

115. The "messenger/angel of YHWH" in Judg 2:1-5 appears to be a spiritual being, especially in light of other uses of this phrase in Judges (6:11; 13:2-23).

116. B. V. Malchow, "The Messenger of the Covenant in Malachi 3:1," *JBL* 103 (1984)

dence of O'Brien above, however, suggests that this is either a heavenly (angel) or human (prophet) figure who will not arise from the Levites but rather be involved in the refining of the Levites. It is difficult to ignore the fact that the description of this messenger as "my messenger" is identical to the name in the superscription to this book, suggesting possibly that the redactor viewed the prophet himself as this messenger.

The timing of his appearance is conditioned by the central event of YHWH coming to his temple (3:1), which is then called "the day of his coming" (3:2). This kind of language does not appear to carry the eschatological weight that is often placed upon it. Hill, for example, identifies it as "pregnant with eschatological implications associated with the Day of Yahweh," but then likens it to similar phrases that denote the presence of YHWH in the Haggai-Zechariah-Malachi corpus, few of which (if any) are eschatological in scope.[117] It is probably this evidence that led R. Smith to highlight the lack of eschatology in Malachi: "He did not speak of 'the day of the Lord.' He made no reference to 'The Messiah.' He has no 'full-blown' system of eschatology. Yet he knows he is living in the 'not yet' era."[118] By this Smith appears to be referring to the oral level in Malachi, rather than to what are considered two additional appendices attached after Mal 3:21 [Eng. 4:3]. The reference to "day of his coming" in 3:2 does not appear to be any more than a reference to the arrival of YHWH in his temple (3:1).

Thus, Mal 3:1 denotes some kind of messenger, whether heavenly or human, who will come and deliver a prophetic message to prepare for the arrival of YHWH. The actual character of this preparation is never spelled out.[119] Then YHWH with this messenger at his side will refine the Levites to qualify them for temple service. The timing of this arrival of YHWH is not specified, but it is related to his return to fill the Second Temple.

252-55; see E. R. Achtemeier, *Nahum-Malachi* (Interpretation; Atlanta: John Knox, 1986) 171-73, who identifies Malachi as a lawsuit of a Levitical priest who acts as a messenger of the covenant in the temple; cf. D. G. Clark, "Elijah as Eschatological High Priest: An Examination of the Elijah Tradition in Mal. 3:22-24" (Ph.D. diss., University of Notre Dame, 1975).

117. Hill, *Malachi*, 272.

118. Smith, "Shape of Theology," 26.

119. See Glazier-McDonald, *Malachi*, 136-39 for the significance of this language in preparations for the arrival of royalty.

Malachi 3:23-24 [Eng. 4:5-6]

For many scholars, however, the ambiguous features in Mal 3:1 are filled out in 3:23-24 [Eng. 4:5-6], a pericope that is treated as a later addition to the book of Malachi, functioning either as an early interpretation of the book itself or as a pericope inserted by canonical scribes who were seeking to forge together either the more limited Book of the Twelve (cf. Hosea 14 and Mal 3:22-24) or the broader Torah and Prophets.[120] However, it is difficult to deny lexical connections between 3:23-24 and 3:1, evidence that leads Petersen, who is sympathetic to these canonical views, to admit that the "individual who wrote it seems interested in identifying the messenger."[121]

Malachi 3:23-24 thus appears to be clarifying 3:1, and it does so in three ways. First, it identifies the "messenger" as "Elijah the prophet." This choice is interesting in light of our discussion of 3:1, for there we showed that the two figures who come as messengers for YHWH with a prophetic tone are angels and prophets. It is well known that the Hebrew prophetic stream was regularly associated with the divine council — that is, the angelic host (1 Kings 22; Isaiah 6; Jer 23:18, 22) — but Elijah's association is even more pronounced, for he did not die and was taken up in a chariot of fire accompanied by horsemen. Here we see a fusion of the two "messenger" traditions: a heavenly-human prophetic figure.[122] Second, this passage identifies the timing of this preparation as "before the coming of the great and terrible day of YHWH." What was originally a reference to God's return to the temple now has taken on an eschatological dimension (Joel 3:4 [Eng. 2:31b]; cf. Joel 2:11; Jer 30:7; Zeph 1:14).[123] Third, the activity of preparation is now spelled out as the prophet is called to a ministry of either repentance or reconciliation.[124] Whether 3:22-24 was an original part

---

120. See G. L. Keown, "Messianism in the Book of Malachi," *Review & Expositor* 84 (1987) 443-51, here 445; Petersen, *Zechariah 9–14*, 232-33; P. L. Redditt, "Zechariah 9–14, Malachi, and the Redaction of the Book of the Twelve," in Watts and House, eds., *Forming Prophetic Literature*, 245-68, here 266-67; Hill, *Malachi*, 363-66.

121. Petersen, *Zechariah 9–14*, 230.

122. Slightly different is Berry, "Malachi's Dual Design," 290, who sees the messenger as combining the roles of priest, prophet, and divine emissary (angel). The Elijah pericope, however, he does admit "involves the introduction or identification of the messenger who acts in more of a divine than human role" (291).

123. See Hill, *Malachi*, 377; Glazier-McDonald, *Malachi*, 264-65.

124. For this debate and its basis in the ancient versions, see Glazier-McDonald, *Malachi*, 255-57; Hill, *Malachi*, 378-81.

of the book of Malachi[125] or a later addition to the book,[126] this passage plays a significant role in our interpretation of the book, for it functions to clarify what was at one point nebulous.

Summary

The book of Malachi, therefore, is silent on the royal stream of leadership. Its focus is on the priestly and prophetic streams instead. The present priestly leadership is corrupt, but this does not disqualify this stream from a role in the community. A refined priestly group will be created through the actions of a prophetic figure, which at first appears to be the prophet himself (Malachi), but in the end is identified as Elijah, who is both heavenly and human messenger, and who will return and usher in the appearance of the refining God. The timing of this appearance may have originally been in the near future, if 3:1 referred to the role of the prophetic voice of the book of Malachi (1:1), but it was interpreted in 3:22-24 [Eng. 4:4-6] as a future event that possessed a far more severe and cataclysmic tone.

Conclusion

The books of Haggai-Malachi offer us a perspective on messianic expectation in the final phase of prophetic tradition in the Old Testament. They reveal an initial burst of renewal of the messianic streams of pre-exilic Judah as royal, priestly, and prophetic figures ascend to places of influence. The temporal focus of Haggai and Zechariah 1:7–6:15 is assuredly in the imminent future. This hope, however, is carefully nuanced beginning in Zechariah 7–8, which reveals that fulfillment awaits the covenant obedience of the people and leadership. Although the hope is kept alive by the introduction of the royal figure in Zech 9:9-10, chs. 9–14 represent a serious threat to royal hopes as the royal figure resigns, ceding rule to an inappropriate shepherd. The only way forward will be through a future punishment of this shepherd leadership. Although the focus clearly shifts to YHWH by ch. 14, all hope for the royal and priestly houses is not lost, even if it means peni-

125. Glazier-McDonald, *Malachi*, 243-70; O'Brien, *Malachi*, 79.
126. Hill, *Malachi*, 363-66; Petersen, *Zechariah 9–14*, 227-33.

tential cleansing and possibly a genealogical shift to a different royal and priestly clan. Concerns over the validity of the priestly stream are voiced in the book of Malachi. The way forward is linked to the appearance of a heavenly-human messenger who is identified as the prophet Elijah in the closing pericope of this corpus. Thus, in the end, hope for the reemergence of king and priest is carried forward by the prophetic stream, which looks to a distant future day for the hoped-for renewal.

The interrelationship among these three functionary types is highlighted by a common phrase shared by all three in this final phase of prophetic witness. In Haggai-Malachi, royal, priestly, and prophetic streams are all called *mal'āk YHWH*: Hag 1:13 (prophet), Zech 12:8 (king), and Mal 2:7 (priest). Outside of these three references *"mal'āk YHWH"* (which is used fifty-four times in the Old Testament) is never used for a human figure; elsewhere in the Old Testament it is always used for a heavenly being.[127] Zechariah 1–8 stands apart from the rest of the Haggai-Malachi corpus as the one section that uses *mal'āk YHWH* to refer to a heavenly being. There a *mal'āk YHWH* appears at the outset of the vision series and then at the heart of the vision series in Zechariah 3, where he addresses the role that all three functionaries will play in a future kingdom.[128] In this same section the *mal'āk YHWH* addresses each of these three functionaries, showing their heightened role within the divine council. It may be that one of the key uniting features of the Haggai-Malachi corpus is the identification of all "messianic" streams as *mal'āk YHWH*, confirming their close identification with YHWH, by whom they are truly "anointed," and suggesting heavenly access if not also origin for these figures who are represented in the present by the traditional royal, priestly, and prophetic lines.[129]

---

127. Cf. E. W. Conrad, "The End of Prophecy and the Appearance of Angels/Messengers in the Book of the Twelve," *JSOT* 73 (1997) 65-79; Conrad, "Messengers in Isaiah and the Twelve," 83-97. Conrad links this to the waning of prophecy, whereas it appears to be related to the heightening of all three functionary streams.

128. Interestingly, this vision is often seen as an addition to the original series of seven, a view bolstered by commonalities between it and other later pieces in 1:7–6:15; see preceding footnote.

129. On this heavenly figure coming in human form in Malachi, see N. G. Cohen, "From *Nabi* to *Mal'ak* to 'Ancient Figure,'" *JJS* 26, no. 2 (1985) 12-24.

The Messiah in the Qumran Documents

Al Wolters

The topic of messianism in the Dead Sea Scrolls is a minefield of contested claims. Scholars disagree on a whole range of issues, some of them quite basic. For example, did the Qumran sect expect one Messiah or two? Can we speak of a Messiah only when the Hebrew term משיח occurs? If not, what elements need to be present to justify speaking of a messianic figure? Is there a consistent pattern with respect to messianic expectations in the Qumran materials, or can we speak only of different strands that were never integrated into a single conception? Then there is the momentous question of the relation between the messianic expectations reflected in the Dead Sea Scrolls and the expectations that the New Testament writers see fulfilled in Jesus Christ. Running through the disputes about these and similar foundational questions are more detailed philological disagreements about how to restore damaged texts and how to understand rare and unvocalized Hebrew and Aramaic words.

Clearly, it is a dangerous enterprise for anyone to venture into this minefield. For the purposes of this paper, I will take as my guide two relatively recent books on the subject by leading Qumran specialists. The first is John J. Collins, *The Scepter and the Star: The Messiahs of the Dead Sea Scrolls and Other Ancient Literature;*[1] the second is Michael O. Wise, *The First Messiah: Investigating the Savior Before Jesus.*[2] These books are very different and in some respects represent opposite poles on the spectrum of

1. (New York: Doubleday, 1995).
2. (San Francisco: HarperCollins, 1999).

scholarly work on messianism in the Dead Sea Scrolls. Collins is one of the acknowledged authorities on this topic, and his monograph is perhaps the standard book-length treatment of the subject today. He gives a balanced and judicious survey of both the relevant texts and the scholarly literature surrounding them. Wise, on the other hand, though also a recognized Qumran specialist, presents an audacious proposal of his own in which a single messianic figure, in many ways foreshadowing Jesus Christ, is the interpretative key to a whole range of Qumran documents. By surveying the salient features of these two monographs, I will endeavor to give some sense of the current state of scholarship on this topic. My own contribution will consist largely in some incidental criticisms of a methodological and exegetical kind, the latter specifically with reference to my own research on the book of Zechariah.[3]

I begin with three preliminary remarks about Collins's monograph. (1) Although an important feature of his book is the way he situates the evidence from the Qumran scrolls within the broader context of what we know about contemporary Judaism as a whole, my assignment calls for me to focus my remarks on the former. (2) Like most scholars, Collins assumes that the scrolls discovered in the Judean Desert belonged to a distinct Jewish sect, which is probably to be identified with the Essenes, and which probably settled in Qumran, as well as other places in Israel (4-11). (3) Terminologically, he treats as "messianic" any authoritative figure who is the object of eschatological hopes, whether or not the term מְשִׁיחַ is used of him (11-12).

Having defined "messianic" in this way, Collins's main thesis is that we can discern four different kinds of messianic figures in the Dead Sea Scrolls, as in the other Jewish documents that are roughly contemporaneous with them. He calls them four "messianic paradigms" and labels them "king," "priest," "prophet," and "heavenly messiah" (12).

The "king" paradigm refers to the expectation of an eschatological king of the Davidic line. Before the discovery of the Dead Sea Scrolls, the main evidence for this expectation in the two pre-Christian centuries was found in the so-called *Psalms of Solomon* (49). This evidence was signifi-

---

3. I am grateful to both Collins and Wise for commenting on an earlier draft of this paper, especially their comments on my presentation of their own views. Needless to say, although I have taken their comments into account in my final draft, I am myself solely responsible for the latter. I cite their works by giving page numbers parenthetically within the body of the text.

cantly expanded in the Qumran documents. It can be found in the following texts:

(1) The *pesher* or commentary on Isaiah (4QpIsa[a]). Although this document is very fragmentary, it is clear that it refers to an eschatological king, who will play a role in the final battle against the *Kittim* or Romans (57-58). He is given the titles "Branch of David" and "Prince of the Congregation," which allude to messianic prophecies in Isaiah (specifically 11:1) and Ezekiel.

(2) The controversial "Dying Messiah" text (4Q285), probably a part of the War Rule (1QM), which describes the expected eschatological war. The original claim that this text refers to someone who was killed is now widely discounted, but the fragment does refer to a messianic figure, again designated with the titles "Branch of David" and "Prince of the Congregation" (58-60).

(3) The Scroll of Blessings (1QSb), which pronounces a blessing over the eschatological "Prince of the Congregation," who is again described in terms of the messianic prophecy of Isa 11:1-5. He is also described as the "scepter," an apparent allusion to the messianic "scepter" of Balaam's prophecy in Num 24:17 (60-61).

(4) The Florilegium (4Q174) also speaks of the "Branch of David," who will arise "at the end of days." He is also called "the Son of God" (61).

(5) The Patriarchal Blessings text (4Q252) again interprets the messianic text Gen 49:10 as referring to the "Branch of David," who is here also called the "Messiah of Righteousness," the recipient of an everlasting kingdom (62).

(6) The Damascus Document (CD), Manuscript A, mentions the "Prince of the Congregation" (CD 7:19) in the context of a citation of Balaam's oracle about the star and the scepter in Numbers 24, an oracle that was widely understood as a messianic prophecy in ancient Judaism (63-64).

These texts seem to reflect a fairly uniform exegetical tradition (also attested outside of the Qumran documents) that saw the Messiah as the Davidic king predicted in a number of texts in the Hebrew Bible. The portrait of this king that emerges is fairly consistently that of a warrior figure who will smite the wicked and restore the Davidic dynasty. This, too, is part of a broader tradition in contemporary Judaism, reflected also in *4 Ezra* and *2 Baruch*. Collins concludes: "This concept of the Davidic messiah as the warrior king who would destroy the enemies of Israel and institute an era of unending peace constitutes the common core of Jewish messianism around the turn of the era" (68).

Although less common, there is also considerable evidence for the second messianic paradigm in the Qumran materials, that of the eschatological priest. This paradigm is illustrated in the famous phrase "the Messiahs of Aaron and Israel," found in the Community Rule (1QS 9:11), in which the Messiah of Aaron is clearly a priestly figure. However, the evidence for this paradigm is certainly not restricted to that oft-cited phrase. There are also a number of texts where the future royal messiah appears to defer to a priestly figure. One of these is the so-called "Messianic Rule" (1QSa), where a priest takes precedence over the "Messiah of Israel." This is presumably the "Messiah of Aaron." We find similar indications in two texts we have already considered in connection with the Davidic king, namely 4QpIsa^a and 4Q285, as well as others (the War Scroll, 1QSb, the *Florilegium*, CD). "In fact, all the major rule and law books . . . support the bifurcation of authority in the messianic era" (76). Collins writes: "There is, then, impressive evidence that the Dead Sea sect expected two messiahs, one royal and one priestly. This binary messianism had, of course, its biblical precedent in Zechariah's 'two sons of oil' (Zech 4:14)" (77). It is to be noted that the various developmental theories, which posit a stage when only a priestly messiah was expected in the Qumran sect, are not convincing (77-83).

The third messianic paradigm is that of the prophet or teacher. It is this paradigm that we find in the figure who is called "the one who is to teach righteousness in the end of days" in the Damascus Document (CD 6:11) and the "Interpreter of the Law" in both the Damascus Document (CD 7:18) and the *Florilegium* (4Q174). Despite the arguments of some scholars, the future appearance of this figure is not to be interpreted as the second coming of the founder of the Qumran sect, although he too is designated as "Interpreter of the Law" in the Damascus Document (CD 6:7) and is elsewhere frequently called the "Teacher of Righteousness." These were interchangeable titles that were clearly applicable to a variety of people (102-4). It was the future eschatological teacher, not the past historical Teacher of Righteousness, who was in all likelihood identified by the Qumran sectarians with the future "prophet like Moses" predicted in Deut 18:18. However, they may not have been totally consistent, since there is also evidence that they also equated the prophet predicted in Deuteronomy with the priestly messiah (114).

Another possible reference to the prophetic messiah is found in the fragmentary text called "The Messiah of Heaven and Earth" (4Q521), where the משיח whom "heaven and earth will obey" may well be an anointed eschatological prophet, either Elijah or a prophet like Elijah (117-22).

In the light of the parallels that some scholars have drawn between the eschatological teacher and Jesus Christ, it is also worth pointing out that the scrolls do not have an expectation of a messiah who suffers before entering into glory (123-26).

As an introduction to his discussion of the fourth paradigm, that of the heavenly messiah, Collins first deals with the mysterious text that Baillet entitled "canticle of Michael" (4Q491 11). In this text the speaker makes the remarkable claim, "I have taken my seat . . . in the heavens. . . . I shall be reckoned with gods." Although M. Baillet identified the speaker as the archangel Michael, there is considerable evidence that he was in fact a human being (136-39). One possibility is that he is to be identified with the eschatological "Interpreter of the Law" who would "teach righteousness at the end of days." The text is significant, however, not primarily because it may allude to a messianic figure, but because it refers to a human being who is enthroned in heaven in a way that suggests a kind of divinization (146-49).

The one Qumran text that may qualify as illustrating the "heavenly messiah" paradigm is the much-disputed Aramaic fragment known as the "Son of God" text (4Q246), which begins with the words, "'Son of God' he shall be called, and they will name him 'Son of the Most High.'" The phraseology of this fragment has such striking parallels with the infancy narrative in Luke 1 that Collins believes that Luke must have been in some way dependent on it (155). Unfortunately, most of the rest of this fragment is damaged or ambiguous, and there has been a good deal of dispute about the identity of the figure here called "Son of God." Collins himself argues, especially on the basis of verbal parallels with Daniel 7, that a messianic interpretation is most probable. In fact, 4Q246 may represent the earliest example of the messianic interpretation of the "one like the son of man" of Dan 7:13 (155-69).

As background to the possibility that this last text refers to a heavenly messiah, Collins includes a discussion of the interpretation of Daniel's "Son of Man" in two Jewish texts that do not belong to the Dead Sea Scrolls but are roughly contemporary with them, namely the *Similitudes of Enoch* and *4 Ezra*, both dated to the first century CE (177-87). Each of these interprets the "son of man" of Daniel 7 as a preexistent messiah, a transcendent figure of heavenly origin who can be described in quasi-divine terms (187). These common assumptions about the Danielic "Son of Man" bespeak a prevalent exegetical tradition in the Judaism of the first century CE that may well have been shared by the Qumran sectarians (188).

In a final chapter, Collins briefly discusses a series of actual historical figures in the Judaism of the first two centuries CE who could be described as fulfilling a "messianic" expectation in some sense. Some of these arose as prophets, others as royal pretenders, but all were eventually destroyed by the might of imperial Rome, including the second-century Bar Kokhba, who was hailed as the messiah by Rabbi Aqiba, one of the leading rabbis of the day (196-204). Compared to these other royal pretenders, what distinguishes Jesus is that, although he too apparently claimed to be the expected messianic king of Davidic descent, he did not exemplify the military features of this strand of messianic expectation. This non-military aspect of his messiahship, together with his suffering and dying, breaks the mold of the messianic paradigms that were current in the Judaism of his day (204-9).

Looking back over this brief survey of Collins's magisterial treatment of the evidence, I am struck by a number of points that call for comment. The first is how sparse and ambiguous the evidence is. The Qumran Scrolls speak very little of an eschatological messiah — even of a messianic figure broadly defined — and when they do it is always incidental to other concerns and usually subject to multiple interpretations. In short, it is clear that messianic expectation was not central to the religious worldview of the Qumran sectarians, and what little such expectation there was is hard to pin down.

Second, Collins shows convincingly that even this marginal messianic expectation was not monolithic. He is right to speak of different messianic strands. In this way he steers a judicious middle course between the earlier scholarly consensus, which had seen a common messianic expectation in Judaism around the turn of the era, and the more recent reaction to this consensus, which sees no messianic patterns at all. (See Collins's discussion on pp. 3-4.)

Third, it is striking that the one strand that stands out in bold relief and that is both well-documented and widely recognized is the expectation of the Davidic king. It is beyond dispute that the Qumran sectarians, like many of their Jewish contemporaries, understood their Scriptures to predict a future royal messiah who would deliver Israel from its enemies.

Fourth, I would point out that it is somewhat misleading for Collins to speak of four *distinct* strands of messianic expectation. This emerges very clearly from a passage on the first page of his last chapter (195). He first recapitulates the overall results of his investigation in the following words: "In the preceding chapters we have seen evidence for four distinct messianic paradigms in Judaism around the turn of the era: king, priest, prophet, and heavenly messiah or Son of Man." However, the very next sentence reads as follows: "These paradigms were not always distinct." As a matter of fact, at least with reference to the Qumran materials, it seems that they were *often* not distinct. As we have seen, sometimes a messianic figure is both priestly and prophetic (114-15), and the heavenly messiah may also be a king (164, 167, 173).

This raises a fifth point, which I believe is of some significance. The fourth paradigm, that of the heavenly messiah or Son of Man, may not be represented in the Dead Sea Scrolls at all, and in any case is not on a par with the others. The two Qumran texts that Collins discusses in this connection (4Q491 11 and 4Q246) do not provide clear evidence for this category. The first probably does not speak of a messianic figure at all, and it is adduced by Collins mainly as evidence of the heavenly exaltation of a human figure (149). The second *may* speak of a messianic figure of the required type, but this interpretation is disputed by many Qumran scholars, and its possibility can be affirmed by Collins only on the basis of a fairly convoluted argument (155-69).[4] But even if this fourth paradigm did show up clearly in the sectarian documents, it would evidently not be coordinate with the others. The first three are defined on the basis of the societal *office* to which the messiah is anointed, but the fourth is defined by the messiah's cosmological *status*, either earthly or heavenly. There is nothing contradictory, therefore, in the heavenly messiah also being a king — or, for that matter, a priest or a prophet. Consequently, I would argue that the Dead Sea Scrolls give evidence of only three kinds of messianic expectation, those corresponding to the three anointed offices of prophet, priest, and king, and that there is some slight evidence that this expectation may on occasion have been connected with a notion of heavenly exaltation.

---

4. In an email to me dated June 14, 2004, Collins clarifies his position as follows: "I never actually meant the 'throne in heaven' text or the Son of Man text to be taken as referring to a heavenly messiah, although I can see how my book may have been confusing in that regard."

Finally, I would like to raise an exegetical issue related to the book of Zechariah. Zechariah 4:14 speaks of "the two sons of oil who stand by the Lord of the whole earth," and this verse is often cited in connection with the Jewish expectation of the Messiah. Collins, too, speaks of this text in his survey of Old Testament messianic passages (30, 31). As we have seen, he also writes of the expectation of a royal and priestly Messiah in the Dead Sea sect, that "[t]his binary messianism had . . . its biblical precedent in Zechariah's 'two sons of oil'" (77). However, there are a number of problems with this use of the biblical phrase. To begin with, it is not at all clear that Zech 4:14 is a messianic text. The primary reference is usually taken to be the high priest Joshua and the civil governor Zerubbabel, but eminent exegetes have disputed this, partly because the word for oil (יצהר) is not otherwise used for anointing, and partly because Zerubbabel was in fact never anointed. However, quite apart from the text's original referents, there is no evidence that the Qumran sect ever appealed to it to support a "binary messianism," as Collins implicitly concedes (98n.55). In fact, the only place (to my knowledge) where this text is cited in the Dead Sea Scrolls is 4Q254, where it has no discernible connection with the sect's messianic expectation. Besides, if Collins's overall argument has merit, then any biblical text that implies only a *dual* messianic expectation is unlikely to have found favor in a religious group that held to a triple or quadruple expectation.

I turn now to the second book on this subject that I have undertaken to review, that by Michael O. Wise. As I have pointed out already, it is very different from Collins's work. It is written in a popular (not to say journalistic) style and is aimed at a general audience. Although Wise is an acknowledged Qumran scholar in his own right, he wears his considerable erudition lightly and confines most of his scholarly argumentation and documentation to his footnotes, which are sometimes quite lengthy. Furthermore, much more than Collins, he sets out to prove a controversial thesis. In addition, although Collins also makes a few passing references to modern messianic sects, Wise makes the anthropological study of what he calls "crisis cults" one of the foundation stones of his analysis. He refers especially to the nineteenth-century Millerite movement in the United States and to the twentieth-century Branch Davidians led by David Koresh. He interprets the rise and development of the Dead Sea sect in the light of what modern anthropologists have found to be typical of such crisis cults in other times and places.

On many of the basic points in dispute concerning the Dead Sea Scrolls and messianism, Wise takes a different view from Collins. Whereas Collins accepts the consensus view that the sectarians who produced the Scrolls were the Essenes of whom Pliny wrote, and who settled (among other places) at Qumran, Wise makes no reference to the Essenes, and instead associates (although he does not identify) the people of the Scrolls with the Sadducees, disputing the connection that is usually made between Qumran and the sectarians (305n.4). Whereas Collins denies that the historical Teacher of Righteousness is the same person as the eschatological Teacher of Righteousness whom the sectarians expected, Wise affirms this identification. On the other hand, whereas Collins identifies the historical Teacher of Righteousness with the historical Interpreter of the Law, Wise distinguishes them. Whereas Collins is at pains to distinguish four distinct messianic paradigms, Wise takes almost all messianic references found in the Scrolls to refer to the same paradigm. Whereas Collins denies that there is a notion of a suffering Messiah in the Scrolls, Wise affirms that there is. Whereas Collins stresses the discontinuity between the sectarian messianic expectation and Jesus Christ, Wise stresses the continuity. In fact, Wise argues that the Messiah of the Dead Sea sectarians defined the shape of the messianic mold that Jesus, in his own distinctive way, filled. Most importantly, however, Wise claims that the Qumran Messiah was not just a religious ideal; he was an actual historical personage about whom we can know quite a lot.

Wise's fundamental thesis is that the founder of the "crisis cult" that produced the Dead Sea Scrolls, the so-called Teacher of Righteousness, considered himself to be the Messiah predicted in the Hebrew Scriptures, and that many of the messianic references in the Scrolls refer to him — either to him as a historical personage who lived in the early first century BCE or to him as the eschatological figure who was to come again. Wise gives him the name Judah, although it is not clear what evidence this is based on (41). A cornerstone of Wise's argument is that Judah was himself the author of a number of the Dead Sea Scrolls, including 4QMMT (67), the directives contained in CD 6:11–7:4 (42-43), and especially the nine Teacher Hymns that constitute the core of the Thanksgiving Hymns (1QH 9:1–20:7) (44-45). It is especially the latter that allows Wise to reconstruct much of the tumultuous career of the charismatic leader Judah.

In outline, that career was as follows. Judah was a respected priest and wisdom teacher in Jerusalem who had served as a religious adviser to the Hasmonean ruler Alexander Jannaeus, a ruler who had favored the Sadducees over the Pharisees. However, Judah's position changed dramatically upon Alexander's death in 76 BCE. The new ruler was Alexandra, who appointed her son Hyrcanus to the high priesthood. Under this new regime the Sadducees, together with priests like Judah who sympathized with their position, lost their privileged position, and the Pharisees were now in favor at the court. Ousted from his position of privilege, Judah wrote his First Hymn, still in 76 BCE (46), from which it is clear that he was under attack from the Pharisees. "The crisis of the Pharisees' rise to power had forced Judah to rethink everything that he believed. His thoughts about himself had also taken a new direction" (51). He now claimed to be "a prophet given knowledge of wondrous mysteries" (50), which means, says Wise, that Judah had now come to see himself as "*the* intermediary between the nation and God" (51), as someone "of a stature comparable to that of any of Israel's ancient prophets," in fact a new Moses (57). He even began to identify himself as the Suffering Servant of Isaiah (64) and to predict that he would ultimately prevail against his enemies and be reinstated in his rightful place in Jerusalem (65). It was around this same time that Judah coauthored the document known as "Some of the Laws of the Torah" (4QMMT), addressed to the new high priest Hyrcanus, and boldly challenging the Pharisees' understanding of cultic law (67-68). In it he also announced that the eschatological "Latter Days" were at hand, in which the curses of Deuteronomy would fall on the Pharisees and their allies (75). In response, the leading Pharisee of the day, Shimeon ben Shetah, urged Hyrcanus to arrest Judah and have him tried on the charge of false prophecy (79). Judah was duly tried, and Wise uses the words of Judah's Fifth Hymn to reconstruct the speech that he delivered in his defense (96). In it he alluded to "the prophet like Moses" of Deut 18:18 and cast himself in that role. He also applied the words about the Suffering Servant in Isaiah 53 to himself (91-92). Not surprisingly, he was found guilty by Hyrcanus, although the punishment of death was commuted to exile (95).

In the Fourth Hymn, Judah recorded a kind of mystical vision he had around this time, perhaps just previous to the trial (104). In an experience like those recorded in the *Similitudes of Enoch* and *Aramaic Levi,* Judah traveled to heaven. In Wise's words, "He seemed to have believed that he journeyed to heaven, received direct revelation, and returned to announce it to the millennial generation" (116). Furthermore, Wise argues that Judah now even applied the messianic epithet "Wonderful Counselor" (Isa 9:6) to himself (120). It is abundantly clear that Judah saw himself as the Messiah (122), the first one in history to do so (129). Out of the intensity of this messianic self-consciousness, Judah launched a movement that was to become, apart from early Christianity, "the most dynamic and enduring crisis cult of these centuries of Jewish civilization" (131).

Accompanied by a band of followers comprised of perhaps fifty to one hundred men with their families (134), Judah was exiled in 74 BCE to the "land of Damascus," probably the kingdom of Coele-Syria, more specifically the "Wilderness of Damascus" or Trachonitis (138). We can deduce from his Sixth Hymn, written around this time, that Judah and his followers now began to make their living as brigands, an accepted occupation in the ancient world (141-52). He now also began to prophesy that Gentile invaders would come from the north to bring judgment on Jerusalem and its corrupt religious establishment (141). On the basis of the prophetic chronology of the book of Daniel, he calculated that this invasion would take place soon, in a "week" of seven years, sometime between 73 and 65 BCE (157).

We learn from Judah's Seventh Hymn and some other sources that in the first year of his exile many of his followers deserted him (164) and that these apostates subsequently helped Hyrcanus and the Pharisees to launch a treacherous attack upon Judah's community (185). Many sectarians were killed, but Judah himself narrowly escaped (188). A year or two later, however, around 72 BCE (219), he did finally meet a violent end. We can deduce his violent death from a passage in the Damascus Document (CD 19:5-10), in which Judah's followers later identified him with the smitten shepherd of Zech 13:7 (216-19). By that time his band of followers had been reduced to a mere fifteen men and their families (219).

But this was not the end of the story. Although they were reeling with what students of crisis cults have called "disconfirmation distress" — since their charismatic leader had died, and his predictions had not come to pass (221) — Judah's remaining followers came to a conclusion that others in their situation have also frequently reached: their fallen leader had been exalted and would eventually return. We find aspects of this new perspective reflected in the "Community Hymns" that precede and follow Judah's own compositions in the *Thanksgiving Hymns* (222). One of these is the newly reconstituted fragment 1QH 26:2-10, in which the speaker (assumed to be the Teacher of Righteousness himself, i.e. Judah) says, among other things, "I am reckoned with the angels, my dwelling place is in the holy council. . . . I sit on high, exalted in heaven. . . . Who is like me among the angels?" (223). In effect, says Wise, Judah was understood to have been raised higher than the archangels. "He had taken his seat at the right hand of God" (224). Furthermore, Judah was also identified with both the Herald and Melchizedek of the manuscript 11QMelchizedek: the former a figure of the past (explicitly said to be "anointed," i.e., a messiah), and the latter a figure of the future. Of Melchizedek, extraordinary things are claimed. In effect, says Wise, "Melchizedek was the highest angel, and he was coming in the future to atone for the sins of Judah's followers and to establish the Kingdom of God" (230). What is more, by combining the chronological schemes of Daniel and 11QMelchizedek, it was possible to calculate when Melchizedek (alias the Herald, alias Judah) was to return and the eschatological End was to come. It was to be in 34 BCE (233).

The new leader of the small remnant of Judah's followers that remained, the one who was probably responsible for the new interpretation, was called the "Interpreter of the Law" (238). This group composed the "Original Manifesto," the original core of the *Community Rule* (1QS 8:1-16), which became the foundation document of what was henceforth to be called "the Society of the Yahad" (237). Most of this group returned to Judea (239). The tiny group limped along, struggling to survive, until 63 BCE. Then suddenly, after the Roman conquest of Judea, it began to grow rapidly again, no doubt because the Roman conquest could be seen (with some slight adjustment) as the dramatic fulfillment of Judah's prophecy concerning the coming Gentile invasion from the north (239). Between 63 and 34 BCE, the time between the Roman takeover and the expected return of Judah, thousands joined the sect, and the vast majority of the Dead Sea Scrolls were copied (243). Then, when the expected End did not come in 34 BCE, the whole movement collapsed, although a final attempted reinterpretation is recorded in the pesher on Habakkuk (248).

Wise's final chapter is devoted to a comparison of Judah's movement and Christianity. It begins with a list of fifteen parallels between Judah and Jesus, for which Wise acknowledges his indebtedness to the French scholar A. Dupont-Sommer. It is not surprising, in the light of his entire preceding argument, that many of these parallels are quite startling. For example, the last two of the list read as follows: "As growing numbers came to believe that Jesus had been glorified and now sat at the right hand of God, so it had been with Judah. As early Christians anticipated the imminent return of Jesus to judge the quick and the dead, redeem Israel, and initiate a millennium wherein believers would rule the world, so it had been with Judah's followers" (254). Wise goes so far as to say that the sectarians of the Scrolls represented a kind of "proto-Christianity" (256). As a final dramatic illustration of the similarity between the two Jewish religious movements, he points out how the statement in the Gospels that "the dead are raised up, the poor have glad tidings preached to them" (Matt 11:5 and Luke 7:22) finds a remarkable parallel in what Collins had called the "Messiah of Heaven and Earth" text (4Q521). Wise writes: "Both the scroll and the Gospels connect three critical elements: the raising of the dead, the preaching of glad tidings to the poor, and the time of the messiah" (274). So alike are the two messiahs, in fact, that Wise considers it possible to come to conclusions about Jesus by analogy with what we know about Judah. Finally, he makes the following summarizing statement: "In general the analogy with the first messiah argues that much of what the Gospels tell us about Jesus . . . happened along the lines the Gospels present. And the specific analogy of the first messiah is supported by a more universal one, for the fact is that the Gospels present a story typical of crisis cults. Not to speak of specific points and particular details, the story of the Gospels is plausible" (276-77).

As with Collins's book, permit me to make a few general observations of an evaluative kind about Wise's remarkable book. It is a difficult work to assess, because it does not fall into a recognizable genre. It seems to be a kind of hybrid of historical novel and scholarly monograph, aimed at both a general audience and Wise's academic peers. As far as its scholarship goes, it runs the gamut from proposing bold interdisciplinary syntheses to arguing the semantic nuances of Hebrew words to analyzing the redactional layers of sectarian compositions. There is no doubt that Wise's book is a brilliant *tour de force,* displaying an astonishing breadth of erudition and an extraordinary capacity for bringing a vast mass of data into a comprehensive synthesis.

Nevertheless, the book strikes me as far too clever. As a result of piling hypothesis on hypothesis, each of which arguably has some plausibility, Wise erects an amazingly coherent historical reconstruction, but of course its overall plausibility diminishes with every level of supposition. Quite apart from the many detailed and often disputed questions of textual restoration and translation, the whole edifice turns out to be on shaky ground if certain disputed assumptions are not granted — for example, that the central columns of the *Thanksgiving Hymns* (and only they) were written by the Teacher of Righteousness himself, or that the Teacher can be dated to the early first century BCE, or that Judah's movement and early Christianity both conform to the type of a "crisis cult." In addition, a good deal depends on being able to identify biblical allusions in the Scrolls and to grasp the significance, in the mind of a given Scroll's writer, of the biblical context of the text being alluded to. In a word, there is far too much speculation.

As a case in point, I refer to the way Wise argues that later sectarians, after the death of their founding Teacher, expected him to come back to atone for their sins and usher in the kingdom of God. This rests on the rather bold hypothesis that the Melchizedek of 11QMelchizedek is to be identified with the Herald of that same document, who in turn is to be identified with the Teacher. It is possible to make a more-or-less plausible argument in favor of each of these identifications, as Wise does, but their combination is a very shaky foundation for the momentous claim that the Teacher is a credible analogue to Jesus on this point.

It is also of interest to observe that the phrase "the Messiah(s) of Aaron and Israel," which rightly plays such a prominent role in other discussions of Qumran messianism, is conspicuous by its virtual absence in Wise's treatment, no doubt because it does not fit his overall reconstruction. He does mention it in a footnote (323n.9), where he concedes that it cannot plausibly be said to apply to Judah, but then he suggests rather lamely that it may represent a later "Zadokite intrusion." It is also telling that he fails to deal with a number of the other messianic texts that Collins discusses, presumably because they, too, do not fit his overall thesis with respect to Judah.

Another specific criticism I would like to bring forward has once again to do with the exegesis of a text in Zechariah. There is a passage in the Damascus Document (CD 19:8-9) that quotes Zech 13:7b, and Wise adduces it as evidence that Judah died a violent death. He translates the quoted text as follows: "Strike down the Shepherd and the sheep will scatter; but I will *draw back my hand from the Oppressed*" (217; my emphasis). This is a very unusual translation, partly because the verbal idiom in question (השיב יד על) always has a violent connotation elsewhere (usually rendered "turn one's hand against"), but also because the noun that is its object (צערים) is never understood elsewhere to mean "oppressors" (217). Commentators differ on whether it should be understood of the "little ones" (of the sheep), or — probably rightly — of subordinate "shepherds." In a footnote Wise defends his rendering "oppressors" by saying that it "follows the sense required by its equation with *aniyim* of Zech. 11:11" and by appealing to the meaning of the root in Syriac (320n.36). I would argue that this is an example of making a Hebrew word mean something implausible in order to suit one's argument. Unfortunately, this is not the only example where Wise has a tendentious rendering of a Hebrew word. Other examples are his translation of *tokhahat* as "trial" (96, 292n.16) and *urtom* as "heavenly splendor" (108-9).

Having said all this, however, it is undeniably true that speculative hypotheses are the lifeblood of creative scholarship and are indispensable for suggesting new lines of investigation. Thus Wise's audacious synthetic proposal constitutes a provocative challenge to the mainstream of Scrolls scholarship to test the validity of his specific proposals and hypotheses. In addition, his novelistic approach to his historical reconstruction adds an immediacy and vividness of concrete detail to the discussion that is too often sorely lacking in the sober and dry-as-dust world of Qumran scholarship.

Perhaps the greatest contribution of Wise's book is that he shows that it is possible to construe the scattered and fragmentary data of the Scrolls in an entirely new way. His bold and very erudite proposal shows that *all* reconstructions of the teachings of the elusive religious group that produced the Scrolls, whether about messianism or some other doctrine, are necessarily based on a host of assumptions that have less than certain foundations. It has often been said that the work of Scrolls research is like doing a giant jigsaw puzzle. This is true not only of the arduous work of physically piecing together the thousands of Scroll fragments, but also of the necessarily speculative work of trying to reconstitute theoretically a system of thought or coherent doctrine from many disparate statements, often with very little knowledge (if any) about their date, their author, or their literary context. It behooves us to be modest in our claims to know what the Dead Sea Scrolls teach about the Messiah.

The two books by Collins and Wise are representative of the range of scholarly opinion on messianism in the Dead Sea Scrolls, but they are certainly not exhaustive. I have not mentioned Israel Knohl, whose little book *The Messiah before Jesus: The Suffering Servant of the Dead Sea Scrolls*[5] is remarkably similar to Wise's but identifies an entirely different historical figure as the pre-Christian Messiah, or a host of other writers who nuance the available options in various ways. But enough has been said to give some sense of the scholarly lay of the land on this topic.

---

5. (Berkeley: University of California Press, 2000).

Messianic Ideas in the Apocalyptic and Related Literature of Early Judaism

Loren T. Stuckenbruck

Introduction

In this paper I shall consider "Messiah" in early Jewish literature. This area of study is important in relation to our understanding of early Christianity for three reasons. First, it has figured prominently in the way beliefs of Jews in "the Messiah" set the stage for the emerging belief among early Jewish Christian communities that Jesus was God's "Anointed One" or "Messiah." In this light, differences between "Christian" and contemporary "Jewish" understanding have often been construed as confirming the "uniqueness" of the Christian understanding of "Messiah." This concern with Christian distinctiveness has, in turn, fed a polarizing mentality that not only oversimplifies early Judaism but also reduces early Christian views about Jesus as "Messiah" to an unnecessarily rigid spectrum of ideas. Second, a reconsideration of this literature is becoming increasingly necessary, given that our evidence for "Messiah" in non-Christian Judaism has been increased through materials published from the Dead Sea materials during the last dozen years.[1] Indeed, the Dead Sea Scrolls, to

---

1. For an early, but timely, attempt at such a broader investigation, see John J. Collins, *The Scepter and the Star* (New York: Doubleday, 1995). During the first forty years after the discovery of the Qumran cave materials, texts mentioning "messiah," "messiahs," or "anointed figures" or containing related messianic terminology were generally only available through the following texts: 1QS col. ix, lines 9-11; 1QSa col. ii, lines 11-22; 1QSb col. v, lines 20-26; 1QM col. v, lines 1-2; col. xi, lines 7-9; 4Q161 frg. 8-10, lines 11-25; 4Q174 col. iii, lines 10-19; 11Q13 col. ii, lines 15-20; CD col. ii, lines 11-13; xii, line 23–xiii, line 1; xiv, lines 18-19; xix,

some degree, may be thought to provide an added, and previously un-available, interpretive context for contemporary Jewish literature. Third and finally, beyond shedding light on Christian origins, we learn that early Jewish ideas about "Messiah" underwent significant development through to the end of the first century CE. Despite the growing independence of Christian communities, especially in the aftermath of 70 CE, speculative ideas about intermediary figures and agents of God attested in non-Christian Jewish literature continued to shape and parallel convictions about the exalted Jesus in Christian communities. Both communities, overlapping in tradition and devotion to the God of Israel, found in language about a Messiah ways of addressing and interpreting their experiences with religious and socio-political conditions under Roman rule in the Mediterranean world.

Initially, however, it is important to delimit the focus of this review. I do so in several ways: (1) We are looking initially at the term "Messiah" as it occurs in the most important textual witnesses of Jewish literature preserved in Greek (χριστός, a sense translation from Hebrew and Aramaic משיח), Latin *(unctus)*, Syriac (משיחא), and Ethiopic *(maš/sih/h)*.[2] We do

---

lines 7-11; and xix, line 33–xx, line 1. Since 1991, however, further such texts have become more fully available through publications: 4Q246 cols. i-ii; 4Q252 frg. 1 col. v; 4Q285 frg. 5; 4Q369 frg. 1 col. ii; 4Q377 frg. 2 col. ii; 4Q458 frg. 2 col. ii; 4Q521 frg. 2 col. ii, lines 1-2; frg. 8, line 9; and 4Q534 frg. 1 col. i. The scholarly literature on these materials is voluminous. For a nearly full bibliography until 1998, see "Bibliography of Messianism and the Dead Sea Scrolls," compiled by Martin B. Abegg and Craig A. Evans (completed by Gerben S. Oegema), in *Qumran-Messianism: Studies on the Messianic Expectations in the Dead Sea Scrolls* (ed. James H. Charlesworth, Hermann Lichtenberger, and Gerben S. Oegema; Tübingen: J. C. B. Mohr [Paul Siebeck], 1998) 204-14. For the most recent full treatment of the Dead Sea "messianic" texts, see Johannes Zimmermann, *Messianische Texte aus Qumran* (WUNT II.104; Tübingen: J. C. B. Mohr [Paul Siebeck], 1998), which offers a material advance on the still very useful work by A. S. van der Woude, *Die messianischen Vorstellungen in der Gemeinde von Qumrân* (Assen: Van Gorcum, 1957).

2. While a consideration of terminology might seem overly narrow, it cautions against unreflected use of the word "messianic" for passages that nowhere actually refer to a Messiah; see, for instance, R. H. Charles's treatment of the concept of a "Messianic Kingdom" in, e.g., *Jubilees* 1:27-29; 23:26-31 and in *1 Enoch* 6–36; 83–90; and 91–104 in *A Critical History of the Doctrine of a Future Life in Israel, in Judaism, and in Christianity* (London: Adam and Charles Black, 1913) 208-11, 213-20 (*1 En* 6–36), 220-23 (*1 En* 83–90), 235-40 (*Jub*), 250-59 (*1 En* 91–104); see also his *The Revelation of St. John* (2 vols.; ICC; Edinburgh: T&T Clark, 1920) 2:142-43; and D. H. Russell, *The Method and Message of Jewish Apocalyptic* (London: SCM Press, 1964) 285-303.

so, recognizing that there will be other eschatological figures, not designated by these terms, who are envisaged as God's agents. For this reason, the present discussion shall not be a broad consideration of "eschatological redeemer figures" in ancient Jewish thought. Put another way, we are not, broadly speaking, looking for "messianic" figures who may or may not carry the title "Messiah." Nevertheless, the narrower focus on figures actually designated as "Messiah" makes it possible to pose the question of what we are doing in this discussion more sharply: What did early Jewish writers have in mind when they chose *this* designation as a suitable one to describe an agent of God? To be sure, some authors who speak of a "Messiah" or "Anointed One" frequently apply other titles or descriptions for the same figure. However, rather than simply adopting a synthetic approach, even within a given document, we look for clues from within the narrative itself or from the author's use of tradition that explain why "Messiah" has occurred in a particular instance. (2) We are here going to throw the spotlight on literature that is essentially non-Christian Jewish in character. This means that we shall not consider passages in writings that were composed by Christian authors (so *Ascension of Isaiah, Odes of Solomon, Apocalypse of Zephaniah,* and *Apocalypse of Sedrach*). Moreover, we shall neither attend to references to "the Messiah" in Christian additions to originally Jewish documents *(Testament of Adam)* nor consider those which, though heavily indebted to Jewish tradition, are Christian in their present form and convey views that cannot be straightforwardly assigned to non-Christian Jewish tradition *(Testaments of the Twelve Patriarchs)*.[3] (3) Given our interest in Jewish tradition that may have shaped early Christian theology, we shall not consider views of "Messiah" in rabbinic or other later Jewish literature (for example, the so-called *3 Enoch*). (4) We shall inquire into two aspects of "Messiah" where these occur: *nature* and *function,* asking in particular what both have to do with perceptions about the activity of the God of Israel. (5) Finally, we shall ask whether any of the texts considered allow us to draw inferences about the social setting in which hope in a Messiah was expressed.

The focus as delineated leads us to consider four Jewish works, which were composed early enough to either pre-date or be contemporaneous

---

3. For an overview of "Messiah" in these Christian and Christianized documents, see James H. Charlesworth, "Messianology in the Biblical Pseudepigrapha," in Charlesworth, Lichtenberger, and Oegema, eds., *Qumran Messianism,* 21-52 (esp. 41-49).

with the growing early Christian movement before the Bar Kochba revolt. These shall be considered in the approximate sequence of composition: *Psalms of Solomon, Similitudes* of *1 Enoch, 4 Ezra* and *2 Baruch.*

Psalms of Solomon

Preserved in Greek and Syriac manuscripts from the tenth to sixteenth centuries,[4] this collection of eighteen psalms was written within a generation of Pompey's capture of Jerusalem in 63 BCE and its aftermath, which saw the overthrow and humiliation of Hasmonaean rule (see especially 2:1-5, 11-14; 8:14-22; and 17:11-18). The psalms are categorically critical of the Hasmonaeans, who are blamed for law-breaking activities in the home and the temple that exceeded even what the Gentiles do (cf. 1:4-8; 2:3-5; 8:8-13). The community behind the psalms believed that Pompey's activity, despite being a means by which God was punishing such "sinners" who had set up illegitimate rule (17:6), had introduced even further impurity and Gentile practices among Jews in Jerusalem (17:13-15, 18b-20), so much so that the pious fled and were scattered "over the whole earth" (17:16-18a). Knowing something about these events, especially as they are depicted among the psalms themselves, takes on particular importance since it is precisely in relation to these that what is said about the Messiah takes shape.

All four references to "Messiah" (Greek χριστός; Syriac *mšyh'*) occur in chs. 17 and 18. They may be listed as follows:

17:32(36) — "There is no unrighteousness in his days in their midst, for all (will be) holy and *their king (shall be the) Messiah Lord.*" (καὶ βασιλεὺς αὐτῶν χριστὸς κύριος; *wmlkyhwn mšyh' mry'*)

---

4. The most thorough description of the textual witnesses is still to be found in Joseph Ziegler, *Sapientia Salomonis* (Septuaginta Vetus Testamentum Graecum XII, 1; Göttingen: Vandenhoeck & Ruprecht, 1962) 7-65. Though the priority of the Greek evidence has been maintained by many scholars who hold that the Syriac version was a translation from the Greek, Joseph L. Trafton has put forth a detailed case favoring the view that the Syriac text groups represent an independent translation from a Semitic (Hebrew) *Vorlage* and thus merit consultation for text-critical problems; so Trafton, *Syriac Version of the Psalms of Solomon: A Critical Evaluation* (SBL Septuagint and Cognate Studies 11; Atlanta: Scholars Press, 1985).

The heading to 18 — "Psalm of Solomon *concerning the Messiah Lord.*"
(ψαλμὸς τοῦ Σαλωμων ἔτι [emend to ἐπὶ?] χριστοῦ κυρίου; no heading in Syriac)

18:5 — "May God purify Israel for the day of mercy with blessing, for the day of election *in the return of his Messiah.*"
(ἐν ἀνάξει χριστοῦ αὐτοῦ; Syriac damaged)

18:7 — (the generation to come, v. 6) . . . "under the disciplinary rod *of the Messiah Lord* in the fear of his God, in wisdom of spirit and of righteousness and of strength."
(χριστοῦ κυρίου)

The present discussion will thus consider chs. 17 and 18, respectively.

In ch. 17, "Messiah Lord" is the title given to a figure whose activities are described in vv. 21-43. The psalmist petitions God to raise him up as "king" of Israel "in the time which you see (or know)." This anointed figure is to be the antithesis of the religio-political rule under the Hasmonaeans: He will be a (legitimate) descendant of David, and is "to rule over Israel your servant" in an ideal way. In the role of a king, this agent of God will "purify Jerusalem from gentiles," dispossess Jewish "sinners from their inheritance," and annihilate "unlawful gentiles" (vv. 22-24). In their place, he will restore to the land (ἐπὶ τῆς γῆς) "a holy people, whom he will lead in righteousness, and will judge the tribes of people who have been sanctified by the Lord his God" (v. 26; cf. vv. 28, 43).

Two main features mark the rule and character of this Messiah: (cultic) purity and justice, on the one hand, and power and might, on the other. First, the "Messiah Lord" is to restore Jerusalem to the pure and prominent state it enjoyed at the beginning of the (here idealized) Davidic monarchy (v. 30). This state will be achieved as he judges not only those people who have been restored (vv. 26, 43), but also the remaining peoples and nations "in the wisdom of his righteousness" (v. 29). This judgment is the pre-condition for a proper order of things. Ultimately, the nations (v. 30), as well as Israel (cf. 7:9), will be subject to his "yoke," and the persecuted righteous who have been scattered throughout the earth (cf. 17:18) will be brought as gifts by the nations "to see the glory of the Lord" (vv. 30-31; cf. Isa 43:4-7). Unequivocally, all the re-gathered people of Israel will be holy (v. 32), leaving no room for "sinners" and corrupt "officials," who will be driven out (v. 36; cf. vv. 23, 27). By the same token, this messianic figure will be "pure from sin" (v. 36) and powerful "in the holy spirit" (v. 37).[5] His "words"[6] will be more refined — that is, they will be in a purer state (note the comparative expression πεπυρωμένα ὑπέρ) — than even the choicest gold and will be comparable to words of holy ones (ἁγίων) in the midst of sanctified peoples (v. 43).[7] It is possible here that the purity of the Messiah's activity is emphasized through a comparison with angels whose worship of God is considered ideal (cf. Ps 89:5-7).[8] Perhaps, then, the Messiah is not only expected to rule as king but also to perform priestly functions. This may be especially the case if the psalmist's description of the Messiah's work is formulated as an antithesis to the Hasmonaean dynasty that, since the rule of Aristobulus I (105-104 BCE), incorporated into one person the claim to be "king" and "high priest."[9]

Second, the author expects the Messiah to exercise power and authority over the nations of the earth. One manifestation of this rule is the destruction of "unrighteous rulers" and "the unlawful nations (ἔθνη παράνομα)" (vv. 22, 24). This retribution against the enemies of God's people might leave the impression that the Messiah is essentially a warrior figure — that is, one who will deliver Israel through military conflict. Indeed, it is at least true in principle that the author claims he "will crush all their substance with an iron rod" (v. 24), which borrows language from Ps 2:9. However, this may in fact be a description of the effect rather than the means, since it is "by the word of his mouth" that this will be accomplished (v. 24; cf. v. 35: "he will strike the earth with the word of his mouth forever"). Thus, unlike the Hasmonaeans, this king will not rule through military might. In emphasizing this very point, the psalmist has probably been inspired by Isa 11:4: "he shall strike the earth with the rod of his mouth, and with the breath of his lips he shall slay the wicked."[10] Significantly, this

5. The Greek witnesses read ἐν πνεύματι ἁγίῳ, while the fragmentary Syriac has *q]dyš*, i.e., "[h]oly" and not "(spirit of) holiness").

6. In the place where the Greek uses two terms for "words" at the beginning and end of v. 43 (ῥήματα and λόγοι), the Syriac has only one term, *ptgm*.

7. For a possible parallel, see 4Q521 frg. 2 col. ii, line 2: "he [i.e., his Messiah] will not depart from the precepts of the holy ones (ממצרת קדושים)."

8. Concerning the exemplary worship of angels in other Second Temple documents, see the *Songs of the Sabbath Sacrifice* (at 4Q400 frg. 2, lines 1-9), *Musar le-Mevin* (4Q418 frg. 55, lines 8-11), and *Jub* 1:17-22.

9. Cf. Josephus, *Antiquities* 13.11.1; see the discussion in Emil Schürer, *The History of the Jewish People in the Age of Jesus Christ* (rev. by Geza Vermes, Martin Goodman, and Fergus Millar; 3 vols.; Edinburgh: T&T Clark, 1973-87) 1:217, 603.

10. So, correctly, Martin Hengel, *Gewalt und Gewaltlosigkeit* (Calwer Hefte, 118;

annihilation of Israel's enemies does not mean that the Gentiles as a whole are to be destroyed. On the contrary, the psalmist does not consider all Gentiles inimical: the Gentiles are to serve God's anointed one (v. 30; cf. *1 En* 52:4), for "he will have mercy on all nations who are before him in fear" (v. 34; cf. *2 Bar* 72:2-4).[11] Presumably those Gentiles who have not oppressed or subjugated Israel will be included in the new order; though they will not be converted as such, they will nevertheless play a positive, if clearly subordinate, role.[12]

Having reviewed the Messiah's character and activities in *Psalms of Solomon,* we may consider the question of who the author thought he would be. The title "Messiah Lord" in 17:32 (and 18:7) does not in any way imply that his position approximates that of the God of Israel. Neither is it correct to suppose that we have here a deliberate or inadvertent Christianization of a Jewish tradition.[13] If anything, we may instead have to do with a very early use of Ps 110:1, in which the second "lord" in the phrase "the Lord said to my lord" is being used of the king, so that a double title is used (as occurs in also Dan 9:25 [מָשִׁיחַ נָגִיד; Theod. χριστοῦ ἡγουμένου]).

Stuttgart: Calwer Verlag, 1971) 36. The motif of a messianic figure slaying the wicked under the influence of Isa 11:4 is attested in 4Q285 frg. 5, line 4 (cf. also *2 Bar* 40:2). The association of Isa 11:4 with the "shoot of Jesse," in turn, led the Targum Isaiah to identify this figure as "a king . . . from the sons of Jesse" from which will come "a Messiah from Israel," no doubt under the influence of Num 24:17; see William Horbury, *Jewish Messianism and the Cult of Christ* (London: SCM Press, 1998) 92-93.

11. A similar combination of passivity and military language may be found in John's Apocalypse, the Christology of which juxtaposes "the Lamb standing as slaughtered," on the one hand, with the activity of the warrior Christ, on the other, "who rules the nations with an iron rod" (cf. Rev 2:27; 12:5; and 19:15); for a recent attempt to address this tension in the Apocalypse, see Loren L. Johns, *The Lamb Christology of the Apocalypse of John* (WUNT 2.167; Tübingen: J. C. B. Mohr [Paul Siebeck], 2003).

12. This is not unlike the place of the nations in Deutero-Isaiah (Isa 42:6; 49:6, 22-26; 60:1-3, 12), for whom the option is either to serve God (i.e., God's people) or to be destroyed. Perhaps *Pss Sol* 17:34 implies the view that the nations will actually worship God in recognition of God's rule (cf., e.g., Pss 86:9; 96:9-10).

13. Some have argued (e.g., Joseph Klausner, *The Messianic Idea in Israel from Its Beginning to the Completion of the Mishnah* [trans. W. F. Stinespring; London: Allen and Unwin, 1956] 321) that in 17:32 an original genitive ("the anointed *of* the Lord") was corrupted by a Christian scribe. In 18:7, the expression χριστοῦ κυρίου may be translated as either "of the Messiah/Anointed of the Lord" or "of the Messiah Lord," but its rendering depends on what one makes of the expression in 17:32. On the other hand, there is no way to translate the double genitive in 18:5 other than "his [i.e., the Lord's] Messiah."

It is not surprising, then, to find that throughout the psalmist makes clear that the Messiah is himself dependent on and subordinate to God, whose activity is ultimately, and immediately, in view. Although the Messiah is a royal figure, ch. 17 is framed by the proclamation that the Lord, the God of Israel, is "our king forever more" (vv. 1, 46). Moreover, in the main body of the psalm, it is God who will raise up David's descendant in his own time (v. 21), and it is God who will make him strong with a holy spirit (v. 37). Indeed, the Lord "is his [i.e., the Messiah Lord's] king" (v. 34). Because of this, the Messiah shall place his hope in God (v. 34; cf. also v. 39) and "shall glorify the Lord in a prominent (place) of the earth" (i.e., Jerusalem; v. 30). The Messiah Lord's kingship over the returnees to Jerusalem will be righteous because he has been "instructed by God" (vv. 31-32a).

The Messiah is not "divine." He has neither heavenly status nor any apparent preexistence. The sinlessness with which he is to be endowed (v. 36; cf. Heb 4:15) functions here to make him an ideal, righteous ruler who sets matters aright in accordance with God's timing and purposes for Israel (cf. Acts 1:6-7). From the psalmist's perspective, he is a *future* agent of God's activity. The main thrust is thus summed up nicely at the conclusion of the psalm: "May God hurry up (to give) his mercy to Israel, may he rescue us from the pollution of profane enemies; the Lord himself is our king forever more."

In ch. 18 the references to the Messiah are very brief and not developed. While the points described in relation to ch. 17 may be inferred for the superscription and v. 7 (cited above at the beginning of this section), the one new element may seem to be in v. 5: ". . . for the day of election in the return (ἀνάξει) of his Messiah." It is unnecessary from this to infer a preexistence, as the psalmist likely has in view the return of legitimate rule by a descendant of David whom God will set apart to fulfill Israel's hope for a theocracy.

Similitudes of *Ethiopic* or *1 Enoch* (chapters 37–71)

Similitudes is a pseudepigraphic "vision of wisdom" given to Enoch that comprises chs. 37–71 of the earliest collection of Enochic compositions commonly called *1 Enoch*. Whereas the antiquity of the remaining parts of *1 Enoch* has not been questioned, the relative date of the *Similitudes* has been subject to some debate. This is so because of J. T. Milik's claim that this work, no fragments of which were found among any of the Dead Sea materials, was an essentially Christian book produced during the latter part of the third century CE.[14] Unconvinced that *Similitudes* shows any trace of Christian composition, many have been more inclined to assign a date of its production to sometime between the latter part of the first century BCE and 100 CE.[15] Indeed, the absence in *Similitudes* of any overt response to Christian tradition, especially in relation to the "Son of Man" figure, seems to push its traditions back into a period before the identification of Jesus with the apocalyptic "Son of Man" as recorded in the Gospels was sufficiently widespread.

Similitudes contains two brief references to a "Messiah" or "Anointed One": 48:10 and 52:4:[16]

48:10 — "On the day of their trouble [i.e., that of the kings of the earth and the wealthy landowners; cf. v. 8] there will be no rest on the earth, and they shall fall before him and shall not rise; and (there is) no one who will take them with his hands and raise them, for they have denied the Lord of the Spirits and his Messiah. Blessed be the name of the Lord of Spirits!"

14. J. T. Milik, *The Books of Enoch: Aramaic Fragments of Qumrân Cave 4* (Oxford: Clarendon Press, 1976) 4, 58, 78, and esp. 94-98 (around or just after 270 CE).

15. These earlier and later dates have been argued, respectively, by Jonas C. Greenfield and Michael E. Stone, "The Enochic Pentateuch and the Date of the Similitudes," *HTR* 70 (1977) 51-65; and Michael Knibb, "The Date of the Parables of Enoch: A Critical Review," *NTS* 25 (1979) 344-57. For a discussion of the debate, see George W. E. Nickelsburg, *Jewish Literature Between the Bible and the Mishnah* (Philadelphia: Fortress, 1981) 221-23. Allusions to an invasion of Judah by Parthians and Medes in 40 BCE (1 *En* 56:5-8) or to the loss of farmland to rich landowners (much maligned in *Similitudes*) during the reign of Herod the Great are not specific enough to be much help. Nickelsburg rightly emphasizes that, at the very least, traditions contained in *Similitudes* were known around the turn of the common era. Drawing attention to the identification of Enoch with the Son of Man at the end of *Similitudes* (1 *En* 71:14), he cites Wisdom of Solomon's allusion to Enoch, a prototype for the persecuted righteous who will become judges over their enemies (4:10-15; cf. 4:16–5:23). Most important for the early date, however, remains the *absence* in *Similitudes* of any overt response to Christian tradition, especially in relation to the "Son of Man" figure.

16. Translations are my own, based on the text published by Michael A. Knibb, *The Ethiopic Book of Enoch* (2 vols.; Oxford: Clarendon Press, 1978) 1:136-37, 142 and 2:134, 136, which in this passage does not differ in any essential details from the texts negotiated by Ephraim Isaac in his essay "1 Enoch," in *Old Testament Pseudepigrapha* (ed. James H. Charlesworth; 2 vols.; Garden City: Doubleday, 1983-85) 1:36-37.

> 52:4 — "And he [i.e., the interpreting angel] said to me, 'All these things which you have seen serve the authority of his Messiah so that he may be mighty and strong upon the earth.'"

These passages occur within the "second parable" (chs. 45–57). Near the beginning of this vision (46:1-8), a figure designated "the Son of Man" — also called "the Chosen One" and "the Righteous One" — has been introduced as the agent of God (called "Head of Days" and mostly "Lord of the Spirits") to execute judgment against the wicked who through wealth have oppressed the righteous (46:1-8). In all likelihood, the "Messiah" referred to in 48:10 is thought to be the same figure. Just prior to 48:10, the author in v. 6 anticipates that a "Chosen One" (identified with "that Son of Man" in v. 2) will be disclosed by God's wisdom to "the holy and righteous ones" whom he will deliver. This figure is preexistent, as he has been "concealed since before the creation of the world" (v. 6), which is parallel to "that Son of Man" who in v. 3 was named before the Lord of the Spirits "before the stars of heaven were made." When the righteous ones are delivered, the wicked kings of the earth and the landowners will be given over to "the chosen ones" for punishment (v. 9). Thus the denial mentioned in v. 10 is a summary way, as elsewhere in the parable (45:1-2; 46:7), of characterizing the activities of the wicked; to oppose those who are righteous is nothing less than a denial of the Lord of the Spirits and his Messiah. The phrase "and his Messiah," this time added to "Lord of the Spirits" as the object of denial (cf. 45:1-2; 46:7), reflects the influence of Ps 2:2: "The kings of the earth set themselves, and the rulers take counsel together, against the Lord and his anointed" (NRSV).[17] However, it is striking that the author has not invested this designation with any further detail. No activity as such is ascribed to God's agent when he is called "his Messiah."

The same brevity and lack of detail apply even more to the reference in 52:4. Here, as in ch. 48, God's Messiah may be implicitly identified with "the Chosen One" (52:6, 9), while the "Son of Man" title does not occur in this part of the vision (i.e., in 52:1–57:3).[18] A connection with the "Son of

---

17. Cf. similarly in Rev 11:15 and 12:10 (cf. 20:6). This christological addition to a statement about God is elsewhere, perhaps also under the influence of Psalm 2, reformulated in relation to "the Lamb" (Rev 5:13; 7:10; 21:22; 22:1, 3).

18. However, "the Chosen One" in *1 En* 62:1 is also called "Son of Man" (*1 En* 62:5). The application to the Chosen One of tradition from Isa 11:4b and Psalm 110 in *1 Enoch* 62 (where in v. 2 "the spirit of righteousness is poured out upon him and the word of his mouth kills the

Man" tradition from Dan 7:13-14 may nonetheless be influential here. The seer's vision of mountains of various metals in the west (52:2) is explained by the angel as phenomena that serve "the authority" of "his Messiah," where the Ethiopic term for "authority" *(seltan)* approximates the Aramaic שלטן in Daniel 7:14, where it denotes the power given to the "one like a son of man."[19] Immediately following in the passage, the angel discloses that these same mountains will dissipate into fluid "before the Chosen One" (v. 6) — that is, the weapons fashioned through these metals will be useless in saving the wicked from judgment "when the Chosen One will appear before the Lord of the Spirits" (v. 9).

These passages allow for several observations. First, the reference to "Messiah" in ch. 48 implies that God's designate is an ideal ruler figure who stands in stark contrast with the wealthy and oppressive kings of the earth and mighty who possess land. Though neither 48:10 nor 52:4 states anything about his activity, the Messiah's domain is conceived as terrestrial. However, it is striking that *Similitudes* makes no explicit attempt to link this figure with a Davidic lineage. This apocalyptic scenario does not envision the restoration of the monarchy, as in *Psalms of Solomon*. Second, the texts say nothing directly about what sort of figure God's Anointed One is supposed to be — that is, whether he is human, angelic, or divine. Something, nonetheless, can be noted if the author of 48:10 is identifying God's Messiah with the "Son of Man" and "Chosen One" mentioned earlier in the chapter. In this case, the author must have regarded the Messiah as preexistent and, as the Chosen One, yet to be revealed in the future. If in the wider context of the second parable (chs. 45–56) the Messiah is identified with the "Son of Man" and "Chosen One," then more can be said: he is a figure exalted to sit on God's throne to judge and to dispense wisdom

---

sinners" and in v. 3 "he sits on the throne of his glory") may suggest that he is being understood as a judge in the royal messianic tradition; see, e.g., J. Theison, *Der auserwählte Richter. Untersuchungen zum traditionsgeschichtlichen Ort der Menschensohngestalt der Bilderreden des äthiopischen Henoch* (Studien zur Umwelt des Neuen Testament 12; Göttingen: Vandenhoeck & Ruprecht, 1975) 111-13, 114-24; and Matthew Black, "The Messianism of the Parables of Enoch: Their Date and Contribution to Christian Origins," in *The Messiah: Developments in Earliest Judaism and Christianity* (ed. James H. Charlesworth; Minneapolis: Fortress, 1992) 145-68 (here 159), who emphasizes beyond Theison the influence of the Isaianic Ebed-Jahweh tradition on the Chosen One as well (esp. Isa 49:2-3, 7; 52:13).

19. As suggested, though with caution, by James C. VanderKam, "Righteous One, Messiah, Chosen One, and Son of Man in 1 Enoch 37–71," in Charlesworth, ed., *The Messiah*, 169-91 (here 171-72).

(45:3; 51:3; 55:3); he has a human and angel-like appearance (46:1); he removes the wicked (human and demonic) from positions of power (45:6; 46:4-7; 48:8-10; 52:6-9; 53:5-7; 55:4); and — without parallel in any earlier or contemporary Jewish literature — he can even be worshiped alongside God "by all those who dwell upon the earth" (48:5; cf. 46:5). Third, since these functions are co-opted into a profile for the Messiah only by extension, we may suggest that the activities and status ascribed to the eschatological vice-regent in *Similitudes* do not seem to have resulted from a writer's speculation about God's Messiah per se (which does not appear in an absolute form).[20] He may be a composite figure of many titles, but it is questionable how much the title itself has shaped the author's understanding. The formative background for this speculation lies much more in Dan 7:9-14 and related traditions (in addition to biblical tradition, also the seated man-like figure recording judgment in *Animal Apocalypse; 1 En* 90:14, 17). In short, it is not *as a Messiah* that God's eschatological agent does all these things, but rather as the angelic and heavenly "Son of Man" whom the author further anchors in tradition by applying the "messianic" designation.

4 Ezra (= 2 Esdras 3–14)

This pseudepigraphon, attributed to Ezra thirty years after the destruction of the first temple in 586 BCE (cf. *4 Ez* 3:1), consists of a series of seven dialogues or visions composed around the turn of the second century CE, that is, in the aftermath of the destruction of the second temple in 70 CE. These visions, though framed by Christian compositions *5 Ezra* and *6 Ezra*, respectively, with few exceptions preserve non-Christian Jewish tradition. The document does not survive in its original language, and so the most important textual witnesses to *4 Ezra* are preserved for us in Latin and Syriac manuscripts. These, in addition to the evidence from Georgian, Ar-

---

20. For this reason one should not, conversely, hasten without further evidence to construe the mention of a "Chosen One" in other texts (such as "the Chosen One of God," **בחיר אלהא**, in 4Q534 frg. 3 col. i, line 10) as a reference to a "messiah." Thus Craig Evans rightly adduces allusions to Isa 11:4 in the 4Q534 fragment (lines 6-10) as more important than the designation itself; see Evans, "Are the 'Son' Texts at Qumran Messianic? Reflections on 4Q369 and Related Scrolls," in Charlesworth, Lichtenberger, Oegema, eds., *Qumran-Messianism*, 135-53 (here 144-45).

menian, and Ethiopic translations, furnish enough evidence to determine more original Jewish traditions behind the occasionally Christian intrusions into the texts.[21] In *4 Ezra* several passages are concerned with a "Messiah" (Lat. *unctus;* Syr. *mšyh'*) figure: 7:26-44 (from the third vision); 11:36–12:34 (from the fifth vision); and, by extension, 13:3–14:9 (from the sixth and seventh visions).

4 Ezra 7:26-44: The Temporary Appearance of the Messiah

The Messiah is first referred to in the third vision during the course of the interpreting angel's speech that responds to the seer's queries. Ezra has continued to question in 6:38-59 why God's covenant people do not possess the world as they should, while other nations, who have no special relationship with God, are allowed to dominate Israel (esp. 6:55-59). The angel counters, first by asserting the necessity of danger and hardship (7:3-9) and distinguishing between present and future experience and then by affirming that all, whether righteous or wicked, are accountable to the Law. This dialogue sets the stage for the angel's description of a time to come when things will not be as they are now: a city and land, previously unseen and hidden, will be disclosed, and wonders will be seen (7:26-28). This time lies in the future, when a figure called "my son the Messiah"[22] and those who are with him (i.e., the righteous dead) will be revealed,[23] while the remaining ones (the righteous) "shall rejoice four hundred years" (v. 28). The passage then continues by making what might seem to be an unusual claim:

---

21. Below, I cite the English translation by Bruce M. Metzger, who takes many of the differences between the versions into account in his translation and notes; see Metzger, "The Fourth Book of Ezra," in Charlesworth, ed., *Old Testament Pseudepigrapha,* 1:517-59.

22. Here the Latin reading *filius meus Iesus* is surely secondary, and so the Syriac (*bry mšyh'*, close to similar readings in the Ethiopic, Georgian, and Armenian) is to be supported; see Michael E. Stone, *Fourth Ezra: A Commentary on the Book of Fourth Ezra* (Hermeneia; Minneapolis: Fortress, 1990) 208.

23. I am not certain that this revealing of the Messiah implies his preexistence, as is the case in *Similitudes* in relation to "the Chosen One" (*1 En* 48:6) who "was hidden . . . before the world was created." Preexistence for the Messiah is a more likely concept in the later visions of *4 Ezra* (see below; cf. esp. 13:26).

> And after these years my son[24] the Messiah will die *(morietur filius meus christus)*, and all who draw human breath. And the world shall be turned back to primeval silence for seven days, as it was at the first beginnings; so that no one shall be left. (7:29-30)

The author divides time into two ages, one of this world and one of the world to come (7:50; cf. 4:26; 6:7, 20, 25-28; 7:112-15). The revelation of the Messiah will occur as the first of several events that bring this age to a close. Nothing is explicitly stated about a kingdom that this Messiah is to inaugurate; however, that he is expected to rule is implied by the specification of a limited number of years, during which conditions for the righteous will give cause for rejoicing. The surprising element here is the mention of the Messiah's death, which, though attested in later Jewish traditions,[25] is unprecedented here. Unlike Christian conviction with regard to Jesus' death, this event is not apparently the result of any persecution or suffering[26] and carries with it no salvific or atoning significance. Instead, coupled with the death of the remainder of humanity, it serves as a "ground clearing" of this age that prepares for the judgment that leads to life in the world to come. The Messiah's death, then, helps to mark the closing of this age.

The hiatus between the old age and judgment is underscored by a space of time, seven days of primeval silence, which signals the correspondence between *Urzeit* and *Endzeit* shared by many apocalyptic writers. The judgment itself then occurs as the last event of this age, when there is a general resurrection of both the righteous and wicked (7:32; cf. Dan 12:2). As such, the judgment does not happen all at once; rather, it is envisioned as a drawn-out process of "a week of years" (7:43). Significantly, it is "the Most High," not the Messiah, who "will be revealed upon the seat of judgment" (7:33) to pronounce punishment upon many and

---

24. On this expression in conjunction with "Messiah," see the discussion of *4 Ezra* 13 below.

25. Concerning these, see, e.g., George Foot Moore, *Judaism in the First Centuries of the Christian Era: The Age of the Tannaim* (3 vols.; Cambridge, MA: Harvard University Press, 1927-30) 2:370-71.

26. This means that not too much should be inferred from the possibility that here "servant" ultimately lies behind the Lat. "son," insofar as it may have anything to do with the Ebed-Yahweh tradition in Isaiah 52–53. So correctly E. Sjöberg, *Der Menschensohn im äthiopischen Henochbuch* (Lund: Gleerup, 1946) 133-34.

reward to the few (7:138–8:3). The Messiah, aside from setting up a temporary kingdom, is given no further role in any of the subsequent eschatological events.

4 Ezra 11:1–12:36: *The Lion Messiah*

The fifth vision of the seer is interpreted by the angel in relation to the Messiah. The vision itself opens with an eagle with twelve wings and three heads emerging from the sea and subjecting "everything under heaven" to itself (11:6). From the twelve wings eight smaller ones grew; each of the twelve wings and two of the little ones ruled in succession, each disappearing after its reign, until three heads and six little wings remained. After brief reigns, two of the little wings were devoured by the middle head, which then ruled oppressively "over the whole earth" with a power greater than all the previous rulers (11:32). This head disappeared, leaving the remaining right head to devour the left one (11:35). The vision shifts focus to "a creature like a lion" that is stirred from the forest. With a human voice, this lion addressed the eagle on behalf of the Most High. It called the eagle "the fourth beast" that God had allowed to reign in the world and then announced its doom (11:36-46). At the conclusion of the lion's words, the last head disappeared, and two further wings ruled briefly until they disappeared as well (12:1-3).

In the interpretation, the author explicitly acknowledges that the vision is adapted from Daniel (12:11), who, however, was not given the proper explanation for his "fourth kingdom" (Dan 7:7). This kingdom, the eagle "from the sea," is identified as the Roman Empire, while the wings and heads represent its kings. The lion that spoke to the eagle is interpreted as "the Messiah whom the Most High has kept until the end of days, who will arise from the posterity of David" (12:32; cf. Gen 49:9-10 and Rev 5:5). He is the one who, from "his judgment seat" (contrast with *4 Ez* 7:33), will denounce and destroy the ungodly, while at the same time delivering the righteous remnant among God's people. In stating that the remnant will be made joyful, the author refers back to the earlier vision "of which I spoke to you at the beginning" (cf. 7:28).

Several points may be noticed from this vision. First, as in *Psalms of Solomon,* the Davidic pedigree of the Messiah is stressed. Nothing is explicitly said about his nature. The claim that "the Most High has kept [the

Messiah] until the end of days" implies that he is a preexistent figure,[27] or, correspondingly, that he is a heavenly or angelic being. His status as a descendant from David does not contradict the notion of his preexistence;[28] this suggests merely that the future Messiah is also a human being whose activities will not be unleashed until the close of the present age. Second, in contrast to the earlier vision in ch. 7, the Messiah here takes on a more active role in the eschatological events described: whereas God is the one who pronounces judgment in the earlier vision, the Messiah is now the one who occupies "his judgment seat." This is, however, a preliminary judgment, as "the day of judgment," which is yet to come, is described in neither the vision nor its interpretation.[29] Third, in addition to dispensing judgment, the Messiah is to carry out the sentence by destroying the Roman Empire. The Messiah, then, is a military or warrior figure as well.[30] Fourth and finally, he will deliver a righteous remnant of Israel. The remnant refers to those who will live in the age to come. The author of *4 Ezra* does not think the Messiah will restore Israel to its former glory in the way described in *Psalms of Solomon*. He envisions a clear break between the past, which belongs to this age, and the future, which belongs to a different order of things. For this reason, the Messiah, as descended from David, is involved in events that relate to a future that still lies within the present age. When he delivers "the remnant of my people, . . . he will make them joyful *until the end comes*" (12:34).

27. Significantly, the term "hidden" does not occur in any of the versions (in contrast to "the Chosen One" in *1 En* 48:6); the sense of the phrase is less a statement about the Messiah's nature than about the (eschatological) timing of his activity.

28. See Stone's apt arguments, *Fourth Ezra*, 210.

29. There is no inconsistency, therefore, with the scenario in ch. 7, in which God acts as judge, as there the author is concerned with the final judgment. The distinction between the Messiah's judgment (i.e., of the Roman Empire) in ch. 12 and God's judgment of the wicked in ch. 7 has sometimes not been adequately perceived; so recently, e.g., Timo Eskola, *Messiah and the Throne: Jewish Merkabah Mysticism and Early Christian Exaltation Discourse* (WUNT 142; Tübingen: J. C. B. Mohr [Paul Siebeck], 2001) 100. On the consistency of eschatology in *4 Ezra*, see Peter Schäfer, "Die Lehre von den zwei Welten in 4. Buch Esra und in der tannaitischen Literatur," in Schäfer, *Studien zur Geschichte und Theologie des rabbinischen Judentums* (Arbeiten zur Geschichte des antiken Judentums und des Urchristentums 15; Leiden: Brill, 1978) 244-91.

30. As emphasized by Michael E. Stone, "The Concept of the Messiah in IV Ezra," in *Religions in Antiquity: Essays in Memory of Erwin Ramsdell Goodenough,* ed. J. Neusner (Studies in the History of Religions 14; Leiden: Brill, 1968) 295-312 (here 302), though at the expense of noting the importance of the Messiah's juridical activity.

4 Ezra 13:1-56: *The Man from the Sea*

In this section, the eschatological deliverer is not actually designated "Messiah." However, his function as one who destroys the enemies of the righteous at a time appointed by God (13:26, 52) makes it clear that the author is thinking of the figure he has called the Messiah in chs. 7 and 12. The dominant designation here is, instead, "son," which in the Latin version is rendered by the term *filius*. Scholars have argued that the messianic background for this term is strengthened in the more ambiguous Greek παῖς ("son," "servant"), which, in turn, goes back to the Hebrew עֶבֶד ("servant"; cf. Ps 89:20-37, esp. vv. 20 and 26-27).[31] This seems, however, a remote way of establishing the messianic profile of the "man." More important may be two further considerations. First, there is the reception of Psalm 2, which at once refers to the conspiracy "against the Lord and his anointed one (מָשִׁיחַ)" (Ps 2:2; cf. 1 En 48:10) and the Lord's decree to the psalmist, "You are my son (בְּנִי); today I have begotten you (יְלִדְתִּיךָ)" (Ps 2:7). The identification of "his [the Lord's] anointed one" together with "my [the Lord's] son" was certainly current in Jewish circles by the turn of the Common Era, as is attested in the Dead Sea documents (esp. 1QSa col. ii, lines 11-12[32]). While 4 Ezra does not explicitly cite Psalm 2, the fixed designation "my son" in the sixth vision (13:32, 37, 52; cf. 14:9) would be consistent with this, and, as such, it is possible that the author knew the identification of "my son" and "anointed one" based on the biblical tradition. In this light the double designation "my son the Messiah" in the Syriac version of 7:28

---

31. So, e.g., Ulrich B. Müller, in *Messias und Menschensohn in jüdischen Apokalypsen und in der Offenbarung Johannes* (Studien zum Neuen Testament und seiner Umwelt 6; Gütersloh: Gerd Mohn, 1972) 90; and John J. Collins, *The Apocalyptic Imagination* (New York: Crossroad, 1987) 166-67, 244.

32. The reading יוֹלִיד instead of יוֹלִי, as argued by the original editor of 1Q28a, is a more accurate construal of the letters: "when [God] will be[g]et the Messiah"; cf. D. Barthélemy, in D. Barthélemy and J. T. Milik, *Qumran Cave 1* (DJD 1; Oxford: Clarendon Press, 1955) 117-18. Evans, "Are the 'Son' Texts at Qumran Messianic?" 141-52 argues similarly that 4Q174 (col. i, lines 10-13), 4Q246 (col. i, line 9–ii, line 1), 4Q534 (frg. 3 col. i, lines 10-11), and 4Q369 (frg. 1 col. ii, lines 6-10) all convey tradition that associates the Davidic descendant with "sonship" in relation to God. Of these texts, 4Q246 has special affinity with the sonship terminology in 4 Ezra 13, as the authors of both documents depict God's Son in terms that draw heavily on the "one like a son of man" tradition in Daniel 7; see Zimmermann, *Messianische Texte*, 167-70: 4Q246 is evidence that in pre-Christian times the "son of man" from Daniel 7 could already be understood as "Son of God" (170).

takes on a special importance. Second, and even more salient, is the author's use of tradition from Daniel 7 without making an explicit claim about the protagonist's Davidic pedigree. The "man from the sea" is an imaginative interpretation of Daniel's "one as a son of man," which places the author in a position to claim more about the nature of this eschatological figure than in the previous visions. The interpretation of this "man" as "my son" reflects a fusion of ideas: the heavenly "one like a son of man" in Daniel 7 is ultimately appropriated by the author, not as the heavenly Son of Man (as is the case in *Similitudes*), but as God's "Son" in whom the symbolic significance of "the man from the sea" is not lost.[33] The role of God's eschatological agent in *4 Ezra* 13 is thus universalized; beyond ch. 12's focus on the Roman Empire, the judgment and destruction that he metes out from Mt. Zion embrace all nations and inhabitants of the earth who assemble against him (13:33-39; cf. Psalm 2). In his destruction of Israel's enemies, the "man" of the vision reflects what has been associated with "Messiah" in earlier tradition. While he is militaristic, his function as a warrior, similar to *Psalms of Solomon* (17:24, 35), is qualified by the fact that he accomplishes this without conventional military instruments and draws on tradition from Isa 11:4:

> And behold, when he saw the onrush of the approaching multitude, he neither lifted his hand nor held a spear or any weapon of war; but I saw only how he sent forth from his mouth as it were a stream of fire, and from his lips a flaming breath, and from his tongue he shot forth a storm of sparks. (*4 Ez* 13:9-10)

The author's use of Isaiah 11 is more elaborate than that of *Psalms of Solomon*. The result described, however, is every bit what one could expect from military engagement: the multitude is completely burned, leaving only "the dust of ashes and the smell of smoke" (13:11).

Thus, the identification of "my son" and "man" from ch. 13, on the one hand, with the "Messiah" from chs. 7 and 12, on the other hand, is implicit, based on tradition-historical considerations and on the prominence of a figure in the parallel scenarios of eschatological events in the document. Why is this implicit? For the author, the concept of "Messiah" re-

---

33. As we have seen above, the fusion between "Son of Man" and "Messiah" is more explicit in *Similitudes*.

mains in the strict sense one concerned with a human designate of God descended from David. Because the author wished to emphasize the preexistent nature of this figure even more than in the previous visions (esp. 13:26; cf. 13:32, as 7:28), "Messiah" was in itself no longer sufficient; he found it necessary to use more comprehensive, far-reaching, though still related, designations. The interplay of the human imagery in the vision and the language of divine sonship in the interpretation feeds the author's claim that eschatological events will involve more than simply the restoration of a Davidic kingdom.[34]

2 Baruch

The author of 2 Baruch composed his work soon after 4 Ezra, that is, after the destruction of the Second Temple and perhaps at the turn of or during the early part of the second century CE. 2 Baruch has much in common with its predecessor, including its use of the Babylonian destruction of the First Temple as the analogy through which to interpret the more recent catastrophic events at the hands of Rome.[35] There are, however, many differences in the way the author of 2 Baruch treats common themes. Not surprisingly, this applies also to those passages that refer to the Messiah. The text is preserved in an important Syriac manuscript from Milan (dated sixth to seventh century CE), which claims that the version is a translation from Greek. The Greek is extant, however, only through a small fragment, while a more secondary version exists in an Arabic version.[36] The original language may have been either Hebrew or Aramaic.

References to God's eschatological "Messiah" or "Anointed One" occur in three groups: (1) 29:3 and 30:1 (within a section, chs. 26–30, which describes eschatological calamities and the messianic age); (2) 39:7 and 40:1 (within chs. 35–40, a forest vision and its interpretation); and (3) 70:9

---

34. Despite my reservation simply to brand "one like a man" as "the Messiah," I agree with John Collins's observation that ch. 13 reflects a conceptual development that moves beyond that of chs. 7 and 12; cf. Collins, *The Apocalyptic Imagination*, 166-67.

35. See further Collins, *The Apocalyptic Imagination*, 178.

36. See A. F. J. Klijn, "2 (Syriac Apocalypse of) Baruch," in Charlesworth, ed., *Old Testament Pseudepigrapha*, 1:615-16. The English translations given here follow those of Klijn, with the exception that, for clarity's sake, I have preferred the term "Messiah" to his equivalent rendering, "Anointed One."

and 72:2 (within chs. 53–76, a vision of clouds and its lengthy interpretation). We discuss these texts in turn.

2 Baruch *29:3 and 30:1:*
The Messiah's Revelation and Return

Chapter 26 begins with a description of eschatological "tribulation," which is to be a lengthy process divided into twelve periods. After recounting the worldwide calamities associated with each of these periods, the author goes on to claim that protection will be reserved for those who are "found in this land" (29:2). It is then that "the Messiah" (Syr. *mšyh*ʾ) "will begin to be revealed," a motif we have already noticed in the first reference to the Messiah in *4 Ez* 7:28 and in what happens to "the Chosen One" in the *Similitudes* (*1 En* 46:6). This disclosure ushers in an age of bliss characterized by abundance of food, fertility, wonders, and good health for the protected righteous ones of the land. The author has here added the Messiah to an already known tradition of apocalyptic speculation about a period of future bliss and reward (see *Book of Watchers* in *1 En* 10:17-22 and *Book of Giants* in 1Q23 frgs. 1 + 6 + 22),[37] making his appearance the means by which this period is initiated.

In 30:1, a further, spectacular event is associated with the Messiah's appearance, also referred to as a return "with glory": the resurrection of those who "sleep in hope of him." Unlike the general resurrection of both the righteous and wicked in *4 Ez* 7:32, this event is limited to the righteous who "will enjoy themselves" (*2 Bar* 30:2), while "the souls of the wicked will waste away" and undergo torment (30:5). The "returning" of the Messiah may be a hint that the author considers him to be a descendant from David (cf. *Pss Sol* 18:5) and for the author probably implies that he is preexistent.[38] In *2 Baruch* 29–30, the presence of the Messiah is enough to

37. For a publication and discussion of this combined group of fragments, see L. Stuckenbruck, "1Q23 (Re-edition)," in *Qumran Cave 4 XXVI: Cryptic Texts and Miscellanea, Part 1* (ed. Stephen J. Pfann et al.; DJD 36; Oxford: Clarendon Press, 2000) 50-52.

38. Scholarly opinion is divided on how to interpret the motif of the Messiah's "returning." P.-M. Bogaert, *Apocalypse de Baruch: Introduction, traduction du Syriac et commentaire* (2 vols.; Sources chrétiennes 144-45; Paris: du Cerfs, 1969) 1:416 argues that this return is an even more future event that has in view his resumption of glory and his resurrection. Along these lines, therefore, Ulrich B. Müller has argued that this part of the sen-

generate the events described. The text does not attribute any activities to him; what happens in relation to him is ultimately regulated by the God of Israel.

2 Baruch 39:7 and 40:1:
"My Messiah" as the Fountain and the Vine

In response to his despondence over the destruction of Jerusalem and the Temple, the seer is given a vision of a forest. He sees a large forest surrounded by "high mountains and rugged rocks" (36:2; cf. 39:2). At the appearance of a vine watered by a great fountain, the forest is drowned and uprooted, with the exception of one cedar tree (36:5). In a fashion similar to the lion episode in 4 Ezra 12, the vine then speaks to the cedar, reproving it for its wickedness, and decrees for it a period of "sleep in distress and rest in pain" until the time for an eternal torment comes (2 Bar 36:7-11).

In the interpretation, the forest is interpreted as four world kingdoms (cf. Dan 7:2-8), each of which, being increasingly evil, is destroyed in turn. The last of these kingdoms will be in power through "a multitude of times," and the unrighteous will seek refuge in it (2 Bar 39:5-6). The duration of this kingdom is measured, and when the time of its end draws near, "the dominion of my Messiah, which is like the fountain and the vine, will be revealed" (39:7). The remaining cedar from the vision represents a ruler, who — while the rest have been destroyed — is taken alive to Mt. Zion, where a court proceeding conducted by "my Messiah" against him takes place. After convicting this remaining archenemy of his evil deeds, the Messiah "will kill him" (cf. Isa 11:4b; 4Q285 frg. 7, line 4[39]). The Messiah's dominion then commences; it is to last for a limited time, that is, "until the

---

tence (i.e., "when he returns in glory") must be a Christian addition; cf. Müller, *Messias und Menschensohn*, 142-44. It should be noted, however, that the interpretation that construes the Messiah's "return" in relation to his preexistence derives from a consideration of the wider narrative context (cf. 39:7) and thus contrasts with that of *Pss Sol* 18:5, where preexistence is not in view (see above).

39. As is now well known, this fragment preserves a citation of Isa 10:34 and goes on to describe the messianic figure — called "the branch of David" (line 3) and "the prince of the congregation" (line 4) — who slays an inimical figure (זהמיטו) with language that alludes to Isa 11:4.

world of corruption" is complete.[40] The author at this point does not go on to describe what will ultimately happen after this. As in *4 Ezra*, the Messiah's reign is intended as a prelude to the end.

2 Baruch 70:9 and 72:2:
"The Messiah" as Slayer of Israel's Enemies

The main actor in the eschatological events is God "the Most High," who orchestrates a series of catastrophes among the nations of the earth (war, earthquake, fire, and famine) and delivers over — expressed through a *passivum divinum* — all who have escaped with their lives "into the hands of my Servant, the Messiah" (70:9). As the following passage in 72:1-6 shows, the primary function of the Messiah is to destroy the wicked ones, that is, those who are inimical to Israel; as in chs. 39–40, and unlike *4 Ezra* 12 (and 13), nothing is said about his rescue of the righteous. However, whereas in chs. 39–40 the Messiah convicts and slays the single ruler symbolized by the cedar, according to 72:2 his role is more comprehensive: he convenes all nations, sparing some and killing others.

Three things may be noted about the Messiah's activity in this passage. First, destruction is not the lot for all Gentiles, but rather is confined to those nations which "ruled over" Israel.[41] The same is similarly implied in the way the nations are treated in *Pss Sol* 17:34 (see above and n. 12). Second, the Messiah's profile as a warrior is not mitigated by allusions to biblical tradition (as in *Psalms of Solomon* 17 and *4 Ezra* 13). The nations to whom Israel has been subjected "will be delivered up to the sword" (*2 Bar* 72:6). Just who will do the killing is not specified. The "sword" is, however, a general way of referring to conflict by material means and occurs in earlier apocalyptic documents as the means by which revenge is taken out upon the wicked (cf., e.g., *Jub* 5:7, 9; *1 En* 62:13; 90:34; and 91:12; in the latter two the sword being wielded by the righteous). Third, the Messiah will sit down "on the throne of his kingdom" (*2 Bar* 73:1), inaugurating a reign, the

---

40. A similar idea, though explained differently, is found in 1 Corinthians 15, in which Paul draws on a combination of Pss 8:6 and 110:4 to argue that the reign of Christ will last until "all his enemies" (i.e., "every ruler and every authority and power") have been subjected "under his feet," before the kingdom is handed on to "God the Father" (1 Cor 15:24-28).

41. So Charlesworth, "Messianology in the Biblical Pseudepigrapha," 35.

bliss during which is described in details inspired by Gen 3:16-18 and Isa 11:6-8 (*2 Bar* 73:1b–74:4). As in *4 Ezra* 7 and 12 and in *2 Baruch* 30, joy accompanies his reign and here sums up the emotion awaiting those who will be rewarded for their righteousness.

Conclusion

Our survey of "Messiah" in four non-Christian Jewish writings has encountered a very broad profile: an eschatological ruler, chosen by God to act decisively against the wicked on behalf of the righteous of God's people Israel. Beyond this, diversity takes over. The texts considered reveal the degree to which this messianic speculation varied from author to author and even within the documents themselves. There is no indication that the variation within documents was considered problematic in the transmission of the text, so that copyists, beyond isolated instances, seem not to have attempted to either systematize or harmonize what passages relate about God's anointed one. We have considered a number of motifs held in common by more than one of these writings in relation to a "Messiah" figure: Davidic lineage, preexistence, effects of his disclosure or coming; warrior activity; the interpretation of certain biblical texts (esp. Psalm 2; Daniel 7; and Isaiah 11); and other designations that apply from the narrative contexts (e.g., "Son," "Son of Man," "Chosen One"). While in this discussion we have had occasion to note where parallels between these traditions exist, it is striking that the motifs are neither found in all the literature nor, if there, handled in the same way. Thus, beyond their immediate literary presentations, these compositions resist any attempt to streamline or synthesize their respective ideas,[42] ideas that are integral to the particular concerns of the authors and their communities and that also depend on their respective approaches to the tradition-historical building blocks they had to hand.

Thus, at least in relation to this material, James Charlesworth is correct to say that the question "Why did Jews not recognise Jesus was the Messiah?" is misconstrued;[43] this question easily assumes a high degree of

---

42. Thus the synthetic and thematic overviews of ancient Jewish messianic ideas are in danger of leaving a misleading impression; so, e.g., Schürer, *The History of the Jewish People*, 2:488-554.

43. Charlesworth, "From Messianology to Christology: Problems and Prospects," in Charlesworth, ed., *The Messiah*, 3-35 (here 13).

coherence in Jewish thought, as well as presupposing that early Christian communities, which thrived in culturally and geographically diverse parts of the Mediterranean world, would have shared a common understanding.[44] I find it hard to imagine that Jewish readers of Daniel 7, *Psalms of Solomon*, or any of the other documents considered here would have tried to negotiate the texts around a basic core tradition — not found in any one of our passages — about God's eschatological Messiah. What we do have here, however, is a series of documents composed near the turn of the Common Era by Jews who were inspired by biblical tradition and subsequent patterns and traditions of interpretation to express their hope in a world restored to being totally in the control of the God of Israel. Such a dynamic hope drove their descriptions of eschatological events to be "creatively biblical" at every turn. We should not be surprised, therefore, if figures called "Messiah" participate in at least some of the apocalyptic reformulations of this hope.

44. If we allow for such diversity in both early Christian and Jewish communities, there is no reason to suppose that, beyond the reconciliation of "Messiah" by Christians to the experiences of Jesus, Jewish and Christian ideas were necessarily very distinct from one another; the road from a Davidic Messiah in *Psalms of Solomon* to Jesus the Messiah in John's Apocalypse who, as the Lamb and Davidic Lion of Judah, holds Rome to account for its oppression of the faithful, is on one level not very far. Broadly speaking, Jewish ideas about "Messiah" certainly shaped those of Jesus' followers. At the same time, *the ways of achieving the views that were shared* among the texts reviewed here can hardly be said to be coherent among themselves, not to mention how these were reapplied and readapted by Christians. I am therefore less inclined to speak as confidently as William Horbury about "The Coherence of Messianism"; see Horbury, *Jewish Messianism and the Cult of Christ*, esp. 64-108, who is very aware of the diversity of the sources.

PART II
NEW TESTAMENT PERSPECTIVE

Jesus as Messiah in Mark and Matthew

I. Howard Marshall

It would be difficult to undertake the task of delineating the presentation of Jesus as Messiah in Mark and Matthew without making some comparison between the two Gospels; and the common assumption, which I share, that Matthew utilized Mark in the composition of his own Gospel further encourages such an approach. The term "Messiah" in its Greek translation "Christ" figures in both Gospels, seven times in Mark and sixteen times in Matthew, but our concern is with the broader motif of Messianism in relation to the depiction of Jesus. There is a general recognition today among scholars that, while the Gospels contain a number of words or phrases used as designations of Jesus, the presentation of him takes place through the medium of narratives in which these designations find their proper contexts. The Gospels contain christological statements, but the Christology is revealed to the readers by the medium of a developing story. I shall argue that the Christology is concerned to a considerable extent with what Jesus does, and that a variety of motifs contribute to an understanding of him as Messiah. The question whether Jesus is the Messiah of Jewish expectations gives way to a consideration of the way in which Jesus transforms these expectations by what he says and does. Although there is continuity with Old Testament and Jewish expectation, from now on Messiahship is understood in terms of what Jesus did. Thus the apparently simple Jewish question "Are you the Messiah?" can only be answered in the time-honored manner of the philosopher who responds with, "Well, it all depends on what you mean by . . . ," and in this particular case it is not so much a question of choosing among a set of existing options as of recognizing that a number of existing elements have been brought together in a new blend that is fundamentally shaped by the creativity of Jesus the Messiah.[1]

The Gospel of Mark

The Prologue

Mark's starting point is "the good news about Jesus the Messiah" (Mark 1:1).[2] Whether Jesus is further described in this opening quasi-title as "Son of God" is a moot point; a significant minority of versions and commentators regard the phrase as a later addition, and I am inclined now to agree with them.[3] Thus Mark is concerned primarily with Jesus and his significance as the theme and author of good news, a fact that is illustrated by the way in which he is the subject or central concern of virtually every pericope. The title is of course Mark's own wording, and therefore what we have here is an editorial comment revealing his own understanding.

What happens was planned by God and foretold by him through a prophet. In the first part of a complicated citation, somebody, presumably God himself, announces that he will send a messenger ahead of "you" who will prepare your way. In the original prophecy (Mal 3:1) God is sending a messenger to prepare the way, and then he himself (God) will suddenly

---

1. In addition to works cited below, see M. De Jonge, *Christology in Context: The Earliest Christian Response to Jesus* (Philadelphia: Westminster, 1988); B. Witherington III, *The Many Faces of the Christ: The Christologies of the New Testament and Beyond* (New York: Crossroad, 1998).

2. Biblical citations are normally from the TNIV (New Testament) and NIV (Old Testament).

3. Significantly, the conservative but textually well-informed TNIV relegates it to the margin. It is retained by NRSV, but bracketed by NA. It is accepted by R. T. France, *The Gospel of Mark* (Grand Rapids: Eerdmans; Carlisle: Paternoster, 2002) 33; R. A. Guelich, *Mark 1–8:26* (Dallas: Word, 1989) 6; R. H. Gundry, *Mark: A Commentary on His Apology for the Cross* (Grand Rapids: Eerdmans, 1993) 33; rejected by R. Pesch, *Das Markusevangelium* (2 vols.; Freiburg: Herder, 1976) 1:74; J. Marcus, *Mark 1–8: A New Translation with Introduction and Commentary* (New York: Doubleday, 2000) 141. M. D. Hooker is uncertain in *A Commentary on the Gospel according to St Mark* (London: A & C Black, 1991) 34; but in M. D. Hooker, "'Who Can This Be?' The Christology of Mark's Gospel," in *Contours of Christology in the New Testament* (ed. R. N. Longenecker; Grand Rapids: Eerdmans, 2005) 79-99, she is inclined to omission. The case against its originality is fully presented by P. M. Head, "A Text-Critical Study of Mark 1.1 'The Beginning of the Gospel of Jesus Christ,'" *NTS* 37 (1991) 621-29.

come to his temple.[4] Here in Mark, John is this messenger sent by God. But there is a change of pronoun from "before *me*" in the text of Malachi to "before *you*," and thus the prophecy originally addressed to the people is now seen as addressed to the person whose way is to be prepared by the messenger. The second part of the statement then apparently identifies the messenger with the voice in the desert who calls to people, "Prepare the way for the Lord, make straight paths for him," and thus the person who is to follow him is the Lord himself (as in Malachi). This strongly suggests that, if the statement is addressed to Jesus, he is identified as the Lord or he is the Lord's representative.

The identification of Jesus as Lord is not taken further at this point, and indeed this term does not figure to any great extent in the story.[5] Nevertheless, John's own testimony is that he is to be followed by somebody more powerful than himself and worthy of immense respect. Whereas John merely baptizes with water to grant forgiveness of sins, Jesus will baptize with the Spirit to the same effect. His power will be greater in that he will do something that corresponds to baptizing with water but will be "baptizing" with the Spirit. Again, the point is not explicitly followed up in that Jesus is not recorded in Mark as baptizing with the Spirit; the only baptism that we hear of is Jesus' own "baptism"/death in which the disciples will share, and it is in Acts that we hear that the disciples will be baptized with the Spirit (Acts 1:5). It is implicit in John's message that those who respond to his message will be ready for the Stronger One when he comes and will attach themselves to him.

Without any introduction, Jesus appears on the scene and undergoes John's baptism. No explanation is given as to why the person who (as we know) is the Stronger One who will baptize with the Spirit should himself undergo the baptism that is meant to prepare people for his own coming. Instead, the focus is on the fact that the event is transformed by an experience of Jesus himself in which he sees that the heavens are opened. The Holy Spirit descends upon him, so that he is endowed with the Spirit, like

---

4. See M. J. Boda's contribution to this volume, "Figuring the Future: The Prophets and Messiah," 68-71 above.

5. Nor does the thought of a people prepared for the coming of the Lord/Jesus by the preaching and baptism of John figure in the story; it is only in John 1 that we hear of people coming to Jesus after having heard the testimony of John. And the message of Jesus repeats that of John; preaching of repentance is not superfluous because John has already done it and people have already responded.

the Messiah in Isa 11:1-4, and implicitly equipped to baptize people with the Spirit.[6] A heavenly voice, which can only be the voice of God, declares, "You are my Son, whom I love; with you I am well pleased." The heavenly voice identifies him (a) with the Son of God addressed in Psalm 2 who is the Messiah,[7] and (b) with the Servant of God in whom God delights (Isa 42:1); this latter figure is a future deliverer and is to be understood as the Messiah (although there is no reference to David in this part of Isaiah and the term "king" is not used). Since the Servant in Isaiah is above all a person who is given a task of restoration to perform, the event here is to be understood as an identification and commissioning of Jesus to fulfill this role. Although, then, the actual term "Messiah" does not figure in the story, yet the concept of messiahship is implicit. In fact, it is the categories of Sonship and Servanthood that are explicit. It may be enough by way of explanation to say that for Christians by the time of Mark the equivalence of these categories was self-evident and taken for granted. Furthermore, in the light of this fact, it will be apparent that, however John may have understood his role, Mark could apply the Malachi prophecy to the coming of Jesus, who, by the time of the writing of the Gospel, was known as Lord to his followers.

The baptism is directly followed by the testing in the wilderness. The significance of this is that Jesus is tested to see whether he will obey the Spirit and be faithful to his calling. He triumphs.[8]

The Story of the Mission

The actual work of Jesus now begins. He announces that God had set a time for things to happen and that this time has now arrived.[9] The rule of

---

6. The coming down can be interpreted in the light of Isa 64:1 as the tearing of the heavens for God to come down and assist his people, and in the light of Isa 63:14 LXX as God coming down in the person of the Holy Spirit. See P. H. Y. Ryou, "Apocalyptic Opening, Eschatological 'Inclusio': A Study of the Rending of the Heaven and Temple Curtain in Mark's Gospel, with Special Reference to the Motif of 'Seeing,'" unpublished doctoral thesis, Glasgow, 2004.

7. For this identification see L. T. Stuckenbruck's contribution to this volume, "Messianic Ideas in the Apocalyptic and Related Literature of Early Judaism," 106 above.

8. J. B. Gibson, "Jesus' Wilderness Temptation according to Mark," *JSNT* 53 (1994) 3-34.

9. More precisely, that God has appointed a period of time to elapse at the end of which he will act; it has now run its course.

God has come; this is good news, but it comes true only for those who repent and believe. This announcement could be regarded as simply prophetic, in which an observer, informed by God, announces what God is doing. However, it is to be understood as the performatory language of one who is authorized to carry out the purpose of God. Since, where the term is actually used, the Messiah is the one who will rule on behalf of God, this understanding is present here. It will be confirmed in what follows that what Jesus does goes beyond mere announcement by a commentator or newscaster. Indeed, this is the important point. Mark is showing us what a messiah, or rather, what *the* Messiah does, and it is not what would have been expected.

It is also important to note at this stage that the announcement of God's rule calls for repentance as well as the revival of hope. The messianic hope in *Pss Sol* 17:29 very definitely includes the purging out of the sinners among the Jewish people as well as the overcoming of their external enemies.[10] And it will become clear that Jesus' understanding of his task is primarily concerned with the former.[11]

The opening incident in Capernaum (Mark 1:21-39) states three things that will be illustrated and developed in what follows. First, one main activity of Jesus is teaching and proclaiming. Second, his other main activity is the overcoming of demons and illness. Third, as a result of these two activities Jesus is identified as the Holy One of God.[12] The demons know what is as yet unknown to human beings.

a. Teaching is of primary importance. In chs. 1–8 Mark uses roughly one-third of his space for teaching that covers a rich variety of topics. Jesus is most commonly addressed by friend and foe as "Teacher"; there is no corresponding term for addressing him as a doer of mighty works.[13] This activity may fit in with the understanding of the Servant of Yahweh as a teacher (cf. perhaps Isa 50:4) but gives the people the impression that he is a prophet. The teaching consists of brief statements and dialogues with the exception of the two more lengthy sections in Mark 4 and 7:1-23.

What is interesting from our point of view is that in the teaching we do not hear again explicitly of the rule of God until Mark 4:11, 26, 30; and

10. Stuckenbruck, "Messianic Ideas," 94-96 above.
11. The call of the fishermen is not so much a call to repentance and conversion (although it must presuppose such a response) as a call to share in the work.
12. So also in Luke 4:34; cf. John 6:69; but not in Matthew, who omits the incident.
13. Contrast Matthew's use of "Son of David" in connection with healings.

the term "Christ" will not reappear until Mark 8:29. According to Mark 4 the secret of the kingdom of God has been given to the disciples, but Jesus scarcely refers to it directly. The two parables where he does refer to the kingdom of God (Mark 4:26, 30) indicate that it is present and growing and will become powerful but say nothing about its nature. More importantly, the opening parable must be taken to indicate that the kingdom grows as the word is proclaimed and is accepted by people who respond to it like good soil. One might assume from the references to Satan's kingdom that by implication Jesus is advancing the kingdom of God or his own kingdom over against Satan's.

b. The other two-thirds of Mark's space is devoted to mighty works.[14] No less than twenty pericopes deal directly or indirectly with the mighty works done by Jesus and describe a mixture of exorcisms, healings of illnesses and disabilities, and so-called nature miracles. There is a blend of general accounts of such activity and specific examples. The continuing story indicates that Jesus delivers people from illness and disability as well as from demonic possession. But the latter is especially prominent (cf. Mark 1:32, 34, 39; 3:15; 5:15-18; 6:13; 7:26; cf. 9:38), and it indicates forcibly the supernatural dimension of the mission. This is clarified by reference to the kingdom/rule of Beelzebul, which is the power behind this aspect of human suffering. At the same time sinners who need forgiveness and victims of the power of evil are alike the objects of the mission. The promise of forgiveness associated with John continues with Jesus.

c. This material shows in different ways who Jesus is, or in what capacity he is behaving.

The healing of a paralytic gives Jesus himself the opportunity to declare that the Son of Man has authority to forgive sins (Mark 2:10). It is not immediately clear why this form of self-reference is introduced at this point. As the text stands, the explicit point made by Jesus is that the Son of Man has authority to forgive sins on earth; it would follow that this is either a new point about the powers of the Son of Man or a contested one. But the implicit point would be that Jesus is the Son of Man, although this is simply assumed without argument. The statement might be unpacked

---

14. Roughly 190 verses deal with mighty works and 100 with teaching. This might suggest that the mighty works are more important in Mark's narrative. However, Mark 1:27, 38-39; 6:12-13 would suggest that the mighty works are closely integrated with the teaching, and when Jesus himself takes the initiative, it is to teach rather than to heal or exorcise, although he responds promptly to requests for healing and other mighty works.

as: "But I want you to know that I am the Son of Man and in that capacity have authority to forgive sins." So it might be that the authority of the Son of Man to forgive is taken for granted, and the real point is to identify Jesus as the Son of Man who can forgive sins by demonstrating that he can also heal the paralyzed man. There is the deeper point that perhaps the healing of a paralyzed man, whose situation may have been thought to be a penalty for sin, could take place only if he was first forgiven, and therefore the healing is the appropriate means of demonstrating that he has been forgiven and that Jesus has the authority to forgive.[15]

Likewise, the Sabbath incident is used to argue that the Son of Man is lord of the Sabbath (Mark 2:28), and again this looks like either a piece of fresh news about the Son of Man or a contested statement. In both of these cases the authority to act on behalf of God is at issue.

There is a chain of references in which people possessed by demons state who Jesus is, initially "the Holy One of God" (Mark 1:24), then "the Son of God" (Mark 3:11). Such statements stand over against the alternative explanation that he is possessed by an evil spirit and empowered by Beelzebul, a statement that Jesus counters by replying that he is driving out demons by the Spirit. The man possessed by Legion also knows him to be the Son of God (Mark 5:7), and this is followed by the ambiguous statement that the Lord has done the exorcism, which is promptly restated to say that Jesus has done the exorcism (Mark 5:19-20). In his version Luke edits the statement about the "Lord" to refer specifically to "God" (Luke 8:39).[16] It could, however, be deliberately ambiguous, in which case we would have evidence that Mark was capable of ambiguity and might expect to find other examples of the same thing happening. The raising of Jairus's daughter again must carry the unspoken implication that the power of God has been at work.

All along we have the way in which news about Jesus spreads (Mark 1:28, 45) and in which the spread of this news is actually encouraged by him (Mark 5:19), as is evidenced by the size of the crowds who flock to see and hear him. Yet this is crossed by the way in which Jesus does not want mighty works to be made known (Mark 1:44; 5:43; 7:36; 8:26) and attempts,

---

15. Cf. C. D. Marshall, *Faith as a Theme in Mark's Narrative* (Cambridge: Cambridge University Press, 1989) 78-90.

16. Mark 1:34 does not state what the demons knew; Luke 4:41 makes it explicit that they knew Jesus to be the Christ.

unsuccessfully, to silence the demons (Mark 1:25, 34; 3:12). Is the point simply to emphasize that nothing, not even the command of Jesus, could prevent the spread of news about the sensational impression that he was making? And is there perhaps an element of selectivity in that Jesus is under constraint to cover a wider geographical area rather than to concentrate on one particular place (Mark 1:38-39)?

More explicitly we have the two pericopes in which the question of Jesus' identity is raised and answered by human actors in the story. The climax at Caesarea Philippi produces strange answers. In what sense can Jesus "be" John the Baptist, who has apparently just recently been put to death? The only realistic sense would seem to be: "you are somebody *like* John," were it not that Herod had voiced the unlikely thesis that John had been resurrected. Herod could have been sufficiently ignorant not to know that Jesus was born before John was killed and could have assumed that Jesus had appeared out of nowhere. Mark's readers, of course, were better informed. R. T. France speculates whether Herod was expressing crudely the idea that whatever spirit animated John had now passed into Jesus.[17] This is conceivable, since we also have the equations of John and Jesus with the Elijah who was to return, alongside the more nuanced statement in Luke that John would act "in the spirit and power of Elijah" (Luke 1:17), the prophet who more than others did mighty works. "One of the prophets" presumably means a prophet like one of the old prophets. "You are the Messiah" (Mark 8:29) is a recognition that what Jesus is doing is bringing in the rule of God, that he is the agent and not the commentator.

But then why does Jesus tell them not to tell anyone and proceed to talk about the suffering and resurrection of *the Son of Man?*[18] The best explanation is still that Mark envisages Jesus as carrying out a program that differs from that of the Messiah as traditionally understood. Therefore, to be known as the Messiah or Messiah designate is to invite the kind of response that we get in John 6:14-15, where the crowds want to make him king by force. There may be a trace of this in Mark 6:45 and 8:9-10, where Jesus dismisses the crowds.[19] Further, Jesus' repeated teaching to his disciples that he must suffer, be killed, and be raised from the dead is not the kind of thing

---

17. France, *Gospel of Mark,* 253.

18. The exclusive use of "Son of Man" in this connection is consistent throughout the rest of the Gospel right up to Mark 14:41.

19. France, *Gospel of Mark,* 270-71, is doubtful whether Mark was aware of this nuance.

that one proclaims to the public at large (as opposed to threats to go on hunger strike or readiness to be a martyr). Jesus is conscious of a divinely appointed fate that is his chief concern and from which he must not be diverted. As has often been said, who he is — that is, what he came to do — cannot be understood apart from the story of his suffering, because he came to suffer. Therefore, it cannot be his aim to be known simply as a performer of mighty works or even as a teacher. He has to grapple with evil and be temporarily overpowered by it. Only disciples can begin to understand this, and if they find it difficult to do so, how much more so will the crowds.

If we are dealing with the Messiah of Jewish expectation, could Jesus have defended from Scripture the thesis that the Messiah must suffer? One possibility lies in the view espoused by F. J. Matera that certain of the Psalms were seen as messianic, including those which refer to opposition to the psalmist and his sufferings. Psalm 22 in particular is a psalm of David and could have been interpreted in this way, as indeed it was later understood by *1 Clement* and Justin.[20] Another route that was certainly followed lay in the identification of the Messiah with other Old Testament figures. Mark later makes it clear that the rejection and suffering of Jesus are to be seen as typified by or fulfilling the pictures of the rejected stone in Psalm 118, and the Servant in Isaiah 53. But here Jesus brings the Son of Man back into the picture.

Certainly "Son of Man" in Mark 8:31 would make excellent sense simply as a self-reference in a situation where an "I" statement would be embarrassing.[21] Nevertheless, in Mark 9:12 Jesus refers to *what is written* about the Son of Man, that he must suffer. Granted that there is no clear statement about a Son of Man suffering in the Old Testament, we do have the statements in Dan 7:5, 7, 19, 21, 25, where eventually the saints are identified as the prey of the beasts and the kings represented by them; the implicit identification of the figure like a Son of Man with the saints (Dan 7:14-18 and 27) could suggest that the Son of Man endures oppression,[22] and the description of resurrection in Daniel 12 could lead

20. F. J. Matera, *The Kingship of Jesus: Composition and Theology in Mark 15* (Chico, CA: Scholars, 1982) 127-35. The alternative interpretation of the use of Psalms 22 and 69 is, of course, that Jesus is seen as the righteous sufferer.

21. This statement is generally taken to be an example of indirect speech, as it certainly is taken to be in Matthew. Nevertheless, it is perfectly intelligible as direct speech (so H. B. Swete, *The Gospel according to St Mark* [London: Macmillan, 1898] 168; Mark 9:9 is not a parallel because it is a command), and is perhaps better so understood.

to the interpretation that the Son of Man is killed and yet rises from the dead to reign (along with the other oppressed saints).[23]

But if we find suffering present in Daniel 7, then we have opened up the way to a recognition that Jesus' use of "Son of Man" in connection with his sufferings is more than a euphemistic way of speaking about himself, that it expresses his consciousness that he fulfills this specific role with all that it involves.

We must not make the mistake of thinking that for Mark (or even, as I would hold, for the historical Jesus) the realization that Jesus must suffer did not come about until halfway through the story.[24] For Mark it is already there in Mark 2:20; 3:6; 6:14-29. There have been hints of death earlier, but now for the first time it becomes and remains thematic. Jesus is understood as seeing himself as the suffering Son of Man who understands his role all the more clearly in the light of the Psalms and Isaiah 53.

Whether we understand the statements as authentic or *vaticinia ex eventu*, it is entirely comprehensible on either scenario that Jesus should be represented as foreknowing what was to happen to him and as finding the basis for it in Scripture.

Following the prophecy of Jesus' suffering and resurrection, it is psychologically fitting that there is a promise of the future coming of the Son of Man in the glory of *his* Father (Mark 8:38). This assumes that the Son of Man is a/the Son of God. Parallel with this is the prophecy of the kingdom of God coming with power after the suffering and weakness, and then there is a proleptic revelation of Jesus as the Son of Man in glory as a confirmation that the promise will be fulfilled. It is appropriate that the baptismal statement is repeated and that it affirms Jesus as the Son of God rather than as the Messiah (Mark 9:7); implicitly he is distinguished from Elijah and Moses.[25] By accepting the way of the Son of Man, Jesus has committed himself to obey the will of God, and God confirms and upholds him as his obedient Son.

---

22. M. D. Hooker, *The Son of Man in Mark: A Study of the Background of the Term "Son of Man" and Its Use in St Mark's Gospel* (London: SPCK, 1967).

23. Cf. C. M. Tuckett, *Christology and the New Testament: Jesus and His Earliest Followers* (Louisville: Westminster John Knox, 2001) 112-13.

24. Our concern in this essay is primarily with the Christology of the Evangelists and not with the historical question of how Jesus understood himself and his destiny.

25. Clearly, for Mark, Jesus is superior to Moses and Elijah.

The Way to the Cross

The next little section forbidding the rejection of a non-disciple casting out demons assumes that such a person must be on the side of "us," and it states that to give a disciple a cup of water "in my name" because you belong to the Messiah will lead to reward (Mark 9:38-41). Here, then, Jesus is implicitly identified as the Messiah. By this statement Jesus implicitly accepts what Peter had confessed at Caesarea Philippi.[26] It could be that the usage here is influenced by post-resurrection usage, when "Son of Man" would have been replaced by "Christ" (cf. 1 Pet 4:16).

The conversation with the rich man (Mark 10:17-31) implies that Jesus is the representative of God in that he can formulate commandments that stand alongside the law. Despite the fact that it was God who gave commandments, nevertheless here Jesus authoritatively does so.[27]

In the context of the story as a whole, James's and John's assumption that the Son of Man will sit in glory (Mark 10:35-45) is based on Mark 8:38 with its reference to Daniel 7. They also have to learn, not so much that the Son of Man is to die (they have already been told that), but that his death is a voluntary piece of service through which the many are ransomed. The Servant motif emerges here, regardless of whether Isaiah 53 is the direct background.

Bartimaeus addresses Jesus in a new way as Son of David, which looks messianic (Mark 10:47-48). This is the first such address from an outsider. The call for healing may simply be because Jesus already has a reputation (cf. the Zacchaeus story for his fame having gone ahead of him), but this does not explain the title. It may be simply of a piece with the varied demonic cries, which express the authority of Jesus using different idioms. There is also the possibility of influence from a tradition of David's son, Solomon, as a miracle worker.[28] The incident of the colt may again identify Jesus as "Lord" (Mark 11:1-3); this could hardly be the meaning for the audience in the village, and a reference to God is possible. This

---

26. Although Jesus did not explicitly acknowledge Peter's statement and proceeded to speak in terms of the Son of Man, there are no grounds to suppose that he rejected the identification of him as the Messiah.

27. Cf. Gundry, *Mark*, 560-61. I owe this point to an unpublished paper by S. J. Gathercole.

28. K. Berger, "Die königlichen Messiastraditionen des Neuen Testaments," *NTS* 20 (1973-74) 1-42.

is perhaps supported by Mark 11:9 where the crowds salute the one who comes in the name of the Lord, that is, simply with the authority of God.[29] Mark is unlikely to be saying that they were mistaken because in fact it was the Lord himself coming rather than somebody "in his name." The coming of Jesus and the coming of the kingdom stand in parallel; each interprets the other.

The repeated use of David forms the background or occasion for the question in Mark 12:35-37. Is the Messiah the Son of David? We can assume that the Davidic descent of Jesus was taken for granted by the time of Mark. Moreover, the passage cannot be intended as a denial of Bartimaeus's confession. The problem is rather that the question posed is not "How can David call his son Lord?" but rather "How can David's Lord be his son?" The answer to the former question would be that God exalted his son; an answer to the second could be that the Lord who came from heaven became incarnate by Mary and entered David's line by adoption through Joseph. But this is hardly even hinted at in Mark, who never mentions Joseph.

Mark 13 looks forward to the coming of somebody after a period of horror. People are looking forward to the coming of the Messiah, and false prophets will make false identifications of him (Mark 13:21-22). At last the Son of Man will come (Mark 13:26-27), and it is implicit that he is the Messiah. The use of Son of Man is appropriate here, because the Daniel 7 prophecy is being alluded to; there is no Old Testament reference to a second coming or return of the Messiah. No one knows when it will happen, not even angels or the Son, a statement that does not necessarily identify Jesus as the Son, but the context demands that he is (Mark 13:32). The point is that the person closest to the Father does not know.

At the trial of Jesus, a claim to destroy the temple and build another in three days is attributed to him, but falsely, a comment that may be intended to deny that he said this, or to imply that this was a misunderstood or muddled statement (Mark 14:57-58). In the light of 2 Sam 7:13 (cf. Zech 6:12-13), as taken up in 4QFlorilegium, rebuilding the temple is a task that would be undertaken by the Messiah.[30] The report of what Jesus is supposed to have said is followed up by the high priest's question to Jesus concerning whether he is the Messiah and the Son of God. Jesus replies Yes (to

---

29. That Jesus has this authority is implied in Mark 11:27-33.
30. O. Betz, *What Do We Know about Jesus?* (London: SCM, 1968) 87-92.

both questions) and then adds that they will see the Son of Man at the right hand of God and coming with the clouds (Mark 14:61-62). Here Jesus uses the phrase that he has frequently used and seems to prefer; he adds a point that will confirm and vindicate what he has said; and there is an implied threat of judgment.

Pilate's concern is whether he is the king of the Jews (Mark 15:2). The implication is that the Jewish authorities told Pilate that this was what Jesus claimed to be. Jesus' reply is apparently, "So you say. It's not how I would put it." The priests and others understand this as a paraphrase of "Messiah" (Mark 15:32).

Finally, the centurion understands Jesus to be the Son of God (Mark 15:39). It seems clear that for Mark this means "*the* Son of God," not "a Son of God," and that it is related to the rending of the veil of the temple in Mark 15:38 as an acted parable of the destruction of the temple. In its context, the rending of the veil has been understood as the act of God or of Jesus, but either way it is probably to be seen as part of the vindication of Jesus.[31]

No further Christology follows. The account of the empty tomb with which the Gospel, as we have it, concludes announces the resurrection of Jesus the Nazarene, who will meet his disciples in Galilee, and nothing more.[32]

Putting Things Together

1. One thing that stands out immediately is the centrality of the three concepts of Messiah/Christ, Son of Man, and Son of God. Other associated concepts are Holy One of God; Son of David; King; Lord; Servant of Yahweh; Stone; and Righteous Sufferer.

These concepts are already interrelated in the Old Testament. This is most obviously the case with King and Messiah. Further, the privilege of the King is that he is treated by God as his Son. The Danielic "one like a son

---

31. See France, *Gospel of Mark*, 656-58, and Gundry, *Mark*, 949-51, for these contrasting views. H. L. Chronis, "The Torn Veil: Cultus and Christology in Mark 15:37-39," *JBL* 101 (1982) 97-114, is followed by Tuckett, *Christology*, 116, who holds that the rending of the veil symbolizes the way in which God is now visible, but visible "precisely in the figure of the dead Jesus hanging on a cross"; this seems rather too subtle.

32. I tend to agree with those scholars who think that Mark 16:8 is not the intended end of the Gospel.

of man" has messianic features, and the identification of the Son of Man with the Messiah can be seen in some of the intertestamental literature.[33] The Servant of Yahweh has some kingly features (Isa 42:1-4).

2. Mark himself identifies Jesus as "Christ" (Mark 1:1), which in the light of what follows must retain titular sense. This is confirmed and illuminated as the story develops. Peter recognizes that this is so after a series of events. Jesus implicitly accepts the designation when he talks to his disciples about themselves being attached to him as the Messiah (Mark 9:41). He engages in dispute with the scribes over the inadequate understanding of the Messiah as Son of David, and seeing the Messiah as an exalted figure. He knows of the hope of a future coming of the Christ and of the possibility of false claimants. The high priest is aware of the speculation that Jesus is the Messiah and asks him point blank whether he is. Jesus says Yes and adds a sign by which they will know. Not surprisingly, then, the members of the Sanhedrin scoff at him on the cross, implying that he cannot be the Messiah or else he would come down. Their scoffing makes it clear that they (and Mark) understand Messiah to mean king of Israel. Consequently, references to Jesus as a king belong in this circle of ideas. However, the term is used of Jesus only in the trial before Pilate and then in the titulus on the cross. It is the Roman equivalent for Messiah. And here it is misunderstood in a political sense.

What Jesus does and what happens to him is crucial in showing how the term "Messiah" is to be understood. He announces the dawn of the kingdom of God, and by his proclamation and his deeds he inaugurates it. He has been commissioned by God to do so and equipped with the Spirit. He can therefore speak with authority and also act with the divine authority that overcomes demons, disease, and other forms of evil. He is engaged in a conflict with Satan and with his agents, both demonic and human. He comes to rescue the victims of sin and to call sinners to repent. He recognizes that he is called to suffer, but he sees this suffering as the means of ransoming the many and he knows that God will vindicate him. As part of his task he will bring the temple to an end and will create a new one, no doubt understood by Mark as the church. All of this

---

33. So rightly W. D. Davies and D. C. Allison Jr., *A Critical and Exegetical Commentary on the Gospel according to Saint Matthew* (3 vols.; Edinburgh: T&T Clark, 1988-97) 3:531, draw attention to the melding of the figures of the Messiah and Son of Man in *4 Ezra* 13 and *1 Enoch* 48, 52. I would argue that this is already true in Daniel 7.

brings to a climax and to fulfillment what was adumbrated and prophesied in Scripture.

3. The understanding of Jesus as the Son is powerfully present. Unless there was something else climactic in the putative lost ending, the twin designations of Messiah/King of Israel and Son of God dominate the crucifixion.[34] It seems that Mark recognizes the two terms "Messiah" and "Son of God" as essentially conveying the same role, and therefore it may be wrong to prioritize either one over the other.[35] It is also likely that, whatever their origins and their meanings for contemporary Judaism, for Mark they have their Christian meaning, which developed in the light of the person and career of Jesus.

4. Negatively, there has been no evidence that priestly conceptions play a part in the Gospel. It is true that Jesus will bring the temple to an end and build another one, but even in the account of the rending of the veil the motif of him as high priest or priest does not arise. Jesus is the destroyer and builder of a temple, not the officiant within one. The term "Christ" does not appear to have a priestly nuance.

5. The enigmatic factor is the use of the term "Son of Man." One possible understanding is that it is nothing more than a self-designation that adds very little to the picture. That is to say, if in every case where the term is used we were simply to substitute "I," there might be no loss of meaning. Jesus has authority to forgive sins and over the sabbath. He will suffer and be rejected. He will be ashamed of those who are ashamed of him when he comes in his Father's glory. He came to serve and give his life. He will be betrayed. He will come in the clouds with power and glory and gather his chosen people. His judges will see him sitting on the right hand of God and coming with the clouds. Nothing, it can be argued, is added to the force of these utterances by the term "Son of Man," which is a bland self-designation. The fact that nobody except Jesus uses the term finds its only

34. He cannot be called the Son of Man because this is recognized as a self-designation.

35. B. Gerhardsson, "The Christology of Matthew," in *Who Do You Say That I Am? Essays on Christology* (ed. M. A. Powell and D. R. Bauer; Louisville: Westminster John Knox, 1999) 14-32, says: "All groups needed a cluster of appellations to identify Jesus. The different high designations were taken from different contexts and may originally have had different points, but when applied to Jesus they became pliant and shaded into one another to suit their new function. In the long run they became essentially synonymous; all of them signify the 'whole' Jesus" (29).

viable explanation in the fact that this was originally an Aramaic idiom for referring to oneself and that Jesus used it in this way.[36]

However, there are references to him "coming," especially coming with the clouds, and people who know the book of Daniel will recognize an allusion that can come only from there in which there is a reference to a figure like a man. And so they will deduce that Jesus can say these things about himself in virtue of his being the fulfillment of what was understood as a prophecy. It presumably follows, then, that whatever else is said about this Son of Man is true of Jesus. The puzzle is the presence of sayings that refer to the Son of Man's authority on earth and his suffering, where the Danielic background is not obvious. Although I have claimed above that the oppression of the saints in Daniel 7 could have led to a recognition of the suffering of the Son of Man, his function in forgiveness and as lord of the sabbath has no clear basis in Daniel. Here it would seem that the authority of the Son of Man (Dan 7:14) is being extrapolated in a new way.

If Jesus began by using it as a self-description, it would fit in with a distaste for titles and identifications seen in the Gospel. It had the advantage of being ambiguous, especially if the apocalyptic understanding was not a well-known, commonplace one. I therefore continue to maintain that we must recognize the fact that the usage in the Gospels has a double origin in the use of "Son of Man" as a self-reference and as a description of a figure based on Daniel 7 and kept alive in *4 Ezra* and *1 Enoch*. Some may find this coincidence of sources unlikely, but there is no more convincing explanation.

"Son of Man" is used as a messianic term. If the term was understood to be messianic in its Old Testament usage, then Jesus or the early church could use it in this way. The interpretation of Daniel 7 is disputed, but the figure like a Son of Man is certainly given dominion and a kingdom from God, and this kingdom is given as a possession to the saints of the Most High forever after their foes have been defeated. But this is precisely what is said elsewhere about the kingdom of God and the Messiah. Then, once Jesus used it of himself, it would become messianic for his followers be-

---

36. For this type of explanation, see D. R. A. Hare, *Mark* (Louisville: Westminster John Knox, 1996) 37: "Mark apparently regards it as a mysterious name that Jesus uses when he wants to speak indirectly (modestly) about his present vocation, anticipated suffering, and future glory." Hare, however, is prepared to allow that Jesus may have been influenced by Daniel 7.

cause there would be a natural tendency to equate the various terms used of him.[37]

The question "Are you the Son of Man?" does not arise, partly because nobody else ever uses the phrase. This must be significant. Again, the use of "Lord" does not arise, because it is simply a title of respect in the Gospels, and it would seem likely that they are being faithful historically in this respect.

6. Out of all this arises the question of Jesus' relationship to God. For Mark the fundamentals are in position with the recognition of Jesus by God as his Son, the bearer of the Spirit, destined to sit at his right hand, proleptically seen in heavenly glory at the transfiguration. He is superior to angels, and there are hints of his sharing the lordship of God. There is no discussion as to whether Jesus is a human being. It is taken for granted that this is what he is, and this is not seen to be incompatible with his role and status. At this stage in christological thinking there would appear to be no threats to the understanding of him as a man and therefore no need to defend it.[38]

In summary, then, we have a concept of Jesus as the one who is understood especially in the light of the Old Testament as Christ, Son of God, and Son of Man; these terms are mutually interpretative, and their significance undergoes a profound transformation in the light of his actual career and behavior.[39]

37. I do not accept the view that only those Son of Man sayings which make statements that could be true of people in general (not necessarily all people) and hence of Jesus in particular go back to Jesus himself, and that Jesus did not understand himself in the light of Daniel 7 (so especially M. Casey, *Son of Man* [London: SPCK, 1979]). Even if this view were correct, Mark understood some or all of the Son of Man sayings in terms of the Danielic Son of Man.

38. For a summary of the evidence, see R. P. Martin, *Mark: Evangelist and Theologian* (Exeter: Paternoster, 1972) 107-8, 120-26.

39. On the messianism of Mark, see further E. K. Broadhead, *Naming Jesus: Titular Christology in the Gospel of Mark* (Sheffield: Sheffield Academic Press, 1999); J. D. Kingsbury, *The Christology of Mark's Gospel* (Philadelphia: Fortress, 1983); E. S. Malbon, "The Christology of Mark," in Powell and Bauer, eds., *Who Do You Say That I Am?* 33-48; R. C. Tannehill, "The Gospel of Mark as Narrative Christology," *Semeia* 16 (1980) 57-96.

The Gospel of Matthew

Within the limits of this essay, it is not possible to go through Matthew in the same kind of way as we have done with Mark, tracing the story of Jesus in detail through the Gospel, and to some extent it would be repetitious and even tedious to do so.[40]

My theory about Matthew (and *mutatis mutandis* about Luke) is that it is a case of "all this and much more." Matthew takes over much of Mark and alters it in significant respects, as well as adding other material.[41] The result is a filling out of the picture. The basic story is structured in the same way, with Matthew bringing out even more sharply the division into the two sections in which Jesus preaches about the kingdom (Matt 4:17) and then instructs his disciples that he must suffer (Matt 16:21) and does so.

First, however, we note some omissions and changes of emphasis. One minor point is that the phrase "the Holy One of God" has disappeared, along with the rest of the story in which it stands (Mark 1:21-28; Matthew has used some of the phraseology elsewhere); evidently Matthew did not think it important to retain it. More important, the commands to secrecy have largely disappeared (though see Matt 8:4 par. Mark 1:43-45; Matt 12:16 par. Mark 3:12). This is true of the references in Mark 1:25 (where the whole story has gone), Mark 5:43 (where the story generally is abbreviated), and Mark 7:36. Matthew simply records the spread of Jesus' fame, and the subtleties of Mark's presentation are absent.

As in Mark, there is a clear understanding of Jesus as a genuine human being, but since there is no specific vocabulary dedicated to it, this is much more a basic feature of the narrative that is simply taken for granted and therefore in danger of being overlooked. Right at the outset, however, the genealogy traces the forebears of Jesus back to Abraham and thus indicates that he is a member of the Jewish people as well as specifically belonging to the kingly line of David (Matt 1:1, 2, 17).

---

40. R. T. France, *Matthew: Evangelist and Teacher* (Exeter: Paternoster, 1989) 279-317, is an excellent summary organized mainly by christological designations. See also C. S. Keener, *A Commentary on the Gospel of Matthew* (Grand Rapids: Eerdmans, 1999) 53-68. For a narrative approach, see T. L. Donaldson, "The Vindicated Son: A Narrative Approach to Matthean Christology," in Longenecker, ed., *Contours of Christology*, 100-121.

41. For a detailed discussion of Matthew in relation to Mark, see P. M. Head, *Christology and the Synoptic Problem: An Argument for Markan Priority* (Cambridge: Cambridge University Press, 1997).

In terms of designations for Jesus, Matthew's Christology is not markedly different from that of Mark, with the same use of "Christ," "Son of God," and "Son of Man." But there are differences or changes of emphasis.

Jesus as Messiah and Son of David

Whereas Mark began his Gospel simply by designating its subject as "Jesus Christ," Matthew has his birth narrative in which the significance of both of these terms emerges more vividly. As in the case of the other three Gospels, the opening material is of great importance in anticipating what is to follow in the rest of the story. It also makes clear to the readers who the subject of the Gospel is by sharing with them information that was apparently not known to the contemporaries of Jesus during his mission.

Here at the outset the name "Jesus" takes on significance by being explicitly associated with salvation, and specifically with salvation from sin (Matt 1:21), although subsequently the motif is no more prominent than in Mark. Neither Matthew nor Mark takes up the concept of salvation in the way that Luke does. Matthew, however, does stress forgiveness more than Mark does and specifically ties it to the death of Jesus (Matt 26:28).[42]

The role of Jesus as Messiah is highlighted from the start by the identification of him as "the Christ" (Matt 1:17, 18) and by the story of the quest of the Magi, in which the straight equation is made between the Christ and the king of the Jews (Matt 2:2-4). As in Mark, the term "king" is prominent in the passion narrative (Matt 27:11, 29, 37, 42), but it is also used at the entry of Jesus into Jerusalem (Matt 21:5; citing Zech 9:9); here Matthew's wording brings out what is only implicit in Mark 11:10, where the crowds look forward to the coming kingdom rather than the coming king. The traditional role of the king or a messianic figure as a shepherd of the people is already present in Matthew 2:6 (where it occurs in the citation of Mic 5:2). Matthew as narrator introduces the motif of compassion for the shepherdless sheep in Matt 9:36 and applies it broadly to the teaching and healing mission of Jesus (cf. Mark 6:34, where it is also used editorially in the context of the feeding of the five thousand).[43] The metaphor of shepherding also figures

---

42. Is it significant that the word "forgiveness" is not used in connection with the activity of John the Baptist (contrast Mark 1:4)?

43. See also Matt 10:6; 15:24; 26:31.

as a motif in the description of the last judgment, where the righteous and unrighteous are separated as a shepherd separates the sheep from the goats (Matt 25:32-33); the function of judgment here is transferred from God to the Son of Man who acts as king and lord (Matt 25:34, 40).

As narrator, Matthew can refer to Jesus simply as "the Christ" (Matt 11:2) in a context where the issue is precisely whether Jesus is the one who was to come. Matthew knows that Jesus is the Christ, but John in prison naturally wonders whether the doer of the mighty works is in fact the Christ. Various other uses combine to make the term more prominent than in Mark and Luke (Matt 16:20; 23:10; 24:5; 26:68; 27:17, 22). It is a more significant part of the vocabulary of the narrator and the characters than it is in Mark.

The centrality of the messianic motif is reinforced by Matthew's distinctive use of the term "Son of David"; it sets the tone right in the very first verse of the Gospel and is used especially in connection with healings performed by Jesus (Matt 9:27; 12:23; 15:22; 20:30-31 par. Mark 10:47-48; cf. also Matt 21:9, 15 for its use at the entry to Jerusalem). Perhaps even more clearly than in Mark, the question in Matt 22:41-46 is not meant to be construed as a denial by Jesus of this designation as inappropriate for himself, but is rather an invitation to ponder the riddle of how David's son can also be his lord. It would be reasonable to associate this term with the greater interest in this Gospel in the relationship between the Jewish people as a people and Jesus. Matthew is concerned with the role of Jesus as the Jewish Messiah who is rejected by the leaders of the people but who takes on a cosmic role after his resurrection.

Moreover, the role of the Son of David is seen to be significantly rewritten in the light of Jesus' compassionate actions for the needy.[44] The Davidic Messiah turns out to be less of a kingly ruler in his earthly career than might have been expected; we may compare the way in which the apparently political imagery in the hymns in Luke's birth narrative gives way to a more spiritual understanding of the Messiah's role in the course of that Gospel.

The exalted position of Jesus is further underlined by the very much greater frequency of use of the address "Lord" (Kyrie), which is the normal

---

44. C. Burger, *Jesus als Davidssohn: Eine traditionsgeschichtliche Untersuchung* (Göttingen: Vandenhoeck & Ruprecht, 1970) 90-91; L. Goppelt, *Theology of the New Testament* (Grand Rapids: Eerdmans, 1981, 1982) 2:220-21. We do not need to go into the origins of this presentation, which Burger regards as being an entirely Matthean redaction of his Marcan material.

address by sympathetic, committed people to Jesus, sometimes corresponding to the use of "Rabbi" in Mark.[45] Although very often "Lord" need be no more than a basic title of respect, the frequency of usage and the contextual indicators suggest that there is a rather greater degree of reverence in its use. Several people who come to Jesus are said to show reverence to him *(proskyneō);* this is the appropriate attitude to a king shown by the magi (Matt 2:2), and something of the same aura may surround the subsequent uses.[46] This motif reaches its climax in the final, postresurrection scene where Jesus is worshiped by the Eleven and proclaims his absolute authority.

Jesus as Son of Man and Son of God

We saw that in Mark the term "Son of Man" is broadly messianic. Matthew has the term more frequently than Mark, basically because he has more sayings of Jesus available to him.[47] The general tendency that results is more of a stress on the identity of Jesus as a figure who is rejected on earth (Matt 8:20; 11:19; 12:32) and as the coming Son of Man (Matt 10:23; 13:41). In the former case Matthew is following the tradition found in both Mark and Q, where the Son of Man is a figure who has authority on earth but whose authority is not accepted, and in the latter case he reflects the concept of the coming Son of Man in Daniel 7. But Matthew also adds it editorially in Marcan passages (Matt 16:13; 16:28; 24:30; 26:2) and on occasion substitutes the first-person pronoun (Matt 16:21; contrast Mark 8:31; cf. Matt 5:11 with Luke 6:22); the identity of Jesus as the Son of Man is quite clear.

Similarly, the use of additional source material leads to the much greater prominence of "Son of God" in Matthew. The title is prominent in the temptation narrative, where it is precisely as Son of God that Jesus is tempted to disobey God and turn aside from his mission (Matt 4:3, 6; cf. Luke 4:3, 9). In Mark the designation is used of Jesus only by non-human

---

45. Uncommitted people address him as "Teacher" in Matthew.

46. Cf. Matt 8:2; 9:18; 14:33; 15:25; 20:20; 28:9, 17. The term is also used in Mark 5:6 and, after the resurrection, in Luke 24:52. In each of the Synoptic Gospels there are isolated examples of people falling on their knees before Jesus (Matt 17:14; Mark 1:40; 10:17; Luke 5:8).

47. Matthew has 30 usages, 13 taken over from Mark, 8 shared with Luke, 4 editorial additions, and 5 in passages peculiar to this Gospel. Cf. I. H. Marshall, "Son of Man," in *Dictionary of Jesus and the Gospels* (Downers Grove, IL: InterVarsity Press, 1992) 776-77.

actors before the crucifixion, but in Matthew the disciples worship Jesus as the Son of God after the stilling of the storm (Matt 14:33), and Peter's confession at Caesarea Philippi includes this phrase (Matt 16:16). Moreover, Matthew includes the explicit statement of Jesus about the relationship of the Father and the Son and the latter's role in revelation of the Father (Matt 11:25-27; cf. Luke 10:21-22). For Matthew, then, the recognition of Jesus as Son of God by human beings occurs more powerfully than in Mark, where it does not emerge until the confession of the centurion after the death of Jesus (Mark 15:39).[48]

This is backed up by the fact that Jesus refers to God as Father very much more frequently. Care is needed here, however. Alongside the numerous references to God as "my [sometimes 'my heavenly'] Father" (17) there are also about as many references to 'your Father' (21). This indicates that Matthew brings out the new relationship with God enjoyed by the disciples along with Jesus much more fully than does Mark. Consequently, this usage may reflect a developing theological understanding of God (the Father) in a heightened awareness of the personal relationship of believers generally to God as Father rather than a narrowly christological development; nonetheless, it remains significant. The personal relationship of both Jesus and his disciples to the Father is much more openly and fully expressed in Matthew than in Mark.

There has been some discussion as to whether the concept of Messiah or that of Son of God has priority in Matthew's Christology.[49] The debate is probably futile, and we should recognize that both lines of thought are essential for a full understanding of the role and status of Jesus.[50]

48. In one or two places Matthew uses the term "the Son" rather than "the Son of God" (or equivalents); see Matt 11:27a, 27b; 24:36; 28:19. Since the Son of Man has God as his Father (Matt 16:27), J. P. Meier, *The Vision of Matthew: Christ, Church and Morality in the First Gospel* (New York: Paulist, 1978) 82-83, 172, wants to argue that "the Son" is not necessarily equivalent to "the Son of God" here but rather has connections also with "Son of Man," especially in Matt 24:36. But it would be patently redundant and awkward to include "of God" in Matt 11:27 and 28:19. The case for 24:36 might seem to be more plausible but is exposed to the objection that, whereas "the Son" is a current synonym for "the Son of God," the term "Son" is never found elsewhere as a contraction for "Son of Man."

49. For the latter view see especially J. D. Kingsbury, *Matthew: Structure, Christology, Kingdom* (2nd ed.; Minneapolis: Fortress, 1989); cf. J. D. Kingsbury, *Matthew as Story* (Philadelphia: Fortress, 1986).

50. See, for example, J. K. Riches, *Matthew* (Sheffield: Sheffield Academic Press, 1996) 88-93.

At the outset, Jesus is principally the messianic Son of David, or perhaps we should say the Davidic Messiah, thus emphasizing his role in relation to Israel; and his divine origin and authority are stressed rather than his
sonship. Nevertheless, his sonship is present. It is implicitly expressed in the
announcement of the birth of Jesus and then becomes explicit in the quotation from Hos 11:1 in Matt 2:15. The pregnancy of Mary is brought about by
the Holy Spirit rather than by a human husband (or any other human being), and the fact that the child is to be called "Immanuel" ("God [is] with
us") indicates that in some way he is to be identified with God; the role of be-
getting is carried out by God through the Spirit, and thus God is involved in
what we would call "parenting." Then in Matt 2:15 the Evangelist himself applies the saying in Hos 11:1 to Jesus, where the Lord himself says, "Out of
Egypt I called my son." This confirms that Matthew sees the birth of Jesus as
the birth in this world of the Son of God; he then recounts how God himself
directly addresses Jesus as his Son at his baptism. Matthew's account (like
that of Luke) thus provides an explanation for the saying at the baptism,
which comes without any warning or preparation in Mark's account.

At the very end of the Gospel, Jesus is named in a trinitarian formula
as the Son, thus emphasizing his cosmic status for the world after the resurrection, and his personal relationship to the Father has become evident.
Matthew's concept of sonship shows a notable kinship to that of John.

Jesus as Servant, Wisdom, and New Moses

But this exaltation lies in the future, and over against it must be placed the
identification of Jesus as the Servant of the Lord who works quietly and
gently rather than by raising his voice (Matt 12:18-21; citing Isa 42:1-4). This
is confirmed by the claim of Jesus to be gentle and humble (Matt 11:29; cf.
21:5) and by his invitation to the weary and heavy-laden to come to him
and find rest (Matt 11:28-30).[51] We have already noted that as Son of David
Jesus performs merciful acts. The citation of Isa 53:4 (Matt 8:17), which is
related to the healings done by Jesus, further enlarges the understanding of
his Servant-role.

---

51. For a full exploration of the significance of the term "Servant of the Lord," including especially its connections with justice, see R. Beaton, *Isaiah's Christ in Matthew's Gospel*
(Cambridge: Cambridge University Press, 2002).

According to D. Hill, Matthew gives content to the concept of Jesus as Son of God by his development of servanthood.[52] A corrective to any one-sided understanding of Jesus as Servant, however, is offered by R. Beaton, who has reinvestigated Matthew's use of Isa 42:1-4 and drawn out the way in which he uses Isaianic material to describe the functions of Jesus in a rather more varied way in relation to both justice and compassion, so that Jesus can be characterized as both aggressive and compassionate. This emphasis is worth making over against the constant tendency to play down the judgmental actions of Jesus. The Jesus of Matthew pulls no punches in his strong attacks on the hypocrisy that he sees in some representatives of Jewish religion (Matthew 23), and the threats of judgment in this Gospel are especially severe. At the same time, Matthew stresses the compassion of Jesus as the one who offers relief to the weary and burdened (Matt 11:28-30).

The role of Jesus cannot be ascertained purely by a study of titles and designations. As we have just seen, the ascription of a Servant-role to Jesus is not accompanied by a christological use of the term itself outside the actual citation from Isaiah 42. In particular, his role as teacher and miracle-worker is of central importance and is not tied to any one type of christological designation.[53] Space forbids an examination of how this motif is developed in the course of the narrative. Two further possible aspects of his status that are not expressed in titles require consideration here.

First, there is the question whether the Jewish figure of Wisdom is significant for Matthew's Christology. On occasion Jesus speaks in the manner of a wise teacher, using the kind of sayings found in the Wisdom tradition. In Luke 7:35 he says, "Wisdom is proved right by all her children," and he appears to be an envoy (Gk. child) of Wisdom. However, Matt 11:19 has the same saying in the form, "wisdom is proved right by her actions," which has been taken to imply an identification of Jesus himself with Wisdom.[54] There is also the puzzling problem of the saying of Jesus in Luke 11:49-51 that is said to emanate from "the Wisdom of God" (or perhaps, as TNIV paraphrases, "God in his wisdom") who speaks in the first

---

52. D. Hill, "Son and Servant: An Essay on Matthaean Christology," *JSNT* 6 (1980) 2-16.

53. Cf. Davies and Allison, *Matthew,* 3:718-21.

54. But is the saying really anything more than a comparison between Jesus and Wisdom, or simply a proverbial saying?

person of sending envoys; in Matt 23:34-39, however, this saying is uttered by Jesus himself, who sends his messengers. Does this mean that Matthew silently identified Jesus as Wisdom? But then, if we did not know the parallel in Luke, who would pick up the alleged identification in Matthew? Similarly, Jesus speaks in a style that could be seen as typical of an utterance by Wisdom herself in Matt 11:28-30, although we have no precise parallel elsewhere to confirm this supposition.

These pieces of evidence have been sufficient to persuade some scholars that for Matthew Jesus is seen in the role of Wisdom. Admittedly, there is no use of the term as a title for him, but in view of what has just been said about the lack of the term "Servant," this is not a decisive objection. Certainly this identification would be appropriate in a Gospel that places so much stress upon Jesus as a teacher and emphasizes the divine origin and authority of his sayings (cf. Matt 8:8). It would also be appropriate in complementing the understanding of Jesus as the Son of God; in both cases we have a divine agent who is close to God. Even so, it cannot be said to play a major role in the Gospel compared with the other christological categories.[55]

More significant than the motif of Wisdom is the fact that Jesus may be seen as a counterpart to Moses with an authority that exceeds his.[56] This is particularly evident in the Sermon on the Mount, where the "But I say to you" of Jesus is juxtaposed with what was said to the people long ago (Matt 5:21-22), and obedience to his words is the decisive criterion by which people stand or fall (Matt 7:24-27). The motif is present in other ways also, including some parallel features between Moses and Jesus in the birth story. This understanding of Jesus as a new Moses does justice to the major place that teaching has in the Gospel and fits in with the overall thrust of the Gospel as a work that is especially concerned with the relationship of Christianity to Judaism.[57]

Of crucial importance is the final scene in the Gospel in which the

55. For a "high" estimate of Matthew's Wisdom Christology, see M. J. Suggs, *Wisdom, Christology and Law in Matthew's Gospel* (Cambridge, MA: Harvard University Press, 1970); F. W. Burnett, *The Testament of Jesus-Sophia: A Redaction-Critical Study of the Eschatological Discourse in Matthew* (Lanham: University Press of America, 1981). For a much more restrained view, see Davies and Allison, *Matthew*, 2:295.

56. Davies and Allison, *Matthew*, 3:718-21. More fully, D. C. Allison Jr., *The New Moses: A Matthaean Typology* (Minneapolis: Fortress, 1993).

57. Another possibility is that Jesus is seen as embodying Israel (cf. Matt 2:15).

exalted position of the risen Jesus is graphically depicted in the Christophany placed on a mountain top.[58] Here we do not have the comparatively "cosy" kind of scene in which Jesus kindles a fire and cooks breakfast by the seashore or sits and chats with his disciples over a meal in Emmaus or Jerusalem. Rather, he addresses them using the language of complete omnipotence and is worshiped. There are echoes here of the position of the Son of Man in Daniel 7. A trinitarian formula places him alongside God the Father and the Holy Spirit. There have been hints of this future exalted position earlier in the Gospel. The final scene forms an *inclusio* with the opening one in which the name of Immanuel, "God [is] with us," is to be given to the child (Isa 7:14), and in Matt 18:20 Jesus promises his disciples that where two or three of them are together, he will be with them, in a well-known saying that is remarkably close to a rabbinic statement that promises the presence of the Shekinah to students gathered together round the Torah (*Pirqe Aboth* 3:2, 6). Here the reference is unmistakably to the future spiritual presence of Jesus with the disciples. The Gospel powerfully proclaims the future cosmic, omnipotent, and omnipresent power of Jesus as the Son of God. His presence is equivalent to the presence of God.

Putting Things Together

Although this survey of Matthew has been structured around his use of titles and motifs, it has taken into account the narrative in which they are embedded and which has its own contribution to make to the total picture. It demonstrates that for Matthew the concepts of the Davidic Messiah, Danielic Son of Man, and Son of God combine with other elements to present an understanding of Jesus in which he is a figure of authority as a teacher and as the future judge who fearlessly attacks the sin and hypocrisy that he finds in Israel, but who is also the compassionate healer of sickness, both physical and spiritual. He has a close filial relationship with God as his Father, and the worship that he receives after his resurrection is prefigured in the respect shown to him during his mission. Jesus is seen in comparison with such Jewish figures as Moses and Wisdom, with more to offer

---

58. See T. L. Donaldson, *Jesus on the Mountain: A Study in Matthaean Theology* (Sheffield: JSOT, 1985).

to the people than they ever could. Nor should we ignore the thesis developed by W. Carter that the picture in this Gospel stands in conscious contrast to that of the Roman Emperor and the imperial power and that it demonstrates the superiority of Jesus over against Caesar and anything that he could offer.[59] Tuckett's term "enhancement" aptly characterizes the relationship of this portrayal to that of Mark.[60]

Conclusion

In our examination of both Gospels we have seen that the understanding of Jesus as a person reflects how he behaved and taught so that what results is a reinterpretation of elements from Old Testament and Jewish expectation. The term "Christ" has retained the meaning of the future deliverer and ruler of the people of God when he sets up his kingdom, but has been reinterpreted to accommodate the earthly mission of Jesus, who came as God's representative to combat evil and the forces of Satan in their victimization of humanity, to teach God's ways, to die to deliver people from evil, to rise from the dead, to be spiritually present with his people as they carry out his purpose in the world, and finally to be the king who judges and saves, condemns and rewards. Commenting on Matthew, J. K. Riches observes that "'Son of Man' . . . becomes a kind of portmanteau title which can assume meaning from other titles and also from the narrative of the Gospel itself"; "the various titles interanimate each other."[61] Yet the different designations do not become simply equivalent to one another; rather, each brings its own characteristic contribution to the total picture of the one whose coming is good news for Mark and the incarnation of salvation from sin for Matthew.

---

59. W. Carter, *Matthew and Empire: Initial Explorations* (Harrisburg: Trinity Press International, 2001). This motif is, of course, not confined to this Gospel.

60. Tuckett, *Christology,* 120. See his whole discussion (119-32). On the messiology of Matthew see also D. A. Hagner, *Matthew 1–13* (Dallas: Word, 1993) lxi; U. Luz, *The Theology of the Gospel of Matthew* (Cambridge: Cambridge University Press, 1995); D. Verseput, *The Rejection of the Humble Messianic King: A Study of the Composition of Matthew 11–12* (Frankfurt: Peter Lang, 1986); and D. J. Verseput, "The Role and Meaning of the 'Son of God' Title in Matthew's Gospel," *NTS* 33 (1987) 532-56.

61. J. K. Riches, *Conflicting Mythologies: Identity Formation in the Gospels of Mark and Matthew* (Edinburgh: T&T Clark, 2000) 281.

The Messiah in Luke and Acts: Forgiveness for the Captives

Stanley E. Porter

Introduction

There have been many different concepts of the Messiah in the Old Testament and later Jewish thought.[1] Even though many were not clearly articulated and some were not formalized, they nevertheless helped to set expectations in people's minds. Many of these varying definitions and expectations of the notion grew out of shifting social, cultural, political, and, most importantly, theological situations. Without doubt, political oppression and theological division helped to develop a wide set of expectations regarding God's anointed. Within the New Testament itself, there are a number of at least differing emphases, if not different conceptualizations, of what it means that Jesus was the Messiah, as other papers in this volume indicate. In Luke's Gospel and Acts, in conjunction with the other Synoptic Gospels and the Pauline letters, although there are both affinities and differences, there is an emphasis upon Jesus as the anointed prophet.

1. Useful books include: S. Mowinckel, *He That Cometh* (trans. G. W. Anderson; New York: Abingdon, 1954); *The Lord's Anointed: Interpretation of Old Testament Messianic Texts* (ed. P. E. Satterthwaite, R. S. Hess, and G. J. Wenham; Carlisle: Paternoster, 1995); *Israel's Messiah in the Bible and the Dead Sea Scrolls* (ed. R. S. Hess and M. D. Carroll R.; Grand Rapids: Baker, 2003); and G. S. Oegema, *The Anointed and His People: Messianic Expectations from the Maccabees to Bar Kochba* (JSPSup 27; Sheffield: Sheffield Academic Press, 1998). For a recent summary of many of the issues, with important clarifications regarding messianic terminology, see C. A. Evans, "Messianism," in *Dictionary of New Testament Background* (ed. C. A. Evans and S. E. Porter; Downers Grove: InterVarsity Press, 2000) 698-707.

In the Gospel, Luke draws upon a number of Old Testament passages — especially Isaiah, but not only prophetic sources narrowly defined — that resonated with current Jewish thought to depict Jesus as both the messianic prophet, and hence the eschatological prophet coming in the last times, and the fulfillment of Old Testament prophecy concerning the anointed coming one. In both Luke and Acts, he continues to develop the idea of Jesus as anointed prophet, while also depicting other, and potentially complementary, viewpoints, such as royal son of David.[2]

I am far from the first to suggest that this notion of Jesus as messianic prophet in Luke-Acts is an important christological theme.[3] In fact, it is a theme that has been well developed by a number of recent authors on the topic. For example, Earle Ellis describes the Messiahship of Jesus in these terms: "His whole life, death, and resurrection are one continuing fulfilment of prophecy."[4] Luke Johnson goes further and sees a prophetic structure to the entirety of Luke and Acts.[5] This is not to deny that there are other messianic themes that Luke brings to the fore,[6] or to say that the prophetic theme is the only one he suggests. Some have even suggested that Luke has nothing of his own to say about Jesus as Messiah that is not already found in his sources.[7] I wish to argue that a consistent and fundamental development of Jesus as the anointed prophet stands at the heart of Luke's depiction of Jesus as Messiah, no doubt some of it dependent upon his sources (since, after all, they are depicting the same Jesus), but some of it reflecting his own insights and developed depiction.

---

2. As Dr. Craig Evans has reminded me, the exalted place of David in messianic thought is not a Lukan innovation but is already significant at Qumran. See his "David in the Dead Sea Scrolls," in *The Scrolls and the Scriptures: Qumran Fifty Years After* (ed. S. E. Porter and C. A. Evans; JSPSup 26; Sheffield: Sheffield Academic Press, 1997) 183-97.

3. I grant that it is one important christological theme among many. Numerous works address the Christology of the New Testament. Not all of these treatments are equally helpful, since they tend to conflate christological categories.

4. E. E. Ellis, *The Gospel of Luke* (rev. ed.; NCB; Greenwood, SC: Attic Press, 1974) 11.

5. L. T. Johnson, *The Gospel of Luke* (SP; Collegeville: Liturgical, 1991) 15-17, 17-20; Johnson, *The Acts of the Apostles* (SP; Collegeville: Liturgical, 1992) 10-12, 12-14.

6. It must be conceded that a number of scholars suggest a variety of messianic themes in Luke. For example, D. Bock, *Luke* (2 vols.; BECNT; Grand Rapids: Baker, 1994) 1:29-31; C. L. Blomberg, "Messiah in the New Testament," in Hess and Carroll R., eds., *Israel's Messiah*, 111-41, esp. 117-19, 123-25.

7. The sources are presumably Mark and Q. See I. H. Marshall, *Luke: Historian and Theologian* (Grand Rapids: Zondervan, 1970) 168-69.

Discussion of the messianic nature of Jesus as depicted in Luke-Acts usually focuses around usage of the term χριστός, or "Christ."[8] Fitzmyer has categorized the usage in Luke and Acts in terms of titular[9] and nominal[10] usage. According to his analysis, all of the usage in Luke's Gospel is titular, while the slight majority of the usage in Acts is nominal. As will be shown below, what this indicates is that in the Gospel and Acts the author is depicting and describing the Messiah, to the point where the title becomes associated with and, in fact, part of the name of Jesus. This usage is no doubt important, but what is more important is the context in which such language, and related terminology, is used within the two books. What I want to do is to take an essentially serial approach to the material and highlight those passages that clearly emphasize Luke's view of Jesus as messianic prophet.

The Messiah in Luke

Luke's Gospel was almost assuredly written before the book of Acts. Although this has been disputed by some scholars (in fact, the relationship has been called into question by some),[11] the prologues to the respective works and the way in which Acts finishes, as well as historical tradition, indicate that the Gospel preceded Acts.[12] On the basis of this, it makes sense to treat them in this order.

---

8. Many treatments of christological titles and their meaning can be found in a variety of sources, such as New Testament theologies.

9. See J. Fitzmyer, *The Gospel according to Luke* (AB 28 and 28A; Garden City, NY: Doubleday, 1981) 1:197. Titular usage includes: Luke 2:11 (but see below), 26; 3:15; 4:41; 9:20; 20:41; 22:67; 23:2, 35, 39; 24:26, 46; Acts 2:31, 36; 3:18, 20 (?); 4:26; 5:42; 8:5; 9:22; 17:3; 18:5, 28; 26:23.

10. Nominal usage includes: Acts 2:38; 3:6; 4:10, 33; 8:12 [37, where the best manuscripts do not include the verse]; 9:34; 10:36, 48; 11:17; 15:26; 16:18; 17:3 (?); 20:21; 24:24; 28:31. He notes also that in a few of these passages the word "name" is also used: e.g., 4:10; 8:12.

11. M. C. Parsons and R. I. Pervo, *Rethinking the Unity of Luke and Acts* (SBLMS; Minneapolis: Fortress, 1992).

12. I. H. Marshall, "Acts and the 'Former Treatise,'" in *The Book of Acts in Its First Century Setting*, vol. 1: *Ancient Literary Setting* (ed. B. W. Winter and A. D. Clarke; Grand Rapids: Eerdmans, 1993) 163-82.

Birth Narrative

As Ellis states, "According to some Jewish tradition the prophetic gift ceased at the close of the Old Testament period, but its presence or revival was generally expected in the messianic times."[13] This notion of the "coming one" looks forward to a revival of the prophetic voice.[14] The prophetic revival was sometimes associated with the forerunner to the Messiah (e.g., Elijah) and sometimes associated with the Messiah himself, including one like Moses.[15] The Lukan birth narrative (Luke 1:5–2:40) depicts Jesus' advent as the fulfillment of prophetic utterance. It does this in two significant ways: first, in terms of seeing the coming of Jesus himself as prophetically foretold; and second, in terms of distinguishing Jesus from John as the prophetic forerunner. One need not speculate about a "Baptist Nativity" account lying behind the narrative in Luke 1–2, despite a number of clear parallels,[16] to appreciate that a number of common elements in the depiction of John and Jesus indicate that they have a complementary relationship.[17]

The depiction of the coming of John the Baptist as the forerunner of the Messiah, a part of the prophetic depiction of the Messiah, is clearly made throughout the birth narrative, but not finally established until John's ministry in the desert (see the next section). Some of the significant indicators of John's own prophetic status as forerunner of the Messiah are as follows: in the birth narrative, news of Elizabeth's pregnancy precedes Mary's (Luke 1:13 vs. 1:31); John is described in terms of an Old Testament prophet in the wilderness (1:15); he is to be filled with God's Spirit (1:15);[18] he utters the message of a prophet to repent (1:16-17); he is said to be one who goes before the Lord (1:17); he is described as being in the spirit and power of the prophet Elijah, seen to be the Messiah's forerunner, possibly citing the prophet

---

13. Ellis, *Luke*, 72.

14. Passages referred to by Ellis in this discussion include 1 Macc 14:41 and Josephus, *Apion* 1.41.

15. Ellis, *Luke*, 72. Mention of Moses in Luke and Acts occurs around twenty-nine times. Moses is linked to Elijah in Luke 9:30, 33, in the transfiguration.

16. On this, see W. Wink, *John the Baptist in the Gospel Tradition* (SNTSMS 7; Cambridge: Cambridge University Press, 1968) 58-81, who ably refutes such a hypothesis.

17. See R. E. Brown, *The Birth of the Messiah* (Garden City, NY: Doubleday, 1979) 292-98.

18. See M. Turner, *Power from on High: The Spirit in Israel's Restoration and Witness in Luke-Acts* (Sheffield: Sheffield Academic Press, 1996) 151.

Malachi (3:24 LXX) (1:17);[19] and Zacharias labels him a prophet of God destined to go before the Lord to prepare the way (1:76).[20] In these ways, John is clearly established as the forerunner of the coming one, the Messiah.

The depiction of the birth of Jesus is also seen in terms of prophetic fulfillment. Although his birth is predicted after that of John, his life is seen in terms of being the fulfillment of prophecy as the coming one (Luke 1:32); he is clearly one appointed for a divine purpose (1:31-33); he is depicted in terms of a royal and military triumph, certainly some of the characteristics associated with the Messiah (1:32-33); there are confirmatory prophetic utterances by Elizabeth (1:42-45); there is a "revival" of prophecy by Zacharias (1:67); the shepherds are told of a savior who is born, Christ Lord (2:11);[21] Simeon, who was expecting the Lord's Messiah (2:26), utters prophetically laden words regarding his eyes seeing salvation and a light being revealed to both Gentiles and Israel (2:29-32, echoing passages in Isa 52:10; 42:6; 49:6);[22] and Jesus is received in the temple and adulated by the prophetess Anna as the one anticipated in terms of the redemption of Israel (Luke 2:36-38). These are all elements that go toward establishing Jesus as the eschatological prophet.

Although a certain number of royal or regal elements are also connected with this depiction of Jesus,[23] the prophetic element is also well established, if not at the forefront. After a period of barrenness, both literally and prophetically, the prophetic voice has been heard again. This time it

19. See Bock, *Luke*, 1:83-91; cf. Wink, *John the Baptist*, 42.

20. I take seriously J. A. T. Robinson's hypothesis that the hymn of Zacharias may have originally been written of Jesus, rather than John ("Elijah, John and Jesus," in *Twelve New Testament Studies* [London: SCM Press, 1961] 28-52). Perhaps the passage itself is sufficiently pivotal to contain elements not only of John but also of Jesus (Luke 1:69 regarding the house of David; 1:71, 77 regarding a deliverer of salvation).

21. The phrase χριστὸς κύριος has troubled some scholars. Most are troubled by the lack of the article (e.g., Bock, *Luke*, 1:227; cf. 227-28; Johnson, *Luke*, 50). The more difficult issue is probably the use of κύριος in this construction (note that there are a number of textual variants; see I. H. Marshall, *The Gospel of Luke* [NIGTC; Grand Rapids: Eerdmans, 1978] 110). It may well be that the use in Luke 2:11 without the article is nominal, that is, the angels tell the shepherds that the savior they are to see has the name of "Christ (the) Lord." Proper names often do not appear with the article in Greek (see S. E. Porter, *Idioms of the Greek New Testament* [Biblical Languages: Greek 2; 2nd ed.; Sheffield: Sheffield Academic Press, 1994] 107).

22. See Bock, *Luke*, 1:30.

23. Luke 1:32: "the throne of his father David"; Luke 1:69: "the house of his servant David"; Luke 2:4: Joseph "was of the house and lineage of David"; Luke 2:11: "city of David." See Bock, *Luke*, 1:30.

foretells two individuals, one the forerunner of the other, and the latter being the prophesied Messiah.

John the Baptist and Jesus

John the Baptist continues to be a provocative character within the biblical account and in recent scholarship. Of the many roles that John performed, the most notable being his role as "Baptizer," one that also merits attention is that of prophet.[24] In this prophetic capacity, he looked forward not only to the coming of God in judgment but also to God's anointed agent or Messiah.[25] The appearance of John the Baptist as a prophetic forerunner and then the baptism of Jesus further establish the prophetic messianic character of Jesus. John takes on the character of an Old Testament prophet in his wilderness proclamation (Luke 3:3). This includes his message of repentance and forgiveness of sins (3:3). He finds the basis for this in the prophet Isaiah, whose message regarding making ready and straight the way of the Lord he sees as paving the way for the coming of the salvation of God (3:4-6; citing Isa 40:3-5).[26] John sees this message in terms of his already prophesied (see the birth narrative) task of paving the way for the one of whom he is the forerunner. He recognizes that there is one whom he is anticipating who will be mightier than he is (Luke 3:16). John's announcement of a coming baptism of Holy Spirit and of fire (3:16) has two significant elements,[27] each of them prophetic in nature. His announcement creates a transition between himself as the forerunner and the coming one. The first element is the act of baptizing in the Holy Spirit. The sign of a prophet was to be filled with the Holy Spirit, and the epitome of this prophetic figure was Elijah, the forerunner of the Messiah. The second is the act of baptizing in fire. Elijah was the prophet who called down

---

24. R. L. Webb, "John the Baptist and His Relationship to Jesus," in *Studying the Historical Jesus: Evaluations of the State of Current Research* (ed. B. Chilton and C. A. Evans; NTTS 19; Leiden: Brill, 1994) 179-229, esp. 197-206.

25. See R. L. Webb, *John the Baptizer and Prophet: A Socio-Historical Study* (JSNTSup 62; Sheffield: Sheffield Academic Press, 1991) 219-306, esp. 259-60, 304-6.

26. On dispute regarding the textual version that stands behind John's utterance, see Bock, *Luke*, 1:290-91.

27. See Webb, *John the Baptizer*, 290-95; cf. Turner, *Power from on High*, 170-87, esp. 178-79.

fire on the prophets of Baal at Mt. Carmel in response to their unrepentant sinfulness (1 Kgs 18:20-40). John is here standing as himself an Elijah figure passing the prophetic calling to the prophesied eschatological prophetic figure, who will take up these prophetic functions and separate the wheat from the chaff in judgment (Luke 3:17).

The depiction of John the Baptist in relation to Jesus reinforces both the prophetic role of John as forerunner of the coming one and the role of Jesus as that coming one who is the Messiah foretold and anticipated through the prophetic word and who will come in prophetic judgment.

Jesus and the Nazareth Synagogue

The scene in which Jesus preaches in the synagogue at Nazareth (Luke 4:16-30) has been widely discussed in recent scholarship — and for good reason. As others and I have argued elsewhere, in many ways this passage is programmatic in Luke's Gospel for announcing the mission of Jesus, especially in terms of seeing the Old Testament as motivating the message of the Gospel.[28] This is the first extended use of the Old Testament specifically by Jesus after the beginning of his public ministry. Furthermore, this is the first sermon of Jesus in this Gospel. As a result, it has the character of an inaugural address for his ministry and the explicit proclamation of his Messiahship. Along with this, there are statements by Jesus that interpret the Old Testament quotation and then the response by those who hear this address. In this passage, Jesus enters into the synagogue, takes the scroll with Isaiah in it, and opens it and reads. He cites Isa 61:1-2, with one line from Isa 58:6, in Luke 4:18-19. As Foakes-Jackson and Lake have indicated,

---

28. See, e.g., D. L. Bock, *Proclamation from Prophecy and Pattern: Lucan Old Testament Christology* (JSNTSup 12; Sheffield: JSOT, 1987) 27-37; Bock, "Proclamation from Prophecy and Pattern: Luke's Use of the Old Testament for Christology and Mission," in *The Gospels and the Scriptures of Israel* (ed. C. A. Evans and W. R. Stegner; JSNTSup 104; SSEJC 3; Sheffield: Sheffield Academic Press, 1994) 280-307; M. L. Strauss, *The Davidic Messiah in Luke-Acts: The Promise and Its Fulfillment in Lukan Christology* (JSNTSup 110; Sheffield: Sheffield Academic Press, 1995) 199-260; A. J. Köstenberger and P. T. O'Brien, *Salvation to the Ends of the Earth: A Biblical Theology of Mission* (Downers Grove, IL: InterVarsity Press, 2001) 111-15; and S. E. Porter, "Scripture Justifies Mission: The Use of the Old Testament in Luke-Acts," in *Hearing the Old Testament in the New Testament* (ed. S. E. Porter; Grand Rapids: Eerdmans, 2006) 104-26 (I draw on this paper in some of what follows).

Jesus' reading of this passage from Isaiah as a summary of his mission functions as a substitute for Mark's announcement of Jesus' message in 1:15.[29] The passage reads as follows:

> The Spirit of the Lord is upon me, because of which
>> he has anointed me to preach good news to the poor,
>> he has sent me to proclaim forgiveness to the captives and sight to the blind,
>>> to send out the oppressed in forgiveness [Isa 58:6],
>> to proclaim the acceptable year of the Lord.

(My translation)

Jesus then announces that "Today this Scripture has been fulfilled in your hearing" (Luke 4:21). At first his words are received favorably, but when Jesus clearly appropriates these words for himself (vv. 23-24) and extends his interpretation to those outside of Israel (vv. 25-27), the people in the synagogue become angry with him and want to kill him; so he walks through the crowd and goes on his own way. This episode, and especially the use of the Old Testament passage, has raised a number of questions. Initially, it seems as if his hearers react not to the use of the Old Testament passage or to his saying that it is fulfilled in their presence, but to Jesus' interpretation and application of it to those outside of Israel.[30] It is not Jesus' appropriation but his hermeneutical extension that angered his audience. By examining a number of the issues connected with this passage, we can understand the significance of the passage and the nature of the reaction that it generated. I believe that much of the reason for the reaction stems from the fact that Jesus is thereby appropriating to himself the role of messianic prophet by both reading the prophecy, which uses the term "anoint,"[31] and announcing its fulfillment in himself and his ministry.[32]

---

29. F. J. Foakes-Jackson and K. Lake, "Christology," in *The Acts of the Apostles* (ed. F. J. Foakes-Jackson and K. Lake; 5 vols.; The Beginnings of Christianity 1; London: Macmillan, 1920-33) 1:345-418, esp. 390. An equivalent statement may be found at the close of the Gospel, Luke 24:47.

30. Many scholars have noted apparent differences in the response recorded in Mark. This will be considered below.

31. The noun χριστός is not used in this passage, but the language of anointing of a prophet clearly is.

32. This paper is concerned with Luke's depiction of Jesus. I argue in my earlier paper,

Some have noted that Jesus does not cite all of Isa 61:1-2, but only up to the first clause of v. 2, with the result that the words of judgment that follow are omitted.[33] This apparent omission may not be significant, since it may well be that the theme of judgment is also included in what is being alluded to here, even if the wording is not cited explicitly, since Jesus includes it elsewhere in the Gospel (e.g., Luke 7:22-23; 18:7).[34] Certainly 11QMelch 2, which alludes to Isaiah 61, makes mention of vengeance (2.13), and there appears to have been a view by the Qumran community, and hence within at least certain streams of Judaism, that vengeance and comfort went hand in hand with the coming of the Messiah.[35]

These messianic connections make it more important to note the kind of figure being depicted here. The four major themes that have been proposed are the final eschatological prophet, the Messiah, the suffering servant, and a royal Davidic figure.[36] As I noted in my earlier paper on this passage, "Scripture Justifies Mission," it is probably unnecessary to differentiate strongly between them. In that paper, I instead emphasized the complex figure being described. This was supported by 4Q521 1 ii 1-13, a passage noted for its allusions to Isaiah 61, where the figure who is speaking and appropriating for itself the actions of Isaiah 61 appears to be God. In the Qumran text, the Messiah is mentioned specifically in line 1, with reference to the heavens and earth obeying him. Then, in line 5, the Lord is said to visit the pious. It is the Lord who will "glorify the pious ones on the

---

"Scripture Justifies Mission," that there is good reason for this episode to go back to Jesus himself. If this is so, and there are good reasons for thinking so, then Jesus himself made an explicit claim to Messiahship at the outset of his public ministry, but in terms that he himself defined, including his being the eschatological prophet. This has implications for the development of Christology in the early church. See C. F. D. Moule, *The Origin of Christology* (Cambridge: Cambridge University Press, 1977) 34-35.

33. E.g., Strauss, *Davidic Messiah*, 220.

34. Cf. J. Jeremias, *Jesus' Promise to the Nations* (SBT 24; London: SCM Press, 1958) 45-46, who argues that the reason the crowd reacts so strongly to Jesus is that he had left out the message of judgment.

35. C. A. Evans, *Luke* (NIBC; Peabody, MA: Hendrickson, 1990) 74.

36. These are gleaned from C. A. Kimball, *Jesus' Exposition of the Old Testament in Luke's Gospel* (JSNTSup 94; Sheffield: Sheffield Academic Press, 1994) 111-12, and Strauss, *Davidic Messiah*, 226-33, who provide arguments; they are summarized in Porter, "Scripture Justifies Mission," 113-14. Cf. also Turner, *Power from on High*, 233-38; A. Laato, *A Star Is Rising: The Historical Development of the Old Testament Royal Ideology and the Rise of the Jewish Messianic Expectations* (Atlanta: Scholars Press, 1997).

throne of the eternal kingdom," and who will "release the captives, make the blind see, raise up the downtrodden," and (though this is not certain due to a lacuna in the manuscript) "heal the slain, resurrect the dead, and announce glad tidings to the poor."[37] In other words, there was a tradition in the Judaism of the time in which God himself was the one who was appropriating the proclamation and accomplishment of the actions of Isaiah 61. If the Scroll switches subjects in the lacuna — and this is not certain — then at the least the Messiah is depicted as performing the same kinds of actions that God himself also performs.

No doubt the kind of understanding that Jesus had of his messianic calling was transmitted to John the Baptist, which leads to a third parallel episode between the two. The phrase that I have translated "to proclaim forgiveness to the captives" could be translated "to proclaim release to the captives." This is the way that it is translated in many versions, including the RSV/NRSV and NASB (the NIV/TNIV has "freedom"). This is apparently how John the Baptist understood what Jesus was proclaiming in his messianic role.[38] In Luke 7:18-23, John, who was probably in prison (cf. Matt 11:2), sends two of his disciples to enquire regarding whether Jesus is the Messiah.[39] Jesus responds to the enquiry by summarizing his activities, including quoting part of Isa 61:1. John quite possibly interpreted Isa 61:1-2 in terms of an expected literal physical release of prisoners, such as himself, while Jesus apparently interpreted the passage differently. Jesus' interpretation includes both the physical healing of those who are afflicted, something expected from the Messiah,[40] and the spiritual healing of sinners through forgiveness. Both are evidenced throughout Luke's Gospel. In particular, the same root for "forgiveness" is used in two episodes where Jesus fulfills the Isaianic and messianic expectations. These include the healing of the paralytic man in Luke 5:17-26 (esp. vv. 20, 21, 23, 24), and the forgiveness of the sinful woman in Luke 7:36-50 (esp. vv. 47, 48, 49). This

---

37. See C. A. Evans, *Jesus and His Contemporaries: Comparative Studies* (Leiden: Brill, 1996) 128 for translation; cf. 129, where he discusses whether the last statement does not suggest that the Messiah is now the subject of the verbs.

38. For many of the insights that follow, I am grateful to Dr. Craig Evans, whose response at the Bingham Colloquium led to significant improvements and expansions in this and other parts of my paper.

39. It is unclear whether John the Baptist accepted that Jesus was the Messiah. See Evans, *Luke*, 116.

40. See Evans, *Luke*, 119.

latter episode occurs soon after the visit from John's disciples. In both episodes, the question is raised regarding who has the prerogative to forgive sins. In the first, Jesus directly links forgiveness of sins with healing so that the man can rise and walk. In the latter, Jesus does not link forgiveness to healing, but simply informs the woman that her sins are forgiven. This latter scene gives graphic evidence of Jesus' understanding of his messianic calling to include the forgiveness of those held captive by sin.

Included within Jesus' appropriation of the quotation from Isa 61:1-2 is more than I had space to say in my first paper about how these four proposed figures might be related to each other and to what Luke is doing in depicting Jesus. I believe that the four figures revolve around the notion of the eschatological prophetic Messiah, as indicated by several key factors. The anointing language in Isa 61:1-2 (Luke 4:18) is clearly related to the anointing by the Spirit and proclamation of a prophet.[41] Jesus' own response to the reaction of the crowd is that "no prophet is acceptable in his home town" (Luke 4:24), using the same word for "acceptable" that is used in the quotation of Isa 61:2. This linked response indicates that Jesus saw himself as performing a prophetic role in this passage, being the eschatological prophet proclaimed in the Old Testament quotation. This is consistent with other language in Luke's Gospel in which Jesus is seen as a prophet (e.g., Luke 7:16, 39; 13:33-34; 24:19). Some have questioned whether the anointing language is prophetic because in the Old Testament anointing and the Spirit refer to anointing a king (1 Sam 16:12-13; 2 Sam 23:1-2).[42] However, even the royal Davidic figure is also probably prophetically messianic in nature (cf. Luke 20:41), since enthronement language is common to the Davidic tradition (e.g., 2 Sam 7:12-16; Psalms 2; 110) and the prophetic tradition (Isa 9:2-7; 11:1-10; Mic 5:1-5; Daniel 7, esp. vv. 7, 14).[43] The same can be said of the suffering servant, because of linkage between Isa 61:1-2 and Isa 52:7, the latter of which is the start of the suffering servant song (Isa 52:7–53:12), according to ancient paragraph markers,[44] such that Isa 61:1-3 may be either a suffering servant song or a

---

41. Cf. R. P. Menzies, *The Development of Early Christian Pneumatology with Special Reference to Luke-Acts* (JSNTSup 54; Sheffield: Sheffield Academic Press, 1991) 146-77, esp. 177.

42. Cf. Strauss, *Davidic Messiah*, 230, 227-28.

43. See Evans, *Jesus and His Contemporaries*, 453-54. I wish to thank my former student Richard Van Egmond for bringing some of this material to my attention.

44. Evans, *Luke*, 74.

midrash upon one.[45] Others have questioned whether in Luke's Gospel there is reference to "the" prophet, or only to "a" prophet, with reference to "the" prophet occurring only in Acts.[46] The appropriation by Jesus of the messianic role, and the specific prophetic language used to indicate this figure, suggests that there is more than simply reference to *a* prophet here.[47]

The proclamation of Luke 4 is thus prophetically messianic, in terms of both the citation used and the content of the citation. It depicts one who is anointed by the Spirit of God to proclaim a specific prophetic message. This message inaugurates Jesus' mission and, by his specific appropriation, clearly labels him as the prophetic Messiah.

Peter's Acclamation

In Luke 9, in a passage very similar to Mark and Matthew, Jesus is with his disciples, and he questions them about his identity. The answers they give in some ways summarize the discussion that has been given above. When asked who people say that he is, the disciples answer Jesus by saying: "John the Baptist, Elijah and one of the prophets of old" (Luke 9:19). These are the same answers that are earlier recorded as having been given to Herod regarding Jesus (Luke 9:7-8). When pressed by Jesus for a personal response, Peter answers for them all by saying that Jesus is "The Christ of God" (Luke 9:20). At first glance, it may appear that we have two different categories of response — a haphazard and popular group of wrong answers and the one right answer. This is probably not correct. Bock is probably more accurate when he states regarding the proposed answers that "The basis for each possibility is tied to the prophetic character of Jesus' ministry."[48] As we have already noted, ties have been established with each

---

45. Kimball, *Jesus' Exposition*, 112, referring to Ellis, *Luke*, 97, and J. A. Sanders, "From Isaiah 61 to Luke 4," in C. A. Evans and J. A. Sanders, *Luke and Scripture: The Function of Sacred Tradition in Luke-Acts* (Minneapolis: Fortress, 1993) 46-69, here 49.

46. E.g., O. Cullmann, *Christology of the New Testament* (trans. S. C. Guthrie and C. A. M. Hall; London: SCM Press, 1959) 30; C. F. D. Moule, "The Christology of Acts," in *Studies in Luke-Acts* (ed. L. E. Keck and J. L. Martyn; Philadelphia: Fortress, 1966) 159-85, esp. 162.

47. In fact, I would argue that references to "the" prophet have been in play since the beginning of the Gospel on the basis of the parallels between John and Jesus.

48. Bock, *Luke*, 1:841.

of these — John, Elijah, and the prophets — in terms of Jesus' prophetic and messianic character. In other words, "From Luke's point of view, these responses are not so much wrong as incomplete. In contrast, Peter's reply centers on Jesus' messianic position."[49] This is confirmed by the unique phrasing that Luke uses, affirming that the Messiah is anointed and sent by God.[50] Thus, what Peter is affirming is that a number of prophetic figures have been proposed for who Jesus is. Rather than switching categories altogether, Peter affirms that Jesus is the prophetic Messiah, that is, the Messiah or Christ who comes as fulfillment of the prophets noted earlier, including John, Elijah, or any others (e.g., Isaiah?).[51]

Jesus and the Authorities

Once Jesus is arrested, he is finally taken before the authorities in Jerusalem. At first he is held in custody by the religious authorities overnight so that he can appear before the Sanhedrin. When he is in the custody of the religious authorities, he is mocked and beaten. They also demand that he prophesy regarding who it is that has hit him (Luke 22:64). Luke has wording similar to that in Mark, but Matthew at this point expands it by having the enquirer ask Jesus to "Prophesy to us, you Christ, who is the one that struck you?" (Matt 26:67). Luke retains the Markan form of the account at this point. When Jesus appears before the Sanhedrin, however, the Lukan account is different from that in Mark and Matthew. The Sanhedrin tell him, "If you are the Christ, tell us" (Luke 22:67), to which Jesus says that if he does answer, they won't believe him. At that point, Jesus states: "But from now on the Son of Man will be seated at the right hand of the power of God" (Luke 22:69; citing Ps 110:1). Then the Sanhedrin asks if he is the son of God, to which he replies in the affirmative. At this point, they discount the need for witnesses, since they have heard directly from him.

There has been much recent scholarship regarding Jesus and the accusation of blasphemy made against him in Mark's and Matthew's ac-

---

49. Bock, *Luke*, 1:841. However, one need not continue (as Bock does) by saying that the "regal" category of messianism is now reintroduced from the infancy narrative.

50. L. Morris, *New Testament Theology* (Grand Rapids: Zondervan, 1986) 164.

51. I note that Matt 16:14 records the disciples including Jeremiah with the proposals regarding Jesus. In light of Luke's use of Isaiah (see above on Luke 4), it makes sense for him not to mention any other prophets, leaving the implication that Isaiah is included.

counts.[52] However, that accusation is not explicitly made in Luke's Gospel. Instead, the charge of blasphemy is made against those who were earlier interrogating Jesus (Luke 22:65). This does not mean that Jesus was not charged with blasphemy — he almost assuredly was (see below). But Luke does not use the term directly of Jesus, no doubt to ensure that accusations of irreligious behavior were properly focused.[53] Nevertheless, there are several other differences in the accounts as well. These include Luke's quotation from Dan 7:13 that does not make specific reference to coming with the clouds of heaven, and the change in ordering, so that Jesus' response comes before the question regarding his being the son of God.

Luke, however, is interpreting Jesus' messianism in keeping with his emphases. Several features are to be noted. The first is that the quotation of Ps 110:1 here in Luke 22:69 invokes the discussion in Luke 20:41-44.[54] In this earlier passage, in dialogue with some scribes, Jesus asks them how it is that they say that the Christ is David's son (Luke 20:41). Jesus then cites Ps 110:1 — "the Lord said to my Lord, sit at my right hand, until I make your enemies a footstool for your feet" (Luke 20:42-43), where the point is, as Bock says, that "it is more important to see Messiah as David's Lord than as his son."[55] This would appear to indicate that in Luke 20 and 22 Luke is emphasizing the royal or Davidic messianic characteristics of Jesus. There is no doubt that this is the case. However, two further factors should be considered. The first is that it appears that Luke treats the Psalm quotation as prophetic in nature, since he sees it being fulfilled in Jesus.[56] The second is that, even though Luke does not cite the entire quotation from Dan 7:13 regarding coming with the clouds of heaven, he does refer to the son of man seated at the right hand of power.[57] Not only does this enthronement

52. See Evans, *Jesus and His Contemporaries*, 407-34; D. L. Bock, *Blasphemy and Exaltation in Judaism and the Final Examination of Jesus: A Philological-Historical Study of the Key Jewish Themes Impacting Mark 14:61-64* (WUNT 2.106; Tübingen: Mohr Siebeck, 1998).

53. See Bock, *Luke*, 2:1790.

54. On Psalm 110 in Christian usage, see M. Hengel, *Studies in Early Christology* (Edinburgh: T&T Clark, 1995) 119-225.

55. Bock, *Luke*, 2:1796.

56. See Johnson, *Luke*, 314-15, where he notes that Mark 12:36 refers to the Holy Spirit and Matt 22:43 to the Spirit rather than to David; Johnson, *Acts*, 51-52.

57. See Hengel, *Studies in Early Christology*, 185-89, esp. 187. Hengel notes that Luke "limits himself — consistent with his theology — to the presence of the one who is exalted to the right hand of God and omits the mention of Jesus as the Coming One according to Dan. 7:13." There are other places where Luke clearly indicates Jesus as the coming one, as I

language indicate fulfillment of the Davidic promises of 2 Samuel 7 as well as Psalm 110, but, as noted above, it is also associated with the prophetic tradition of Isaiah 9 and 11 and Daniel 7. As Evans notes, the contexts of Daniel 7 and Psalm 110 are similar, and they were combined in later Jewish exegesis.[58] So, the reference here is to both the royal Davidic and the prophetic Messiah.

The Risen Jesus

After the resurrection, two episodes further reveal Jesus' messianic character in Luke's Gospel. In the first episode, the risen Jesus travels along the road to Emmaus with two men and talks with them about the Christ. After they have expressed their disappointment about events surrounding Jesus' death, the risen Jesus expresses his dismay that they have not believed what the prophets wrote and asks whether it was not necessary (ἔδει) for the Christ to suffer the things recounted. In the second episode, in Jerusalem with a larger group, after eating together with them, he opens his hearers' minds and says that "it is written [γέγραπται] that the Christ should suffer and rise again from the dead the third day" (Luke 24:46).

There are four factors to notice here that confirm the eschatological prophetic messianic role of Jesus in Luke's Gospel.[59] The first is that Jesus refers specifically in v. 25 to what the prophets have said (even if that includes the psalmist, since the psalmist was seen as a prophet by Luke). Jesus refers to the prophetic tradition that had predicted the Messiah's suffering and death (see above on the suffering servant idea) — even if that set of expectations was counter to much messianic expectation of the time.[60] The second is that Luke uses the word "necessary" to depict the things that Jesus underwent as following a prescribed prophetic plan, laid down in advance of the actions that took place. The use of the language of necessity makes clear the prophetic line of continuity from the Old Testa-

---

have noted, and there is the sense in which Luke sees Jesus as the one who has already come, as the episode on the road to Emmaus indicates (see the next section).

58. Evans, *Jesus and His Contemporaries*, 417, 418-19. He cites *Midr. Ps.* 2.9. as combining Ps 110:1 and Dan 7:13.

59. See L. W. Hurtado, "Christ," in *Dictionary of Jesus and the Gospels* (ed. J. B. Green, S. McKnight, and I. H. Marshall; Downers Grove: InterVarsity Press, 1992) 106-17, here 114.

60. Bock, *Luke*, 2:1916.

ment to the events in the New. The third factor is that Jesus refers to what stands written (this form of the verb appears about sixty-seven times in the Greek New Testament). The use of this language indicates specific reference to the Old Testament prophetic tradition, in which passages written in the Old Testament stand written as witnesses and testimony to the established prophetic word of God. The fourth is that the risen Jesus is referring to events that have already transpired, that is, the end of the age has come in the death and resurrection of Jesus. Jesus' citation in v. 47 of what may be seen as a paraphrase of his message of repentance for forgiveness of sins as recorded in Mark 1:15 serves to round out the account, with the Messiah both opening and closing the Gospel.

The Messiah in Acts

Having treated the Gospel of Luke, I turn now to the book of Acts. Although the word "Christ" (χριστός) is used more often in Acts than in the Gospel, half of that usage is nominal in nature.[61] That is, it indicates that the usage has already become associated with the name of Jesus. I wish to concentrate on the titular usage.[62]

Pentecost

Just as the sermon in the synagogue in Nazareth marked the definition and inauguration of Jesus' ministry, so the opening of the second of Luke's two

61. I tend to accept Fitzmyer's analysis of titular and nominal usage, although this has been disputed. Some of the major disputants include H. J. Cadbury, "The Titles of Jesus in Acts," in Foakes-Jackson and Lake, eds., *The Acts of the Apostles*, 5:354-75, esp. 358-59, who argues for titular use; Moule, "Christology of Acts," 174-76; S. S. Smalley, "The Christology of Acts Again," in *Christ and the Spirit in the New Testament* (ed. B. Lindars and S. S. Smalley; Cambridge: Cambridge University Press, 1973) 79-93, esp. 85-88, both of whom find a mix of usage; and most recently Blomberg, "Messiah," 125, who, recapitulating the discussion, argues for predominantly titular usage (questioned by W. W. Klein's response in the same volume, "*Christos:* Jewish Title or Hellenistic Name? A Response to Craig L. Blomberg," in Hess and Carroll R., eds., *Israel's Messiah*, 143-50).

62. I do not mean to imply by this that the messianic sense does not rest with the nominal usage, but that the nominal usage does not reveal its messianic content in the same way that the titular usage does.

volumes begins likewise with a programmatic statement for the book in Acts 2:14-36.[63] This occurs when Peter stands up and addresses the crowd in order to explain the behavior of his fellow disciples, and he explicitly cites Joel 2:28-32 (LXX 3:1-5) in Acts 2:17-21; Ps 16:8-11 in Acts 2:25-28; and Ps 110:1 in Acts 2:34-35.[64] On the basis of his establishment of Jesus as the prophesied crucified and resurrected one,[65] Peter then speaks of him as the Messiah. In Acts 2:30-31, Peter says that because David was a prophet, he could look forward to the resurrection of the Messiah. In Acts 2:36, after citing Ps 110:1, Peter says that all the house of Israel should know that God had made[66] Jesus, who was crucified, both Lord and Christ. This designation was in place from the advent of his ministry, not initiated at the resurrection (see Acts 2:31).[67] Then, in Acts 2:38, after the crowd is pierced to the heart by what they have heard, Peter tells them to repent and be baptized in the name of Jesus the Christ.

This passage continues the prophetic and royal or Davidic messianic figure that was established in Luke's Gospel.[68] The first quotation is from

63. See Bock, *Proclamation*, 205-44.

64. There is also the allusive use of Old Testament language in Acts 2:30 and 31, the latter paraphrasing Ps 16:10. On the text used by Luke, see G. J. Steyn, *Septuagint Quotations in the Context of the Petrine and Pauline Speeches of the Acta Apostolorum* (Kampen: Kok Pharos, 1995) 64-128, who believes that the Septuagint text is followed.

65. There has been widespread neglect of the idea of the importance of the suffering of Jesus in Acts. As I will point out, this is a common theme in the messianic passages that we are discussing. See D. P. Moessner, "The 'Script' of the Scriptures in Acts: Suffering as God's 'Plan' (βουλή) for the World for the 'Release of Sins,'" in *History, Literature and Society in the Book of Acts* (ed. B. Witherington III; Cambridge: Cambridge University Press, 1996) 218-50, esp. 221 and 225-27.

66. The verb gives no indication of when this act took place.

67. Note that there is no article here. Some have posited that an adoptionist Christology is revealed here, whether in Acts itself or in a source used by Luke. For example, R. Bultmann (*New Testament Theology* [trans. K. Grobel; 2 vols.; New York: Scribners, 1952, 1955] 1:27), Cullmann (*Christology*, 216), and Robinson ("The Most Primitive Christology of All?" in his *Twelve New Testament Studies*, 139-53, esp. 140-41) equate Lordship and Messiahship with the resurrection. C. K. Barrett (*A Critical and Exegetical Commentary on the Acts of the Apostles* [ICC; Edinburgh: T&T Clark, 1994, 1998] 1:151-52) thinks that this is not Luke's position, but that it reveals an early source, perhaps the kind of early adoptionist Christology that Paul countered in Rom 1:4 and Phil 2:6-11. Barrett, however, does not believe that Jesus made a public claim to being the Messiah (1:152), which would push back the origins of Jesus' Christology and claim to Messiahship much earlier than some have thought, and certainly to before the resurrection.

68. See Strauss, *Davidic Messiah*, 131-47.

Ps 16:8-11, which refers to the continuation of the Davidic dynasty and hence is a royal psalm. However, as Peter says, David was able prophetically to see that one of his descendants would sit upon his throne, and thus he was a prophet prophesying about the Messiah.[69] The second quotation is from Ps 110:1, which, as we have seen, is an important Lukan (and early Christian) ascension or enthronement psalm, and also a royal Davidic psalm. Similarly to the first example, David is seen by Peter here as a prophet, since he says that "it was not David who ascended into heaven, but he himself says . . . ," thus indicating that David's utterance of the psalm had a prophetic fulfillment in a later, eschatological prophetic figure. The third quotation is reminiscent of the proclamation of John the Baptist in its call for repentance and baptism for forgiveness of sins (cf. Mark 1:15; Luke 3:16-17). As noted above, the message of John is associated with his prophetic role as anticipating fulfillment in the eschatological prophetic Messiah.

Peter's Sermon in the Temple

In this, Peter's second major sermon in the book of Acts, he follows the same pattern as noted in his first sermon, the one given at Pentecost. Here he refers in Acts 3:18 to the things that God announced beforehand by all the prophets, that is, that the Messiah should suffer. This leads him to call for the people to repent of their sins, in anticipation of the sending of Christ Jesus,[70] appointed beforehand for such a purpose (3:20).[71] Unlike the Pentecost sermon, which had a combination of royal and prophetic

---

69. Strauss, *Davidic Messiah*, 137; Johnson, *Acts*, 51-52. Cf. also Acts 4:25-26, where David, by the Holy Spirit, speaks of the rulers gathering against the Christ (Ps 2:1).

70. This usage may well be nominal, rather than titular, especially as there is no article with the noun.

71. Robinson ("Most Primitive Christology," esp. 149-53; followed by R. H. Fuller, *The Foundations of New Testament Christology* [New York: Scribners, 1965] 158-59) argues that there is an underlying primitive Christology in this passage indicating that Jesus, though designated Messiah, had not actually been sent yet as the Messiah, and that there was future expectation regarding his Messiahship. This has been refuted by Moule, "Christology," 167-69; D. L. Jones, "The Title *Christos* in Luke-Acts," *CBQ* 32 (1970) 69-76, esp. 71-73; E. Franklin, *Christ the Lord: A Study in the Purpose and Theology of Luke-Acts* (London: SPCK, 1975) 57. It is worth noting that Robinson's position is in tension with Acts 3:18 and does not best suit the ordering of events as presented by the grammar of the verses involved.

messianic elements, this sermon is clearly focused upon the Messiah as fulfilling what was prophesied. As Johnson states, "Peter strikes one of the central themes of Luke-Acts, that the events in the story of the prophet and the people fulfill the prophecies of Torah (Luke 1:1), most specifically the necessity of the Messiah's suffering before entering his glory."[72] Thus, all the prophets, Peter says, foretold the suffering of the Christ, which elicits human repentance in anticipation of the return of the Christ, who was appointed for such a purpose. Later Christianity did not erase the signs of the early prophetic view of the Messiah;[73] rather, this theme is still readily present.

Paul's Speech in Thessalonica

When Paul arrives in Thessalonica, he finds a synagogue, where he proceeds to teach for three sabbaths so that he can reason from the Scriptures (Acts 17:2). While there, he opens up the meaning of the Scriptures and sets out evidence that the Christ, whom he identifies as Jesus, had to (ἔδει) suffer and rise from the dead (Acts 17:3). Some have questioned the Pauline usage in Acts as out of keeping with that in the epistles by contending that Paul's use in the epistles is nominal,[74] whereas this usage is titular. We should note that Paul's usage in Acts is both titular and nominal. The same in fact is true in his letters, where there is clear identification of Jesus with his Messiahship in, for example, Rom 1:3 and especially 9:5.[75] There are several observations to make about this passage in support of the prophetic messianic hypothesis. The first is that Paul's explaining the Christ comes about as a result of his reasoning from the Scriptures. This implies a prophetic use of the Scriptures, especially in light of the second factor, which is that Paul was explaining Christ's suffering and resurrection from the dead. No doubt Paul was drawing upon passages such as

72. Johnson, *Acts*, 68. He cross-references Luke 24:26-27, 44-46; and Acts 17:2-3 (see below).

73. As believes Robinson, "Most Primitive Christology," 150-51.

74. A representative and highly influential position in this regard is W. Kramer, *Christ, Lord, Son of God* (SBT 50; London: SCM Press, 1966) 203-14.

75. See Moule, "Christology," 174-75. Note that Rom 1:3 has been thought by some to reflect an early christological formulation. This would draw the lines of thought and expression even tighter between Paul and Acts as reflecting earliest Christian thought.

Isaiah 53 that demonstrated that the Messiah had to suffer (seen elsewhere in the Lukan writings as well, such as Luke 9:22; 17:25; 24:26, 46; Acts 3:18).[76] The third observation is that the link between the Scriptures and fulfillment in Christ is drawn by usage of the verb of necessity, "must."

Paul's Defense before Agrippa

There has been much discussion of Paul's speeches, including his speech before Agrippa.[77] For whatever reason, Festus cuts it off right after Paul has laid out a number of considerations regarding the Messiah. First, Paul says that he has stated nothing except what the prophets and Moses said was going to occur (Acts 26:22). Luke here reemphasizes a theme that we have seen throughout the two books, that what has taken place regarding the Messiah has occurred in terms of prophetic fulfillment of what God had said in the Old Testament.[78] The mention of the prophets and Moses is not meant to suggest that they are in opposition to each other; rather, they are complementary, with Moses, representing the Torah, seen to be a prophetic voice. Second, Paul notes that these prophets had specified that the Christ had to suffer but that his resurrection would proclaim light to Jews and Gentiles (Acts 26:23).[79] Once more the Christ is seen as fulfilling prophetic messianic expectations.

Conclusion

Messianic complexity is somewhat clarified in Luke-Acts. This is not because there are not a number of positions that could be argued for regarding presentation of the Messiah in Luke and Acts. Instead, it is because one major and at least one minor emphasis emerge from the discussion. Throughout the two works, the author wishes to present Jesus as the eschatological prophetic messianic figure. That means that the Christ is the

---

76. As noted by Johnson, *Acts*, 305.

77. See S. E. Porter, *The Paul of Acts: Essays in Literary Criticism, Rhetoric and Theology* (WUNT 115; Tübingen: Mohr Siebeck, 1999) 158-61.

78. Johnson, *Acts*, 438.

79. The grammar of the passage is actually stated in terms of verbless protases: "if the Christ is a sufferer, if he is first from resurrection of the dead. . . ."

one who was foretold by the writers of the Old Testament, often in prophetic books but also in other books whose authors became prophets as their writings were seen later to be fulfilled in the ministry, suffering, and resurrection of Jesus. A subsidiary but also important theme is that of the Messiah as the royal Davidic figure. This theme is not as prominent as the prophetic messianic motif, in my view, and in fact is often linked to the prophetic notion, since ideas of ascension and enthronement are often linked in the Old Testament passages cited.

Remembering Jesus:
John's Negative Christology

Tom Thatcher

Any discussion of John's messianic beliefs is essentially a discussion of John's view of Jesus.[1] The first chapter of the Fourth Gospel applies a veritable catalogue of messianic titles to Jesus to make the identity of the protagonist immediately clear. Jesus is Joseph's son (John 1:45), but Joseph's son also happens to be "the Son of God," as well as "the Word," "the Life," "the Light of Humanity," "Christ" (χριστός), "the only-begotten (μονογενής) in the bosom of the Father," "the Lamb of God who takes away the sin of the world," "the Messiah" (μεσσίας), "the one written about in the Law by Moses and in the Prophets," "the King of Israel," and, finally, Jesus' self-designation, "the Son of Man" (1:29-51). Even the most casual reader can scarcely fail to see that John's messianic belief is entirely conflated with the identity of Jesus of Nazareth.

The Puzzle of John's Christology

Because John's Christology is tied to the person of Jesus, one could theoretically outline John's messianic beliefs by going through the text of the

---

1. The terms "John" and "Fourth Evangelist" will be used synonymously throughout this essay to refer to that individual who is primarily responsible for the text of the Fourth Gospel as it exists today. The masculine pronoun "he" will be used in agreement with the gender of the English name "John." For sake of convenience, this essay will closely associate John with the "Elder," the author of 1-2-3 John, under the assumption that these two individuals, if not the same person, held very similar beliefs about Jesus.

Fourth Gospel and highlighting statements by or about Jesus that reflect specific christological themes. These passages could then be distributed across a grid of theological categories that would, when taken together, represent the totality of John's Christology. A convenient starting point for such an inquiry may be found in John 20:30-31, a passage universally recognized as the purpose statement of the Fourth Gospel: "But then also Jesus did many other signs in the presence of his disciples that are not written in this book. But these things have been written so that you may believe that *Jesus is the Christ the Son of God,* and so that *by believing you may have life in his name.*" Similar statements appear in the christological creeds of the Johannine Epistles, which everywhere emphasize that "Jesus is the Christ/Son of God come in flesh" and assert that eternal life is granted to those who accept this claim (1 John 1:2; 2:22, 25; 4:2, 15; 5:1, 5, 13; 2 John 7). Very conveniently for modern readers, John's summaries fit neatly with the Western theological tradition's approach to the mystery of the Incarnation, holding in perfect tension the human and divine aspects of Christ's nature. "Jesus," the human being who came from Nazareth (John 1:45-46) and died on a cross in Jerusalem, was at the same time "the Christ," both in the sense that he fulfilled Israel's messianic hopes and also, on a more metaphysical level, in the sense that he was the divine "Son of God." Eternal life in the name of this individual is promised to those who are able to comprehend this mystery.

But while quick recourse to John 20:31 and the creeds of 1 John offers a simple solution to the puzzle of Johannine Christology, it also obscures the depth of the problem. For a broader look reveals that John's thinking about Jesus appears to be unstable, at least from the perspective of traditional theological categories. For example, although John highlights Jesus' dual nature, he seems uncertain what to do with it, at one moment wallowing in the wounds of Jesus' crucifixion and the taste of his blood (see John 6:53-58; 19:31-35; 20:26-27), at the next presenting "the earthly life of Jesus merely as a backdrop for the Son of God proceeding through the world."[2] As a result of this shifting emphasis throughout the narrative, the Fourth Gospel sometimes exhibits a "low Christology" — one that primarily reflects "OT or intertestamental [Jewish messianic] expectations ... that do not in themselves imply divinity" — and at other times expresses

2. Ernst Käsemann, *The Testament of Jesus: A Study of the Gospel of John in the Light of Chapter 17* (trans. Gerhard Krodel; Philadelphia: Fortress, 1968) 13.

perhaps the "highest Christology" evident in the New Testament, making statements that explicitly "move him [Jesus] into the sphere of divinity."[3] This problem is only one of several that might suggest that John does not have a firm grip on the identity of his main character.[4]

Many modern scholars, overwhelmed by the conflicting christological claims of the Fourth Gospel, have simply torn the text in despair. Most current theories of the composition history of the Gospel of John depend to some extent on its many theological "aporiae" — the apparent gaps, tensions, and paradoxes in John's thinking. In fact, it is fair to say that two of the most significant movements in recent Johannine scholarship, source-critical analysis and the developmental approach, both depend heavily on the inherent ambiguity of John's Christology.

Johannine source criticism has relied heavily on the apparent inconsistency of John's theology. Redaction criticism, the analysis of a biblical text in light of the author's theological and literary development of materials drawn from earlier sources, has been most successful in the study of Matthew and Luke, because the presumed sources behind these texts (Mark and Q, a sayings source) are readily available for comparison and analysis. But in the case of the Gospel of John, as with Mark, obvious sources cannot be so easily identified. One must therefore reconstruct the hypothetical source documents from which John may have drawn material, and these sources must be reconstructed from evidence in the text of the Fourth Gospel itself. Johannine source critics have attempted to develop internal criteria to determine which parts of the Fourth Gospel were derived from these source(s) and which parts reflect John's own editorial revisions and theological tendencies. The christological tensions apparent in the text facilitate this process by allowing scholars to suggest that the Fourth Evangelist utilized sources that did not entirely reflect his own theological perspective. In most versions of this theory, it is argued that the Fourth Evangelist, writing somewhere toward the end of the first century, was responsible for the "high" christological statements in the text, while traces of an older, "lower" Christology reflect the perspective of his sources.

---

3. Raymond Brown, *The Community of the Beloved Disciple: The Life, Loves, and Hates of an Individual Church in New Testament Times* (New York: Paulist Press, 1979) 25n.32.

4. See the convenient survey of the Fourth Gospel's theological tensions in Raymond Brown, *An Introduction to the Gospel of John* (ed. Francis J. Moloney; ABRL; New York: Doubleday, 2003) 238-41, 249-51.

A convenient example of this approach may be found in the work of its most significant recent proponent, Robert Fortna. Fortna proposes two stages in the composition history of the Gospel of John, *"basic document and redaction."* Fortna calls John's basic source document the "Signs Gospel," an early Christian account of seven notable miracles followed by the story of Jesus' passion and resurrection. In Fortna's view, this primitive Signs Gospel was produced in a Jewish Christian milieu "as a missionary tract with a single end, to show . . . that Jesus is the Messiah."[5] As such, it evidenced a low Christology, being content simply to argue that the human Jesus fulfilled Israel's messianic hopes. The Gospel of John betrays a low Christology at exactly those points where John is dependent on this Signs Gospel (SG), due to the fact that John "regards SG . . . as gospel, and treats its language more conservatively than Matthew and Luke treat Mark," quoting the text verbatim and often adding to, but never subtracting from, its contents.[6] The high Christology of the Fourth Gospel reflects John's additions to this primitive text, primarily evident in Jesus' lengthy discourses. As a result, while the narrative portions of the Fourth Gospel, drawn from the older Signs Gospel, reflect the more earthly "Jesus familiar from the Synoptic Gospels," the discourses offer "the more familiar portrait of the [divine] Jesus of universal Christianity."[7] Fortna, along with other source critics, thus solves the christological puzzle of the Fourth Gospel by arguing that the conflicting statements about Jesus' identity must originate in two different places.

Theological tensions also play a key role in the "developmental approach" to the Gospel of John. Advocates of this position argue that the Fourth Gospel as it exists today is the last in a series of revisions of an earlier document that is now lost. Over time, the Johannine Christians faced new challenges and encountered new religious ideas in the world around them. Each new challenge forced them to revise their thinking about Jesus and, in turn, to revise their gospel so as it make it harmonize with these new ideas. The Gospel of John is thus the end product of the series of theological "developments" from which this approach derives its name.

5. Robert T. Fortna, *The Gospel of Signs: A Reconstruction of the Narrative Source Underlying the Fourth Gospel* (SNTSMS; Cambridge: Cambridge University Press, 1970) 77, 225.

6. Robert T. Fortna, "Christology in the Fourth Gospel: Redaction-Critical Perspectives," *NTS* 21 (1974-75) 504; see also Fortna, *The Fourth Gospel and Its Predecessor: From Narrative Source to Present Gospel* (Philadelphia: Fortress, 1988) 7.

7. Fortna, *Fourth Gospel and Its Predecessor*, 1-3.

Advocates of the developmental approach, such as Raymond Brown, highlight christological tensions in the Gospel of John as evidence for this process of theological development. Brown notes that "part of the difficulty in analyzing Johannine Christology . . . is that the [Fourth] Gospel contains statements that seem to have opposing views." He highlights five such apparent contradictions, including Jesus' "equality and subordination in relation to the Father" and "statements capable of being read as Gnostic Christology . . . [alongside] others that would cause trouble for Gnostics."[8] In his most recent treatment of the subject, Brown explains these tensions in terms of a three-stage tradition history. Stage one represents the ministry and teaching of the historical Jesus, which provided the foundational data for all Gospel traditions and all extant Gospels; stage two represents the development of that common tradition to meet the peculiar needs of the Johannine community over time; stage three represents the actual composition of the Fourth Gospel on the basis of the traditional information developed in stage two.[9]

According to Brown, the theological tensions in the text may be explained by the fact that the author of the Fourth Gospel did not personally live through all of stage two, but rather inherited his information about Jesus from the mysterious "Beloved Disciple," an associate of the historical Jesus (John 13:23; 19:26-27; 20:2; 21:7, 20-24). While the Fourth Evangelist was a devoted follower of this Beloved Disciple, he sought to "complement" his mentor's somewhat outdated perspective in order to make it more relevant to his own immediate situation. His example was followed by a later redactor, who added a few further finishing touches to produce the version of the Fourth Gospel that exists today.[10] In the process, Johannine Christology gradually evolved to higher and higher levels, from an earlier view of Jesus as the Jewish Messiah to the later, more fully developed incarnational Christology now evident in the Fourth Gospel. While Brown stresses that he does not wish to emphasize discontinuity between these three stages of development, his analysis nevertheless depends on apparent theological discrepancies in order to reconstruct the history of the Johannine community.[11]

8. Brown, *Introduction to the Gospel of John*, 250.

9. See Brown, *Introduction to the Gospel of John*, 62-78.

10. Brown, *Introduction to the Gospel of John*, 78, 195-96, 251. "Complement" is Brown's term, p. 251.

11. See the similar disclaimer in Brown, *Community of the Beloved Disciple*, 51-54.

In some branches of Johannine scholarship, then, the ambiguity of John's Christology is not only taken as a given, but is in fact exploited as a foundational principle of interpretive method. Source critics and developmental theorists see John's theological aporiae not as a liability, but rather as a window into the composition history of the text. These approaches have yielded fruitful results in exegesis, and for this reason they have played a significant part in Johannine studies for the past fifty years.

Yet despite the success of these methods, one must question their treatment of the data under consideration. Essentially, source-critical and developmental approaches begin with a taxonomy of categories that reflect the Western philosophical and theological tradition. The text of the Fourth Gospel is dissected, and each distinct unit or theme is sorted into one of the familiar christological categories. In the process, it is observed that materials from different sections of the book seem to fall into categories that logically conflict: John 10:3, 26 suggests the "predestination of those who come to Jesus"; but John 3:19-21 "indicate[s] choice."[12] Remarkably, this observation leads to the conclusion that, because these perspectives are irreconcilable, the Fourth Gospel must not represent the christological beliefs of any single individual, but is rather a pastiche of the views of several authors/sources. This conclusion is "remarkable" because it obscures what would otherwise appear to be a more logical solution: that traditional Western theological categories are inadequate to describe John's messianic beliefs, or, indeed, even to describe the way that John constructs a "Christology." Since these categories are obviously not applicable to the data from the text, it would seem more fruitful to abandon them and to assume that John's beliefs about Jesus are coherent at some other level.

The present study will adopt this approach, treating the text of the Fourth Gospel as a unified composition and attempting to describe its Christology in terms relevant to John's own beliefs and situation. Regardless of its composition history, the author/redactor/final editor who produced the version of the Fourth Gospel that exists today clearly was not concerned about the fact that his narrative sometimes advocates a "low Christology" with a "final eschatology" and sometimes a "high Christology" with a "realized eschatology." For the Fourth Evangelist, at least, the text is coherent at some level, and this essay will seek to determine the level at which John's Christology comes clearly into focus. In order to do this, it

12. Brown, *Introduction to the Gospel of John*, 250.

will be necessary to first identify and discuss the generative mechanism of John's messianism, the means by which he created christological ideas and statements, and then to outline the rhetorical objectives of the christological claims of the Johannine literature. While this approach will not produce a comprehensive survey of the content of John's Christology, it will expose the underlying processes that produced that content.

The question of the Fourth Gospel's christological generative mechanism concerns the means by which John constructed his image of Jesus as the Messiah. Obviously, John's thinking was not built on the platform of modern theological categories and the sharp divisions between them, such as "equality or subordination," "human or divine," "election or choice." John did not, in other words, reflect on things that Jesus did and then try to decide whether his words and deeds meant that he was equal to God or subordinate to God, etc. Instead, John refers to the process by which he painted his portrait as a "memory" of Jesus, a "witness" to Jesus' true identity. A coherent theory about the way this witness and memory worked is critical to any study that seriously seeks to understand John's Christology on its own terms.

The question of the rhetorical objectives of John's christological claims concerns the interplay between what John says about Jesus and the historical context in which he made those statements. The Fourth Gospel and 1-2-3 John, like all other texts, were written in response to a specific situation, and the christological claims of those texts should therefore be seen as reactions to external social realities. It is in reference to these social realities, not to modern theological categories, that the apparent tensions in John's Christology become coherent. The theological guideposts of the Johannine books are not, in other words, explicit in the texts themselves. Instead, John's thinking about Jesus as the Messiah finds its conceptual moorings in the real world of his audience.

John's Charismatic Christological Memory Machine

John does not refer to his thinking about Jesus as a "messianic belief" or a "Christology," and he does not talk about Jesus in terms that can be easily reduced to abstract propositions that fit neatly into modern theological categories. He speaks, instead, of his "memory" of Jesus or "witness to" Jesus, the recollection of things that Johannine Christians have known about

Jesus "from the beginning" (1 John 2:7, 24; 3:11). For John, Christian "memory" is not a simple act of recalling information about things that Jesus said or did. Rather, Christian memory is a complex combination of the recall of the historical Jesus, post-resurrection faith, and a Christian interpretation of the Hebrew Bible — all melted together by the heat of the Holy Spirit. This charismatic memory is the generative matrix that produced all of John's statements about Jesus, and what we today call John's "Christology" is the image of Jesus that this memory matrix produced under the specific circumstances in which the Johannine books were written.

John's first explicit indication of the means by which Christians produce images of Jesus appears at the conclusion of his version of the "temple incident," the story of Jesus' disruption of activity in the temple courts during a Passover festival (John 2:13-22). Jesus justifies his radical actions by claiming that practices such as animal vending and currency exchange effectively turn God's house into a market. When the "Jews" ask to see his credentials, he urges them to "destroy this temple, and in three days I will raise it." John quickly clarifies that Jesus was not suggesting that they or he should actually damage the building. Rather, "he said this about the 'temple' of his body. Then when he was *raised* from the dead, his disciples *remembered* that he said these things, and they *believed* the Scripture and the word that Jesus spoke" (2:21-22).

John's main verb here, ἐμνήσθησαν ("they remembered"), is entirely appropriate by any count, for Jesus' actions in the temple would theoretically fall within the finite range of personal experiences that the disciples might bring to mind at a later date. But it is important to stress that their "memory" of the temple incident was not a simple act of recall, as evident from the complementary verbs "was raised" and "believed." Christian memory of Jesus begins with the recall of events from the actual past, but this recollection is interpreted through post-resurrection faith (ἐπίστευσαν). Faith is informative not only for second- and third-generation believers who never actually saw the historical Jesus, but also for eyewitnesses who only later understood Jesus' ultimate destiny. As such, the disciples' "belief" is not a certainty about what happened at the temple (i.e., not "I really do believe that Jesus said this"), but rather a new understanding of the words that Jesus spoke on that occasion in view of messianic passages from the Hebrew Bible. One such passage, Ps 69:9, is quoted directly in John's account: "His disciples remembered that it had been written, 'Zeal for your house will consume me'" (John 2:17). In its original context, this verse describes the psalmist's persecution because of his concern for the temple, and John cites it to explain Jesus' "zealous" actions. Notably, however, John does not cite the specific verse from the Hebrew Bible that the disciples later "believed" on the subject of the "three days" that Jesus would spend in the tomb before the "raising" of his body (cf. Matt 12:39-40).[13] Vague references to "Scripture" are not uncommon in the Fourth Gospel, even when John is citing the Hebrew Bible to prove a key theological point (see 7:38; 17:12; 19:28; 19:36; 20:9). Perhaps in all these cases, as at 2:22, John is pointing his reader not to specific passages but rather to a mode of recall, a way of understanding ambiguous things that Jesus said and did against the backdrop of the sacred text.

The peculiar mode of remembering described at John 2:22 surfaces again some ten chapters later in the story of the triumphal entry (John 12:12-16). The disciples watch in amazement as the crowds wave palm branches and proclaim Jesus "King of Israel." John explains that, "at first, his disciples did not know [ἔγνωσαν] these things. But when Jesus had been glorified then they remembered (ἐμνήσθησαν) that these things had been written about him and that they did these things to him" (12:16). "At first" (τὸ πρῶτον) here must mean "when this happened," and John's assertion that they "did not know these things" must mean that they did not understand the significance of Jesus' actions at that time. This significance became apparent only after Jesus' death and "glorification," subsequent events that clarified their memory of Jesus and their understanding of "the things that had been written about him," specifically Zech 9:9, which is loosely quoted at John 12:15. Here again, John portrays the disciples' "memory" of Jesus as a complex interface between their recollections of things that Jesus did, their awareness of Jesus' ultimate destiny, and a messianic reading of passages from the Hebrew Bible.

These two passages, and others like them, reveal that John's Christology, his image of Jesus as the Messiah, emerges at the intersection of three currents: the recall of things that the historical Jesus presumably did and

---

13. Commentators are generally agreed that John 2:22 does not refer specifically to v. 17, because John seems to be citing Ps 69:9 to explain Jesus' actions in the temple rather than to explain his cryptic remark about rebuilding the temple in three days. See C. K. Barrett, *The Gospel according to St. John* (2nd ed.; Philadelphia: Westminster, 1978) 201; Raymond E. Brown, *The Gospel according to John: A New Translation with Introduction and Commentary* (AB; Garden City, NY: Doubleday, 1966, 1970) 1:116; Rudolf Schnackenburg, *The Gospel according to St. John* (trans. Kevin Smyth; New York: Crossroad, 1987) 1:353.

said; a post-resurrection understanding of Jesus' ultimate destiny; and a messianic interpretation of the Hebrew Bible, not only specific passages but the entire text taken as a whole. The interplay of memory, faith, and Scripture may therefore be viewed as John's christological formula, the generative matrix through which he developed statements about Jesus' messianic identity. Because John's thinking about Jesus was founded on this formula rather than a fixed content of ideas, his Christology must have been dynamic rather than static, capable of reconfiguration as needed and therefore resistant to the narrow categories of the Western theological tradition.

But if John's messianic belief was a generative formula rather than a fixed creed, how would it be possible for his community to maintain any semblance of doctrinal unity and continuity? John solves this problem by stressing that the memory of Jesus is ultimately charismatic. According to the Fourth Gospel, Jesus made a number of specific promises to the disciples just before his death concerning the coming of the "Paraclete" (παράκλητος), a title for the Holy Spirit that is unique to the Johannine literature. It is clear from these "Paraclete sayings," preserved now in John 13–17, that the Spirit will function in the Christian community "as remembrancer and interpreter."[14] Specifically, the Paraclete will "teach you all things and remind you of all things that I said to you" (14:26), "guiding" the disciples "into all truth" by speaking "only what he hears" from Jesus (16:13-14). While the work of the Spirit is personal, this teaching ministry would never, in John's view, lead to innovation or division. As Schnackenburg suggests, the Paraclete "simply continues Jesus' revelation, not by providing new teachings" but only by enhancing and clarifying his words, thus fulfilling the ministry of "a commemorative deepening of that revelation."[15] For John, the Spirit is the ultimate source of the community's Christology, guiding individual believers in their recall of Jesus' deeds and their understanding of those deeds against the backdrop of the Hebrew Bible.

In Johannine terms, then, "Christology" is the image that emerges when a Christian interprets events from Jesus' life through the lens of the

14. F. F. Bruce, *The Gospel of John: Introduction, Exposition, and Notes* (Grand Rapids: Eerdmans, 1983) 305.

15. Schnackenburg, *Gospel according to St. John*, 3:144, 3:83, 3:142; see also 3:138-54; Barrett, *Gospel according to St. John*, 467-68; Brown, *Gospel according to John*, 2:715-16; Rudolf Bultmann, *The Gospel of John: A Commentary* (trans. G. R. Beasley-Murray, R. W. N. Hoare, and J. K. Riches; Philadelphia: Fortress, 1971) 575.

resurrection against the backdrop of the Hebrew Bible under the guidance of the Holy Spirit. Because Christology is guided by the Spirit, it remains consistent from place to place and from generation to generation (see 1 John 2:20-27). Yet because John's Christology is a formula rather than specific content, it remains flexible, capable of adaptation to a variety of situations. The presentation of Christ in the Fourth Gospel and 1-2-3 John reflects one such adaptation to one specific social setting. The contours of that setting will be the subject of the following section.

The Johannine Framework

As noted above, John's Christology is a formula that makes it possible for Christians to construct memories of Jesus under the guidance of the Holy Spirit. Following Culpepper's rule that "theological developments are often precipitated by social crises," this means that the specific christological statements of the Fourth Gospel and 1-2-3 John are products of this generative formula as shaped by John's circumstances at the moment those texts were produced.[16] As such, the Christology of the Johannine literature becomes coherent only when viewed against the backdrop of the "social crisis" that led to the composition of these books. Before proceeding, it will be helpful to briefly identify and outline the most salient elements of this crisis as they impacted John's presentation of Jesus.

John 3:16, perhaps the most well-known verse in the Christian Bible, introduces a key term in the Johannine literature, "the world." In John's vocabulary, "the world" refers to all people who have not accepted John's claims about Jesus. God loves the world, so much so that he sent his Son to give the world eternal life. But the world, failing to recognize this (John 1:10), did not accept Jesus' proclamation and resented his exposé of its evil deeds. Jesus' very presence brings judgment to the world's unbelief (9:39; 12:31), and for this reason the world hates Jesus and rejoices at his death (7:7; 16:19-20). Unfortunately for the disciples, the world will also hate them and seek to kill them (15:18-20; 16:33). In John's view, non-Christians are uniformly hostile to believers, to the point that the relationship between the two groups must always be expressed in dualistic terms such as

16. R. Alan Culpepper, *The Gospel and Letters of John* (Interpreting Biblical Texts; Nashville: Abingdon, 1998) 57.

"love and hate," "light and darkness," "truth and lies." While it is ultimately impossible to know why he felt this way, such evidence suggests that John had experienced persecution from non-believers at some point.

One specific source of this persecution may be evident in John's frequent references to a subgroup within the world of whom he is particularly wary, "the Jews." This designation is inherently ambiguous, since almost every character in the Fourth Gospel, including Jesus, is Jewish by race and religion. In some instances it seems that John is thinking of "the Jews" as the Jewish religious leaders who oppose Jesus (John 5:10; 9:22); yet on other occasions it appears that a "Jew" is any Jewish person who does not accept Jesus' claims about himself (6:41-42; 8:48-59; 10:24-39). Whatever their specific identity, "the Jews," like "the world," are generally hostile to Jesus and the disciples, a fact that comes with little surprise since they are "children of the devil" (8:44-45). From time to time, some Jews seem interested in Jesus' message and miracles, but ultimately they turn against him when he reveals his true identity and agenda (6:14-15, 25-58; 8:30-59). Most scholars today explain these data by following J. Louis Martyn's theory that the Johannine community was a messianic Jewish group that had been banned from the synagogue for their confession of Jesus (see 9:22; 16:2).[17] Removed from the relative safety of the Jewish fold, the Johannine Christians would be left alone to face a hostile and unbelieving world without the rights and privileges granted to Jews in the Roman empire.

Sometime after this excommunication from the synagogue, a heretical sect emerged within the Johannine churches, whom the author of 1-2-3 John calls "the Antichrists." This group is first mentioned at 1 John 2:18, where the Elder warns that "as you have heard that Antichrist is coming, even now many Antichrists have come." Despite the Elder's polemical protests, it is clear that the Antichrists, unlike the world and the Jews, were an *internal* threat to the community. His admission that "they went out from us" (2:19) indicates that even he considered them Christian at one time, and it seems that Diotrephes, the leader of one Johannine church, preferred their doctrine over the older orthodox perspective (3 John 9-10). The Antichrists were probably former disciples of the Elder, Christian

17. J. L. Martyn, *History and Theology in the Fourth Gospel* (2nd ed.; Nashville: Abingdon, 1979) 50-66. Most scholars who take this position today see John's experience as a local phenomenon and therefore do not follow Martyn's attempt to pinpoint a universal excommunication of all Jewish Christians.

teachers who departed from his traditional Christology. Because they were known to, and accepted by, members of John's churches, it was easy for them to secure a following. The Elder therefore goes to pains to specify that true believers must adhere to the traditional perspective, for "whoever denies the Son does not have the Father, either" (1 John 2:23).

The christological statements of the Fourth Gospel and 1-2-3 John were developed from the memory formula described above in response to the claims of the world, the Jews, and the Antichrists. This reactive posture generated what Norman Peterson calls the "anti-language" of the Johannine literature, the use of theological terms and concepts that have been borrowed from orthodox Judaism and Antichristianity but "transformed in contrastive or antistructural ways." John's anti-language leads him to express his messianic beliefs largely in negative terms, producing a portrait of Jesus that clarifies what he is not or what he is "greater than."[18] Specifically, Jesus is not what the Jews and the Antichrists say that he is, and he is in fact greater than anything that either of these groups would admit.

A detailed examination of the full spectrum of John's responses to the claims of the Jews and the Antichrists is beyond the scope of this study. For purposes of illustration, two key themes in John's Christology will be discussed, one that reflects his response to the challenge of the Jews and another that reflects his response to the challenge of the Antichrists. John's ability to generate images of Christ that oppose Jewish claims is evident in his emphasis on Jesus' superiority over Moses, and his ability to generate memories that oppose the Antichrists' claims is evident in his insistence that Jesus came "in water and blood."

More Than Moses

According to John, Jesus is not what the Jews say that he is: he is far superior, not only to their claims about him, but also to their entire religious system. This anti-christological approach expresses itself in a wide variety of ways in the Fourth Gospel, including the "I am" sayings, which draw on

18. Norman R. Peterson, *The Gospel of John and the Sociology of Light: Language and Characterization in the Fourth Gospel* (Valley Forge, PA: Trinity Press International, 1993) 5. Peterson's comments are limited to the Fourth Gospel, but apply equally, in my view, to the christological statements of 1-2-3 John.

metaphors that explicitly compare Jesus to the beliefs and institutions of Judaism ("I am the light of the world"; "I am the good shepherd"; "I am the resurrection and the life"; "I am the vine"), and the many analogies between Jesus and the temple that are currently at the forefront of academic debate.[19] The discussion here will focus on one prominent current in John's anti-Christology: Jesus' categorical superiority to Moses.[20] It is important to stress at the outset that the christological claims of the Fourth Gospel do not necessarily respond to beliefs that most first-century Jewish people *actually* held about either Moses or Jesus; they respond, instead, to beliefs that John *thinks* Jewish people held. As such, this discussion will focus on beliefs held by "the Jews" as a character in the Fourth Gospel and on ways in which Jesus, in John's view, surpasses the expectations of these people.[21]

The Johannine Jews make statements that reveal a wide spectrum of beliefs about the Messiah, and John occasionally suggests that there is some disagreement among them about the specifics of the Christ's identity and mission (John 7:30-31, 40-44). Taken collectively, "the Jews" believe that the Scriptures say the Christ will come from Bethlehem, rather than Galilee (7:42, 52). Some of them, however, are not particularly concerned about his place of birth, because they apparently adhere to the doctrine of a "hidden Messiah," the ancient Jewish belief that the Messiah's identity and origins would remain unknown until he appeared suddenly and dramatically on the public scene as Israel's redeemer (7:27). John the Baptist also seems to hold to some form of this doctrine, telling the Pharisees that

19. For a convenient summary discussion of the Johannine "I am" sayings, see Gary M. Burge, "'I Am' Sayings," in *The Dictionary of Jesus and the Gospels* (ed. Joel B. Green, Scot McKnight, and I. Howard Marshall; Downers Grove, IL: InterVarsity Press, 1992) 354-56. For discussion of John's temple Christology, see Mary Coloe, *God Dwells with Us: Temple Symbolism in the Fourth Gospel* (Collegeville: Liturgical Press, 2001); Alan Kerr, *The Temple of Jesus' Body: The Temple Theme in the Gospel of John* (JSNTSup; Sheffield: Sheffield Academic Press, 2002).

20. For fuller discussion of John's Moses Christology against the backdrop of ancient Jewish beliefs, see the classic study by Wayne Meeks, *The Prophet-King: Moses Traditions and the Johannine Christology* (Leiden: Brill, 1967). A more literary approach to the issue, similar to that adopted here, may be found in Peterson, *Gospel of John and the Sociology of Light*, 80-109.

21. Statements by the Samaritan woman of John 4 have been included here where they seem consistent with messianic beliefs expressed elsewhere in the Fourth Gospel by the Jews (cf. 4:19, 25 with 7:40; 4:29 with 10:21). In point of fact, John does not seem to see a significant difference between the messianic views of Samaritans and "Jews."

"there is one among you whom you do not know" and stating that God had called him to reveal this individual's identity (1:26-31).[22]

Whatever his point of origin, once the Messiah appears the Johannine Jews expect him to perform "signs," attesting miracles that will verify his identity and authority (John 2:18, 23; 3:2; 6:30; 7:31). These signs will not, however, indicate the Messiah's divinity; they are, instead, the signs of an eschatological prophet, specifically the "prophet like Moses" mentioned at Deut 18:18 (John 1:21; 6:14; 7:40). Like Moses, the Messiah will offer his people miraculous provision and healing (6:30; 9:32-33; 10:21) and will also be a revelatory mediator between God and Israel. As such, the Christ will be an exemplary teacher with special miraculous insight (4:25, 29; 7:26; 10:19-21), and he would theoretically have authority to baptize — to purify people and grant them access to an eschatological community of the redeemed (1:19-25). This same prophetic authority would allow the Messiah to criticize and possibly revise the temple cult (2:18). For all these reasons, those Jews who do suspect that Jesus may be the Messiah seek to install him as a theocratic ruler, the "King of Israel," not necessarily a political leader but a new Moses who will lead his people out of oppression (6:15; 12:12-15). Yet, unlike Moses and the Davidic kings, this messianic prophet would "remain forever," never suffering death (12:34).[23]

Overall, these brief glimpses suggest that the Jews, at least in John's view, expected the Christ to fill the shoes of Moses: emerging suddenly from obscure origins with no obvious credentials beyond his unique divine calling (see Exod 3:11); serving as the ultimate prophetic voice of God in the redeemed community; authorizing his pronouncements with miraculous signs, signs that would include supernatural provision and healing. These expectations are especially significant in view of the fact that the Johannine Jews refer to themselves as "disciples of Moses" and insist that they follow Moses' teaching because they know that God spoke to him (John 9:28-29). In response to the Jews' beliefs, two of Jesus' most characteristic traits in the Fourth Gospel explicitly contrast him with Moses. First, whereas Moses was a man who came from this world, Jesus "came down from heaven" (6:38; 13:3; 16:28). Second, because he was earthly, Mo-

---

22. See discussion in Brown, *Gospel according to John*, 1:53.

23. The Jews base this conclusion on "the Law," but it is impossible to determine exactly what verse from the Hebrew Bible they and John have in mind. For possibilities, see the discussion in Brown, *Gospel according to John*, 1:468-69; D. A. Carson, *The Gospel according to John* (Grand Rapids: Eerdmans, 1991) 445-46.

ses could provide only for the temporal needs of his people, whereas Jesus the Christ is empowered to grant eternal life to those who accept him. Because Jesus came from heaven, he can reveal unique information about God that no other person, including Moses, could reveal; because eternal life is granted only to those who accept this unique revelation, the disciples of Moses cannot be saved. Jesus' superiority to Moses is thus a key theme in John's anti-Christology.

Because Moses was of this earth, he operated under the restriction articulated by John the Baptist at John 3:27: "No man is able to receive anything except what is given to him from heaven." Most notable for John, this means that Moses was not permitted to receive a full revelation of God. Alluding to Exod 33:18–34:8, John notes that "no one has ever seen God" (1:18; 1 John 4:12) — Moses desired to behold God's glory, but was permitted only to see his "back" (Exod 33:23). Jesus, on the other hand, was "in the Father's bosom" (John 1:18), and Christ's identity and mission may be summarized by saying that "he came from God and was going back to God" (13:33; 16:28). Jesus highlights the primary privilege of this uniquely intimate relationship at John 8:38: "I say what I saw with the Father" (ἃ ἐγὼ ἑώρακα παρὰ τῷ πατρὶ λαλῶ). Having been in the Father's bosom, Jesus can reveal God to an unprecedented degree. As such, "no one comes to the Father except through me," because Jesus, and Jesus alone, is "the way, the truth, and the life" (14:6).

Because Moses was "from below," he was able to provide only temporal sustenance. Hence, the miraculous food that Moses gave the Jews in the wilderness, manna, quickly "spoiled" (Exod 16:20; John 6:27), and those who ate this bread eventually died (6:58). In a similar way, Moses provided physical healing to those bitten by snakes by "lifting up" the bronze serpent according to God's instruction, yet those who were thus healed ultimately died of other ailments (Num 21:6-9). By contrast, anyone who keeps Jesus' words will never see death (John 3:14-16; 6:51; 10:28). Jesus is, in fact, "the resurrection and the life," meaning that those who accept him will enjoy "eternal life" (11:25-26; 20:30-31). The authority to grant this life is given directly to Jesus, as a son, by the Father (17:2).[24]

---

24. John 11:50-51 implies that "eternal life" results from keeping the commands of the Father as revealed by Jesus, which apparently include accepting Jesus as the exclusive mediator of God's grace (see also 14:10). As such, "life" is given by the Father through the revelation of Jesus.

Because the Law was given through Moses (John 1:17), the Jewish Scriptures bear all the earthly limitations that Moses himself bore. The writings of Moses are therefore categorically distinct from, and inferior to, the teachings of Jesus, following the maxim that "the one who comes from above is over all; the one who comes from the earth is from the earth and speaks from the earth" (3:31). Moses, being from the earth and unable to grant eternal life, could only give a Law that brings judgment and death; Jesus, being from above, could reveal God's "grace and truth" in all its fullness (1:17; 3:14-17). Moses, for example, gave regulations about keeping the Sabbath, regulations that make it illegal for the blind and lame to receive healing on that day (5:10, 16; 9:14-16).[25] Jesus, having come from heaven, bears an authority that inherently transcends anything that Moses said, allowing him both to heal on the Sabbath and to command others to work on that day because "my Father is working until now and I am also working" (5:8, 17). Moses, of course, allowed "work" on the Sabbath in extreme cases, conceding that the Sabbath could be broken if needed to follow the teaching of "the fathers" that a child must be circumcised on the eighth day; Jesus, bearing a higher mandate, is authorized "to make the whole person healthy on the Sabbath" (7:19-23). Claims of this sort lead the Jews to protest, in John's view accurately, that Jesus "said that God was his own Father, making himself equal to God" (5:18). As a result of this unique equality, God's judgment of the world will not be based on the Law of Moses, but rather on acceptance or rejection of Jesus and his teachings (3:17-18).

In John's view, it is logical that Jesus' words should supersede Moses' Law, for the Law in fact pointed to Jesus and when understood correctly speaks about Jesus (John 5:39). Ironically, the Jews, while claiming to be disciples of Moses (9:28), show that they do not trust Moses' words by failing to accept what Moses said about Jesus, leading Jesus to ask at one point, "If you don't believe what that man wrote, how will you believe my words?" (5:45-47). On his best days, then, Moses, like John the Baptist, could only herald the coming of one greater than himself.

The theme of Jesus' superiority to Moses, and its reflection of John's

---

25. Whether or not John 7:53–8:11 was original to the Fourth Gospel, the story of the adulterous woman illustrates the principle at 1:17. As the Pharisees point out, Moses commanded that those guilty of adultery must be stoned; Jesus, by contrast, reveals God's grace by extending forgiveness.

underlying christological formula, is perhaps most explicit in the story of the feeding of the five thousand at John 6. John's presentation of this event specifically sets Jesus' actions against those of Moses through two means. First, while the Synoptics contextualize the miracle by associating it with the mission of the Twelve and the fate of John the Baptist (Mark 6:29-31; Matt 14:12; Luke 9:1-10), John frames the story by noting that "the Passover, the feast of the Jews, was near" (John 6:4). The allusion to Passover connects the feeding to the Exodus, Moses' shining moment as the mediator, redeemer, and provider of Israel. Second, John makes the analogy between Moses and Jesus explicit in the long discourse on the "bread of life" at 6:22-58, a passage designed to demonstrate both the inherent superiority of Jesus' ministry and the inability of "Moses' disciples" to comprehend his messianic identity.

On the day after the miraculous feeding, the crowd catches up with Jesus on the other side of the lake (John 6:22-25). Jesus is not impressed with their exuberance and immediately questions their motives: "You are not seeking me because you saw signs, but rather because you ate of the bread and were filled" (6:26). This statement is inherently ambiguous, because the "sign" in question was in fact the miraculous supply of bread that they had eaten the previous day. But before the Jews can point this out, Jesus proceeds to exhort them: "Do not work for the bread that perishes but rather for the bread that remains to eternal life, which the Son of Man will give to you. For the Father God has set his seal on him" (6:27). Here again, one wonders why the Jews would have to "work" for something that they will receive as a gift. But politely ignoring this problem, they proceed to ask Rabbi Jesus (6:25) what works they must do in order to please God, and he answers that they need only to believe in the one whom God has sent (6:28-29). The Jews, detecting that Jesus claims to be such an individual, then shift the discussion from what *they* must do to what *he* must do. They wish to see an attesting "sign" to verify his claims, and they remind him of one of Moses' most famous signs, the provision of manna in the wilderness (6:30-31). The discussion that follows this request is obviously calculated to demonstrate Jesus' categorical superiority to Moses. Christ is, in fact, so much greater than Moses that any comparison obliterates the Jews' theological taxonomy, making it impossible for them to comprehend Jesus' words and making John 6:32-58 a textbook case of Johannine irony and misunderstanding.

The Jews' remarks in this exchange reveal a theological taxonomy that includes three distinct categories: (1) God (John 6:28); (2) mediators between God and humanity; and (3) gifts of God, which are administered to his people through these mediators. In the immediate context, category 3 (the gifts of God) would include things like Moses' manna and the miraculous bread that Jesus has recently supplied. The Jews' comments to this point in the story reveal their belief that Jesus belongs in category 2. Like Moses (6:31-32), Jesus is a mediator sent by God, as evidenced by their acclamation of Jesus as a "prophet" and their subsequent attempt to proclaim him "king" (6:14-15). In John's view, however, Jesus is completely superior to Moses, not only as a mediator, but also in the sense that he participates *in all three categories at once,* a possibility that the Jews cannot conceive. As the "Son of Man" (6:27), Jesus, like Moses, reveals God to the Jews and provides them with divine gifts. These gifts include miraculous bread. But while Jesus can, like Moses, provide such material sustenance, he can also give the Jews another type of "bread": his own flesh. This flesh is itself a gift that God gives to the world, a "living bread" that provides, unlike manna, eternal life to all who eat it (6:49-51). Jesus can grant this eternal life because he, utterly surpassing Moses, also falls into the Jews' category 1: Jesus himself is "from God," having "come down from heaven" (6:38, 46). Jesus is thus superior to Moses not only in the sense that he is a better mediator between God and Israel who gives better provision, but also in the sense that his identity completely explodes the Jews' way of thinking about God, mediators, and gifts.

The Johannine Jesus is, then, superior to Moses in every conceivable way, doing everything that Moses did and a great many things that Moses could never hope to do. Moses, recognizing this, wrote the Law — the foundational document of Jewish faith and practice — to point the Jews to Jesus. These anti-christological claims are driven by two powerful currents in John's context: his underlying messianic memory formula, which insists that Jesus is the interpretive key to the Hebrew Bible; and his urgent need to defend his claims about Jesus against the attacks of the Jewish community, the "disciples of Moses," of which he had once been a member. It is this emphasis on Jesus' inherent superiority to Moses that generates the "high Christology" that sometimes appears in the Fourth Gospel, statements that elevate Jesus to a point where he seems almost completely abstracted from the realm of human affairs because he, unlike Moses or any other human being, "came down from heaven" and therefore falls into the same category as God.

The Water and the Blood

John's attempt to portray Jesus as superior to the expectations of "the Jews," and, indeed, as superior to Judaism itself, has generated those elements of the Fourth Gospel that reflect a "high Christology" — so high, at times, that "one feels that one has been transported into the [Gnostic] world of C[orpus] Herm[eticum] 13 and the Λόγος τέλειος."[26] Yet, at the same time, John occasionally evidences a very "low Christology," reveling in the physicality of Jesus (John 6:53-58), adamantly insisting that water and blood flowed from his crucified body (19:34-35; 1 John 5:6), and even suggesting that the resurrected Lord could be touched with human hands (John 20:17, 27). As noted earlier, this apparent contradiction has led many scholars to posit multiple sources or editions of the Fourth Gospel. In fact, however, such statements do not conflict with John's claims that Jesus came "from above." Instead, they conflict, explicitly and intentionally, with the teachings of the Antichrists. Viewed as a response to this group, John's emphasis on Jesus' "flesh" appears to highlight not so much the humanity of Jesus as the historical specificity of the revelation of God that he provided.

Because the Antichrists left no literary remains, their views must be reconstructed entirely from the few polemical comments about them in 1-2-3 John. The primary difference between their views and those of John is summarized in terms of two contrasting "confessions." Like the Elder, John confesses that "Jesus Christ came in the water and in the blood," while the Antichrists claim that "Jesus came in water only" (1 John 5:6). As many scholars have observed, the Antichrists' version of the slogan seems to suggest that they adopted a pneumatic Christology. "Water" here most likely refers to the "living water" that Jesus offers his disciples, a metaphor for the Holy Spirit (John 7:37-39).[27] As noted earlier, John believes that all Christians enjoy the Spirit's ongoing guidance in developing memories of Jesus. From John's perspective, the Paraclete establishes a close connection between the human Jesus of the past and the risen Lord who continues to operate in the community, because the Spirit is in fact simply the form in which Jesus himself comes to believers (14:16-18). But it seems that the

---

26. Bultmann, *Gospel of John*, 132.

27. For further discussion of this slogan, see Tom Thatcher, "Water and Blood in AntiChrist Christianity (1 John 5:6)," *Stone Campbell Journal* 4 (2001) 235-48.

Antichrists interpreted Jesus' words about the Spirit in a different way: if the resurrected Lord, through the Spirit, continues to speak and act in the church, there is little need to worry about the life and teachings of the human Jesus. In fact, if the same divine Word that appeared incarnate in the human Jesus continues to speak through believers, there is really not so much difference between Christians and Jesus himself. From this perspective, there would be no point in stressing that "Jesus [the man] is the [spiritual] Christ," for every believer possesses the spiritual Christ in the form of the Paraclete.

Even if John did not substantially disagree with the Antichrists' understanding of the Spirit, he could scarcely ignore their inherent threat to his own authority. By emphasizing the ongoing presence of the spiritual Christ, the Antichrists could freely modify or reinterpret the established Johannine Jesus tradition in light of new revelations. As Rensberger notes, "If the opponents claimed that their ideas were inspired by the Spirit . . . they would not hesitate to offer *new* concepts built up from their basic interpretation of the tradition."[28] From the perspective of the Antichrists, anything that the Paraclete is saying *now* would be just as authoritative as anything that Jesus said back *then,* and of course therefore of equal authority with John's teachings and with the orthodox creeds of the community. The reality of this threat is evident from the very existence of 2 and 3 John, both of which seek to prevent local Christian leaders from going the way of Diotrephes and allowing the Antichrists access to their churches.

John responded to the Antichrists' challenge by emphasizing that Jesus came "in the water and in the blood," meaning that Christ comes to the church both in the form of the Spirit and in the form of the historical Jesus, whose memory lives on in community tradition and in the testimony of the Beloved Disciple. As such, the current experience of Christ finds its moorings in the past, in the deeds and teachings of Jesus of Nazareth. At least three aspects of John's anti-Christology reflect his attempt to shape the memory of Jesus in a way that would counter the Antichrists' claims: an emphasis on the temporal distance between the historical Jesus and the community's present experience of the Paraclete; an emphasis on the physicality of Jesus; and the unique presentation of Mary, Jesus' mother, in

---

28. David Rensberger, *1 John, 2 John, 3 John* (ANTC; Nashville: Abingdon, 1997) 24. See also Brown, *Community of the Beloved Disciple,* 138-42; Gary M. Burge, *The Anointed Community: The Holy Spirit in the Johannine Tradition* (Grand Rapids: Eerdmans, 1987) 218-19.

the Fourth Gospel. All three of these facets merit a complete study, but each will be only briefly reviewed here.

First, while the Fourth Gospel is still often thought of as the "spiritual gospel" because of its emphasis on Christ's transcendent deity, the Johannine literature in fact betrays a greater interest in the historical Jesus than any other primitive Christian text. Against the claims of the Antichrists, John everywhere attempts to portray Jesus as a historical figure, a person who lived and died in the past and whose teachings function as a benchmark for later Christian faith and experience. This emphasis emerges in the Johannine epistles in the repetition of the phrase ἀπ' ἀρχῆς, "from the beginning," which is used to contrast the innovative doctrines of the Antichrists with the teachings of the historical Jesus (1 John 1:1; 2:24). In two passages, the Elder uses the phrase ἀπ' ἀρχῆς to refer to a specific saying of the historical Jesus, the "new commandment" of John 13:34 and 15:12. In John's view, the community's traditional christological creeds and the love command are both authoritative because they originate in the teachings of the human Jesus, rather than in the revelations of the Paraclete. For this reason, the Fourth Gospel appeals to the "witness" of the Beloved Disciple, a member of the community whose testimony must be accepted as final simply because he, unlike the Antichrists, had direct contact both with the Paraclete and with the Jesus who lived in the past (John 21:24).

Second, while John agrees with the Antichrists' emphasis on Christ's heavenly origin, he balances these claims with an emphasis on the physicality of Jesus. Jesus' physical body locates Christ in a specific time and space different from the time and space in which the community now experiences revelations of the Spirit. First John 5:6-8 notes that there are "three witnesses" to the claim that "Jesus is the Son of God," "the Spirit and the water and the blood," and the Fourth Gospel shows that all three of these witnesses originate with the earthly ministry of the human Jesus (John 7:37-39; 19:31-35; 20:21-22). Because the Paraclete was given by Jesus and represents the ongoing presence of Jesus in the community (14:16-18), the Spirit simply reminds the disciples of things that the historical Jesus said and guides their understanding of those teachings (14:26) — even after Jesus' departure, the Spirit can only "take from me and proclaim to you" (16:14). The Prologue to the Fourth Gospel thus emphasizes not only that Jesus came "from above" but also that Christ *came* to this earth to reveal himself at a particular moment in a particular location. The

Antichrists therefore must not forget that "the Word became flesh and tabernacled among us," and that it was only within this human particularity that "we beheld his glory" (1:14).

Third, John's anti-Christology expresses itself in the Fourth Gospel's unique portrait of Mary, the mother of Jesus. Mary is mentioned several times in the Gospel of John, and her two most significant appearances occur in incidents that are unique to the Fourth Gospel yet critical to John's Christology. At John 2, Mary appears at Cana to encourage Jesus to perform the first of his "signs" (turning water into wine), an act that leads his new disciples to "believe in him" (2:1-11). Mary is also present at the cross of Jesus, where she is consigned to the care of the Beloved Disciple and presumably, like that individual, witnesses Jesus' death and sees "water and blood" flow from his pierced side (19:23-35). As a spectator to these two events, Mary can support both of the anti-christological claims discussed in this essay: as a witness to Jesus' signs, she can testify that he came "from above"; as a witness to his death, she can testify that the "word became flesh" in the violent course of human history. Further, as an added bonus for John, Mary is an associate of the Beloved Disciple and adds further weight to the credibility of that individual's "witness." For these reasons, Raymond Brown has suggested that Mary functions in the Fourth Gospel as the Beloved Disciple's female counterpart, a symbol of true discipleship.[29]

In view of John's interest in Mary as a star witness to Jesus' signs and death, two aspects of her characterization in the Fourth Gospel are notable. First, while John tends to focus on specific individuals rather than vague groups of people, he always refers to Mary as "Jesus' mother" and never reveals her actual name. By contrast, Jesus' father is called "Joseph" on two separate occasions, despite the facts that he is not an actor in the story and, in John's view, is not even Jesus' true "father" (John 1:45; 6:42; see 2:1-5; 19:25-27). Second, the label "the mother of Jesus" is especially notable in view of the fact that the Fourth Gospel does not include a Christmas story and generally does not seem particularly interested in the circumstances of Jesus' birth. These two aspects of Mary's characterization suggest that John is less concerned with her specific historical identity than

---

29. Brown, *Community of the Beloved Disciple*, 192-98. Alan Culpepper suggests that Mary and the Beloved Disciple together represent "the beginning of a new family for the children of God" (*Anatomy of the Fourth Gospel: A Study in Literary Design* [Philadelphia: Fortress, 1983] 134).

with the fact that *Christ had a mother* — that he was born and lived at a specific moment in the past. In other words, John's presentation of Mary is one aspect of his anti-Christology, another way in which his messianic formula expressed itself in opposition to the claims of the Antichrists.

The Johannine Christ, then, is a much more historical figure than the Antichrists would like to admit. The Christ did come "from above" and continues to come from above to the community in the form of the Paraclete, yet these ongoing appearances originated in the particular time and space in which the Word was manifested in the body of Jesus of Nazareth. For John, this earlier manifestation set the guideposts for all subsequent encounters with the Christ, so that the community's established christological creeds can function as touchstones for genuine experience of the Paraclete (1 John 4:1-6). Here again, John's anti-Christology is driven by two powerful currents: his underlying messianic memory formula, which insists that any image of Christ must incorporate recollections of the words and deeds of the historical Jesus; and his urgent need to counter the claims of the Antichrists, who wished to minimize the significance of Jesus' temporal ministry. As a result, John emphasizes the raw physicality of Jesus to underscore Christ's historicity and limits the revelatory work of the Spirit to a memory of things that Jesus did and said years ago.

Conclusion

Against the backdrop of the preceding discussion, John 20:30-31 comes into focus at the intersection of two streams in John's negative Christology. Contra the claims of "the Jews," Jesus is "the Christ, the Son of God," who came from above to grant an eternal life that Moses and, indeed, Judaism as a faith system could not provide. This emphasis could lead to a thoroughly spiritualized Christology, one that ignored the historical Jesus in preference for the Christ. The Antichrists seem to have moved in this direction; but contra their claims, John insists that the Son of God is also "Jesus," the one who came "in the water and in the blood" at a particular moment in history (1 John 5:6; see John 19:34-35).

But while John 20:30-31 may be correctly identified as the purpose statement of the Fourth Gospel, it does not span the breadth of John's Christology, nor does it even summarize the content of John's beliefs about Jesus. Johannine Christology is not so much a set of beliefs as an ongoing potential to create memories of Jesus that meet the challenges that would threaten to undermine orthodox faith. The apparent tensions in the Christology of the Fourth Gospel are simply the result of the wide range of particular challenges that faced John at the time the text was produced, and these challenges provide the constellation of points within which John's picture of Jesus takes shape as a unified image.

Divine Life and Corporate Christology: God, Messiah Jesus, and the Covenant Community in Paul

S. A. Cummins

For the apostle Paul, an integral aim and outworking of God's self-disclosure in Jesus Christ is the incorporation of the whole of humanity into Messiah Jesus and his Spirit, and thereby into the divine life that is eternal communion with the triune God. The historical and theological dimensions of such a claim involve at least two key interrelated aspects of Paul's Christology: namely, that Jesus' messianic identity and destiny encompass an Israel-specific life and death transposed into his exaltation as universal living Lord, and that this pattern and path are replicated in the lives of all those who are incorporated into him as the messianic and Spirit-empowered eschatological people of God. This necessarily selective study will explicate this wide-ranging and contentious claim by considering a series of interrelated elements under three headings: "Monotheism and Messiahship in the Judaism Known to Paul"; "Monotheism, Messiah Jesus, and Paul's Conversion and Gospel"; and "Monotheism, Messiah Jesus, and the Eschatological People of God." While reference will be made to various aspects of Paul's letters, the third section will use Gal 2:15-21 and Romans 5–8 as specific sites in which to explore many of the complex and contested issues in view. By this route it will be shown that Paul's understanding of Jesus as Messiah lies at the very heart of his theology, ecclesiology, and eschatology: the Messiah and his faithful followers are agents of the divine life that embraces redemption, reconciliation, and a glorious new creation.

Monotheism and Messiahship
in the Judaism Known to Paul

That early Palestinian and Diaspora Judaism was a diverse and complex phenomenon has been well documented and debated within recent scholarship.[1] Moreover, what is true of Judaism in general is often deemed to be the case regarding its expectations of a coming eschatological redeemer and ruler figure, the Messiah. Hence, scholars have become accustomed to speaking of "Judaisms and their Messiahs."[2] Certainly, as other contributors to this volume have rightly observed, due caution is required regarding simplistic and overly synthesized estimations of the diverse and much disputed evidence. Nonetheless, it may still be argued that early Judaism viewed its history and identity in terms of certain common beliefs and practices (fundamentally, that there was but one God who had chosen Israel), and that its hopes for a Messiah were more widespread and cohesive than is often allowed.

Of course, how strictly Judaism adhered to its belief in one God

1. Among the ever-expanding studies: E. Schürer, *The History of the Jewish People in the Age of Jesus Christ (175 B.C.–A.D. 135)* (3 vols.; rev. and ed. M. Black, G. Vermes, F. Millar, and M. Goodman; Edinburgh: T&T Clark, 1973-87); Lester L. Grabbe, *Judaism from Cyrus to Hadrian,* vol. 2 (Minneapolis: Fortress, 1992); Grabbe, *An Introduction to First Century Judaism: Jewish Religion and History in the Second Temple Period* (Edinburgh: T&T Clark, 1996); Louis H. Feldman, *Jew and Gentile in the Ancient World: Attitudes and Interactions from Alexander to Justinian* (Princeton: Princeton University Press, 1993); John M. G. Barclay, *Jews in the Mediterranean Diaspora: From Alexander to Trajan (323 BCE–117 CE)* (Edinburgh: T&T Clark, 1996); James C. VanderKam, *An Introduction to Early Judaism* (Grand Rapids: Eerdmans, 2001); and Frederick J. Murphy, *Early Judaism: The Exile to the Time of Jesus* (Peabody, MA: Hendrickson, 2002).

2. So Jacob Neusner, William Scott Green, and Ernest S. Frerichs, eds., *Judaisms and Their Messiahs at the Turn of the Christian Era* (Cambridge: Cambridge University Press, 1987). Recent and varied studies on the Messiah include J. H. Charlesworth, ed., *The Messiah: Developments in Earliest Judaism and Christianity* (Minneapolis: Fortress, 1992); John J. Collins, *The Scepter and the Star: The Messiahs of the Dead Sea Scrolls and Other Ancient Literature* (New York: Doubleday, 1995); Kenneth E. Pomykala, *The Davidic Dynasty Tradition in Early Judaism: Its History and Significance for Messianism* (Atlanta: Scholars Press, 1995); Dan Cohn-Sherbok, *The Jewish Messiah* (Edinburgh: T&T Clark, 1997); Gerben S. Oegema, *The Anointed and His People: Messianic Expectations from the Maccabees to BarKochba* (JSPSup 27; Sheffield: Sheffield Academic Press, 1998); J. H.Charlesworth, H. Lichtenberger, and G. S. Oegema, eds., *Qumran-Messianism: Studies in the Messianic Expectations in the Dead Sea Scrolls* (Tübingen: J. C. B. Mohr [Paul Siebeck], 1998).

(monotheism), and what this might have meant for any estimation of Jesus, has been the subject of much scholarly scrutiny of late.[3] On the one hand, it has been argued that a rigorous Jewish monotheism disallowed entirely the ascription of divinity to anyone other than Israel's God. Hence, any such claims concerning Jesus could not have been made from within a Jewish monotheistic milieu but instead would have constituted a complete departure therefrom.[4] On the other hand, a growing number of scholars have suggested that a range of intermediary figures discernible within early Judaism — e.g., angels, exalted human beings, and/or personified divine attributes (word, wisdom, glory), some with messianic associations — held a subordinate divine or semi-divine position, and so in some sense participated in divinity. If, then, the distinction between God and such entities was not absolute, perhaps this provides both precedent and a set of categories against which to evaluate early Jewish-Christian exalted estimations of Jesus.[5] However, following Richard Bauckham, it would appear preferable to adopt a third position. One may readily concur that Jewish monotheism was indeed strict, differentiating the one God from all other reality. From this standpoint, some of the so-called intermediary figures are in fact to be seen as aspects of God's own unique identity (e.g., *his* wisdom, word, glory), and the remainder are to be recognized as the unambiguously creaturely (albeit exalted) servants of God. Yet, on this view, it must then be argued that a high Christology, one which included the early church's worship of

3. Recent notable discussions include Carey C. Newman, James R. Davila, and Gladys S. Lewis, eds., *The Jewish Roots of Christological Monotheism: Papers from the St. Andrews Conference on the Historical Origins of the Worship of Jesus* (JSJSup 63; Leiden: Brill, 1999); and Loren T. Stuckenbruck and Wendy E. S. North, eds., *Early Jewish and Christian Monotheism* (Early Christianity in Context 1/JSNTSup 263; London/New York: T&T Clark, 2004). This summary overview is indebted to Richard J. Bauckham, *God Crucified: Monotheism and Christology in the New Testament* (Grand Rapids: Eerdmans, 1999) 1-5; see also Larry W. Hurtado, *Lord Jesus Christ: Devotion to Jesus in Earliest Christianity* (Grand Rapids: Eerdmans, 2003) 42-48.

4. So P. M. Casey, *From Jewish Prophet to Gentile God* (Cambridge: J. Clarke, 1991); see his more recent "Monotheism, Worship and Christological Developments in the Pauline Churches," in Newman et al., eds., *The Jewish Roots of Christological Monotheism*, 214-33.

5. Cf. C. Rowland, *The Open Heaven* (London: SPCK, 1982); Andrew Chester, "Jewish Messianic Expectations and Mediatorial Figures and Pauline Christology," in *Paulus und das antike Judentum* (ed. Martin Hengel and Ulrich Heckel; WUNT 58; Tübingen: J. C. B. Mohr [Paul Siebeck], 1991) 17-89; C. A. Gieschen, *Angelomorphic Christology: Antecedents and Early Evidence* (AGJU 42; Leiden: Brill, 1998).

Jesus, could thus emerge only "by identifying Jesus directly with the one God of Israel, including Jesus in the unique identity of this one God."[6]

As to the fundamental characteristics of Israel's God, for our purposes it will suffice to stress that Jewish monotheism regarded God as the sole Creator of and Lord over all things, sovereignly accomplishing his creation-wide purposes through his ongoing covenant relationship with Israel, especially in its Torah-obedient and temple-focused pattern of life. We may thus speak of a creational (and covenantal), eschatological, and cultic monotheism.[7] As witnessed throughout the Scriptures, Israel's Creator God has always shown himself to be righteous; he will be faithful to the Abrahamic covenant whose ultimate universal outworking is expected and assured.

It is within this wider context, then, that messianic expectations tended to focus upon a preeminent human agent of God, a redeemer/royal figure in the tradition of King David, who would deliver earthly Israel from its ongoing subjugation under foreign rule and inaugurate the eschatological age and reign of God.[8] This figure and the accompanying eschatological scenario could indeed be envisaged in highly exalted — even apocalyptic — terms. A case in point involves the elevated messianic interpretations of the Danielic "one like a son of man" figure in subsequent Jewish texts and traditions, possibly in 4Q246 and more clearly in *1 Enoch, 4 Ezra,* and *2 Baruch.*[9] Yet, even in these cases where the figure is characterized by angelic and superhuman traits, this is not meant to displace but rather to be coordinated with its role as an earthly and human messianic ruler.[10] (Indeed, Josephus

---

6. Bauckham, *God Crucified,* 4.

7. Cf. Bauckham, *God Crucified,* 9-13; Bauckham, "Paul's Christology of Divine Identity" (unpublished paper) 3; see also N. T. Wright, *The New Testament and the People of God* (Minneapolis: Fortress, 1992) 244-79.

8. On the prevalence, persistence, and general coherence of such messianic expectations in relation to both the Old Testament and early Judaism, see William Horbury, *Jewish Messianism and the Cult of Christ* (London: SCM Press, 1998); cf. the summary estimation indebted thereto in S. A. Cummins, *Paul and the Crucified Christ in Antioch: Maccabean Martyrdom and Galatians 1 and 2* (SNTSMS 114; Cambridge: Cambridge University Press, 2001) 39-42. See also William Horbury, *Messianism among Jews and Christians: Twelve Biblical and Historical Studies* (Edinburgh: T&T Clark, 2003).

9. On which see Cummins, *Paul,* 47-52; cf. the relevant discussions by Wolters and Stuckenbruck in this volume.

10. Horbury maintains that there is adequate biblical precedent to suggest that the Messiah could be seen as the earthly embodiment of an angel-like spirit; *Jewish Messianism,* 86-87, 97-108.

indicates that the religio-political and nationalistic aspects of messianic expectation were widely known in first-century Israel, which resented and resisted Roman rule.)[11] Of further note is the fact that just as Israel as a whole was called God's own "son" (or "child"), so the king-Messiah figure was often viewed in terms of divine sonship in the Old Testament (cf. 2 Sam 7:14; Pss 2:7; 89:27-28) and was variously attested as such at Qumran (4QFlor; cf. 1QSa, 4Q369, and perhaps 4Q246); there are also later Jewish references to a messianic "son of God" (1 Enoch 105:2; 4 Ezra 7:28-29; 13:32, 37, 52; 14:9).[12] Thus, without carrying connotations of divine status, the "son of God"–Messiah connection served to stress the intimacy of the relationship between God and his messianic agent.

In an influential essay, Nils Dahl has argued that for Paul (and the early church overall) the term "Christ" did not receive its content from a previously fixed Jewish messianic concept, but rather from the person, work, crucifixion, and resurrection of Jesus.[13] Yet insofar as the latter must itself be viewed in relation to the former, it may still be contended that Jewish monotheism and messiahship constituted a vital element in Paul's understanding of Jesus as Messiah. Moreover, Jewish understandings functioned not simply by way of "backdrop," but as a monotheism and election that are *themselves* radically and paradoxically reconfigured via Jesus' life and ministry (Dahl's positive and very important point) and Paul's own understanding thereof. That being the case, we must now also reckon seriously with the influence of Jesus' own messianic life and ministry as proclaimed by the earliest church, which Paul first persecuted and then embraced after his own encounter with the risen Jesus.

---

11. N. T. Wright, *Jesus and the Victory of God* (Minneapolis: Fortress, 1996) 481-86, stresses the national and Jerusalem temple–focused dimensions of first-century messianism. Among the many pertinent publications by R. A. Horsley, see his "'Messianic' Figures and Movements in First Century Palestine," in Charlesworth, ed., *The Messiah*, 276-95; and (with John S. Hanson) *Bandits, Prophets and Messiahs* (Harrisburg: Trinity Press International, 1999) 88-134.

12. Collins, *Scepter*, 154-72, considers the evidence for the Messiah as "son of God" (especially 4Q246 and 4Q174), concluding that "the notion that the messiah was Son of God in a special sense was rooted in Judaism" (169). Again, note the pertinent discussions in Wolters and Stuckenbruck in this volume. See also Hurtado, *Lord Jesus Christ*, 101-8.

13. Nils A. Dahl, "The Messiahship of Jesus in Paul," in *Jesus the Christ: The Historical Origins of Christological Doctrine* (ed. Donald H. Juel; Minneapolis: Fortress, 1991) 15-25.

Monotheism, Messiah Jesus, and Paul's Conversion and Gospel

As far as we can tell, Paul himself did not have any direct contact with Jesus' earthly life and ministry. Rather, his initial (if mixed) knowledge of Jesus probably came to him from details acquired during his persecution of the early church, supplied both by the Jewish authorities and by the first followers of Jesus. This knowledge was later significantly augmented (and revised) after he, too, became committed to Christ and had the benefit of the teachings that were transmitted by the Jerusalem-based apostles (cf. Gal 1:18-19; 1 Cor 15:3ff.) and were circulating in the life of the church at large. Certainly his letters give adequate indication that in his own apostolic ministry he both presupposed and drew upon a knowledge of the activities and teachings of Jesus, as evident for example in his employment of oral traditions and early christological formulae in connection with his many churches, which would have been similarly informed.[14]

Paul's pre-conversion knowledge of Jesus would have included an awareness of and response to the earliest church's insistent claim that Jesus was the Messiah, confessed from the outset by both Aramaic-speaking Jewish Christians (Jesus as מְשִׁיחָא [*mašîḥā'*], corresponding to the Hebrew מָשִׁיחַ [*māšîaḥ*]) and then Greek-speaking Jewish-Christian and Gentile converts (Jesus as Χριστός [Christ]).[15] This was a wide-ranging contention that understood Jesus' messiahship as necessarily encompassing both his faithful life resulting in crucifixion and his ensuing resurrection.[16] That is, for the earliest church (and later the converted Paul), Jesus' resurrection confirmed — even as it also transposed — his already existing status and role as the Messiah,[17] even if the true nature and full scope of

---

14. Cf. Michael B. Thompson, *Clothed with Christ: The Example and Teachings of Jesus in Romans 12.1–15.3* (JSNTSup 59; Sheffield: Sheffield Academic Press, 1992); David Wenham, *Paul: Follower of Jesus or Founder of Christianity?* (Grand Rapids: Eerdmans, 1995); Wenham, *Paul and Jesus: The True Story* (Grand Rapids: Eerdmans, 2002).

15. Cf. Martin Hengel, "'Christos' in Paul," in his *Between Jesus and Paul: Studies in the Earliest History of Christianity* (London: SCM Press, 1983) 76-77.

16. Compare, for example, Acts 2:36; 3:18, 20; etc.; early confessional statements, later taken up into Paul's post-conversion writings (e.g., Rom 5:6, 8; 1 Cor 8:11; 15:3); and the wider phenomenon of the early church's experience of the Spirit as "the Spirit of Christ" (Rom 8:9; cf. Gal 4:6).

17. This point is well made by I. Howard Marshall, "A New Understanding of the Present and the Future: Paul and Eschatology," in *The Road from Damascus* (ed. R. N.

this was recognized and achieved only with the resurrection. These crucial interrelated elements are worth reiterating: the earliest church proclaimed a paradoxical messiahship that necessarily embraced Jesus' obedient earthly life and vocation; a humiliating self-sacrificial death; and an entirely unexpected glorious resurrection.

By his own later testimony, the pre-conversion Paul was zealously committed to his way of life "in Judaism" (Gal 1:13-14; Phil 3:5-6) — to the Jewish monotheism, election, and messiahship as outlined earlier — which was now being compromised and jeopardized by this dangerous Jesus-focused messianic movement. The nature and extent of the concern cannot be overestimated. It was not just the immediate worry that a divided and disrupted nation could become all the more susceptible to Roman repression. More fundamentally, it was entirely inconceivable that God would reveal his righteousness, rescue and restore Israel, fulfill the covenant and uphold the Torah, and inaugurate the long-awaited eschatological age through *this* Jesus — a crucified (and thus cursed) messianic pretender, purportedly risen — and his apostate Jewish and now also Gentile followers (Gal 5:11; 1 Cor 1:23; cf. Deut 21:23).[18] The blasphemous implications concerning the very identity of God and the destiny of Israel were scandalous. From such a standpoint Paul's zealous opposition — which he only later viewed as persecution (1 Cor 15:9; Gal 1:13, 23; Phil 3:6) — was understandable.

From the foregoing we may thus conclude that when Paul later tells his Corinthian converts that "though we once knew Christ from a human point of view, we know him no longer in that way" (2 Cor 5:16), he is not stating any lack of interest in the historical Jesus, about whom he would have been adequately informed in the ways just noted. Rather, he is attesting to the stark contrast between his pre- and post-conversion understanding of Jesus as Messiah. While following a life "in Judaism" he had an "according to the flesh" (or an "of man") perspective; as an apostle of Jesus he now had an "of God" outlook, which originated with his remarkable encounter with the risen and exalted Jesus Christ.

In the course of his zealous persecution of the church, Paul is dra-

---

Longenecker; Grand Rapids: Eerdmans, 1997) 54-55; see also Wright, *Jesus and the Victory of God*, 486-89.

18. Cf. A. Hultgren, "Paul's Pre-Christian Persecutions of the Church: Their Purpose, Locale, and Nature," *JBL* 95 (1976) 97-111.

matically transformed when God revealed his son "in him [Paul]" (Gal 1:15-16a).[19] This apocalyptic encounter can be viewed as a radical rework-ing of the Jewish messianic expectations concerning a human redeemer figure noted earlier. Paul the exemplary and fervent Jew now realizes that the one he had been persecuting — in virtue of his pursuit of Jesus' follow-ers — was in fact Israel's (and the nations') messianic Son of God.[20] More-over, the crucified but now risen Messiah Jesus also occupies a role in rela-tion to God that entails a share in divine lordship. Certainly elsewhere Paul explicitly refers to his encounter as having "seen Jesus our Lord" (1 Cor 9:1) and to his former way of life as "loss" compared to "the surpassing value of knowing Christ Jesus my Lord" (Phil 3:7-8). Thus, even in respect to Paul's conversion, Jesus as Messiah, Jesus as Son of God, and Jesus as Lord are al-ready held in close alignment, with the post-resurrection title "Lord" fur-ther radicalizing the Messiah/Son of God designations in a wholly unprec-edented way.[21] Remarkably, the now glorified Jesus is (as Bauckham has put it) being included within the unique identity of God. Paul's astonish-ing new understanding of Jesus strains explication: *this* Jesus, Israel's di-vinely sent *cruciform* Messiah and Son of God, now risen and exalted in glory, who in *this* way discloses who God is even as God himself.

Moreover, Paul can also say that God has revealed this Jesus "in me [ἐν ἐμοί]" (Gal 1:16): the exalted Son of God has reconfigured and is com-pletely constitutive of Paul's entire life, a transformed existence that he can otherwise describe as "Christ in me" (e.g., Gal 2:20) and can also conjoin to the operation of the Holy Spirit inasmuch as "God has sent the Spirit of his Son into our hearts" (Gal 4:6). Paul now embodies a remarkable new existence shaped and sustained by Messiah Jesus. It is this astonishing

---

19. There is some debate as to whether this encounter is best understood as a "conver-sion" or a "call" (cf. Gal 1:15; Isa 42:6; 49:1-6; Jer 1:5). Insofar as the event entailed both dis-continuity and continuity with Paul's former Jewish way of life, both may be kept in view. Nonetheless, given the dramatic change in Paul's life in relation to God, "conversion" itself is an acceptable term. On the latter, see especially Alan Segal, *Paul the Convert: The Apostolate and Apostasy of Saul the Pharisee* (New Haven: Yale University Press, 1990); and Segal, "Con-version and Messianism: An Outline for a New Approach," in Charlesworth, ed., *The Mes-siah*, 96-340. More broadly, see the essays in Longenecker, ed., *The Road from Damascus*.

20. That persecuting the church is tantamount to persecuting Jesus himself (cf. Gal 1:13-16a; Phil 3:6-7; and Acts 9:1-5) is consistent with the "corporate Christology" to be con-sidered below.

21. The account of Paul's conversion and its immediate aftermath in Acts 9 indicates a similar interplay among these three designations (cf. 9:5, 17, 20-22, 27).

christological and pneumatological redefinition of Jewish monotheism that is to be announced as the gospel (the truly "good news") to the whole world, Jew and Gentile alike, from Jerusalem to Rome and beyond.[22] Paul's conversion is accompanied by a call to play a leading role in the spreading of this good news as an apostle to the Gentiles within the wider life of an inclusive and ever-expanding church of God. As his letters amply testify, it will be a costly vocation, entailing a daily dying and rising with Messiah Jesus and his often afflicted people. Yet it will also be marked by the covenantal blessings of a truly divine life, which comes even now with being the glorified messianic eschatological people of God.

Monotheism, Messiah Jesus, and the Eschatological People of God in Paul

The outworking of Paul's transformative encounter with Messiah Jesus, Son of God and Lord, and of his resultant gospel is everywhere evident in his extant letters. Of course, the precise manner in which his understanding of Jesus' messiahship is disclosed therein is much debated. This is due largely to the wide range of complex and interrelated philological, exegetical, and theological elements requiring consideration. In the necessarily selective analysis that follows, it will be argued that for Paul "Christ" denotes "Messiah" and that the term is to be understood in an essentially representative and incorporative way. The extent and manner to which this is variously discernible in the letters themselves, allowing us to appreciate their nature and significance in ways that would not otherwise be possible, will be considered by means of an exegetical and theological analysis of two "test cases," Gal 2:15-21 and Romans 5–8.

---

22. For a summary but pertinent estimation of Paul's gospel, cf. N. T. Wright, *What Saint Paul Really Said* (Grand Rapids: Eerdmans, 1997) 39-62; also Graham N. Stanton, "Paul's Gospel," in *The Cambridge Companion to St. Paul* (ed. James D. G. Dunn; Cambridge: Cambridge University Press, 2003) 173-84. On the provocative resonances of Paul's gospel concerning Christ in relation to Rome, which cannot be explored here, see N. T. Wright, "Paul's Gospel, Caesar's Empire," in *Paul and Politics: Ekklesia, Israel, Imperium, Interpretation* (ed. Richard A. Horsley; Harrisburg: Trinity Press International, 2000) 160-83.

Paul's Incorporative Christ

The bare statistics alone are intriguing: of some 531 instances of Χριστός in the standard critical editions of the Greek New Testament, a dispropor-tionate number of these (approximately 380) are to be found in the Pau-line letters.[23] Even if one excludes, for example, Ephesians and the Pastoral epistles as not being written by Paul himself, there are still about 180 in-stances of the word.[24] Across the Pauline corpus, "Christ" is used fre-quently in the combinations "Jesus Christ," "Lord Jesus Christ," and "Christ Jesus," with the last expression not found anywhere else in the New Testament. Perhaps most notable is the fact that there are about 220 in-stances of Χριστός by itself, almost equally divided between articular and anarthrous forms, which are often deployed interchangeably in a wide range of expressions: for example, "body of (the) Christ," "(the) Christ ac-cording to the flesh," "day of (the) Christ," "in/into (the) Christ," "word of (the) Christ," and "servants of (the) Christ."[25]

The current scholarly consensus still seems to be that Χριστός in Paul has all but lost its titular significance (as "Messiah") and has become "more or less equivalent to a proper name in Paul's letters."[26] Yet given the currency of Jewish messianic expectations, the clearly titular use of Χριστός in the Gospels and Acts,[27] the early church's proclamation of Jesus as Messiah, the pre-conversion Paul's strenuous opposition thereto and his dramatic en-counter with the risen Jesus, it seems *prima facie* probable that Paul would have deployed the term assuming and evoking its messianic associations. In-deed, there appears to be sufficient evidence to suggest that for Paul Χριστός regularly retains the titular sense of Israel's "Messiah" and that much of its significance resides in its representative and incorporative aspects.

23. So Craig Blomberg, "Messiah in the New Testament," in *Israel's Messiah in the Bi-ble and the Dead Sea Scrolls* (ed. Richard S. Hess and M. Daniel Carroll R.; Grand Rapids: Baker Academic, 2003) 111, 125, using UBS[4] = NA[27], and acknowledging that the counts are approximate due to the many textual variants, which, he notes, do not materially affect the general figures.

24. So James D. G. Dunn, *The Theology of Paul the Apostle* (Grand Rapids: Eerdmans, 1998) 196-97 nn. 70 and 76, also observing that the figures are inexact due to the variant readings.

25. From Blomberg, "Messiah," 126.

26. So Dunn, *Theology of Paul*, 197. Influential in this regard is Hengel, "'Christos' in Paul."

27. On which see Blomberg, "Messiah," 114-23.

Certainly Paul knew — and assumed that his Corinthian readers knew — the original meaning of Χριστός as an "anointed one," as his wordplay at 2 Cor 1:21 readily indicates. Moreover, many otherwise skeptical scholars recognize a titular sense to the word at Rom 9:3, 5, wherein Paul rhetorically wishes himself "cut off from [the] Christ for the sake of my own people, my kinsmen according to the flesh . . . from [whom], according to the flesh, comes the Christ." Dunn allows that a similar case could be made for Rom 15:3 and 7; and he conceives it just possible that the distinctive Pauline use of "Christ Jesus" (in contrast to "Jesus Christ") is "a direct translation equivalent of 'Messiah Jesus,' with *Christos* still bearing titular force."[28] Arguably, though, the titular use of Χριστός is also contextually indicated in various other instances, such as 1 Cor 1:13; 10:4; 15:22; 2 Cor 5:10; 11:2-3; Gal 5:24; 6:2: Phil 1:15, 17; 3:7.[29] Additionally, while Paul recognized and confessed that "Jesus is Lord" (cf. Rom 10:9; 1 Cor 12:3; Phil 2:11), he conspicuously fails to write that "Christ is Lord," as might be expected if "Christ" were but an interchangeable name for Jesus.[30]

If Paul uses Χριστός with Jesus' messiahship clearly in view, he also arguably employs it in a manner that indicates its representative and incorporative significance. In the ancient world, not least in Israel, the people were represented by and saw their identity and destiny as being bound up with that of their king. We have already, for example, noted this in connection with Jewish messianic expectations concerning a Davidic Messiah/Son of God figure. It is interesting, therefore, that we find notable and recurring patterns in the way in which Paul deploys prepositional phrases that together suggest that he intends to convey precisely this kind of relationship between Christ and his people. The most striking of these involve (a) the expression "into Christ [εἰς Χριστόν]" (e.g., Rom 6:3; Gal 2:16; 3:27); and (b) the phrase "in Christ [ἐν Χριστῷ]" (e.g., Gal 1:22; 2:4, 17; 3:14, 26, 28).[31] We may also note Paul's use of the possessive genitive, "those

28. Dunn, *Theology of Paul*, 198-99.

29. In all of these instances the word is also articular, though the case does not rest on the presence (or absence) of the article alone, the use of which with proper names can be quite flexible. See the similar list offered in Dahl, *Jesus the Christ*, 17 and 24 n. 11, wherein he detects "messianic connotations," even if he adds that "in no case can *Christos* be translated 'Messiah.'" He also cites, as notable anarthrous instances, 1 Cor 1:23; Rom 15:8; and Gal 3:16. Cf. also Dunn's list, *Theology of Paul*, 199 n. 88.

30. So Dahl, *Jesus the Christ*, 38.

31. For a wider consideration of this and related evidence, see Cummins, *Paul*, 198-

of Christ [οἱ τοῦ Χριστοῦ]" (cf. Gal 3:29; 5:24). From this and other consid-erations,[32] it would appear that Paul's prepositional and syntactical usage is not arbitrary; nor is it adequately accounted for simply by reference to grammatical, syntactical, and idiomatic variation.

Of course, the degree to which Χριστός retained a messianic sense for Paul, and the various ways this is so, cannot be determined on philo-logical grounds alone. Rather, it needs to be made on a case-by-case and cumulative exegetical basis, not least in a way that is alert to the theologi-cal, christological, and ecclesiological aspects of the texts in question. With this in mind, we now consider in more detail Paul's wide-ranging under-standing of "Christ/Messiah" in two passages central to two of his most significant letters: Gal 2:15-21 and Romans 5–8.

Dying and Rising with Messiah Jesus and His People (Galatians 2:15-21)

By any estimation Gal 2:15-21 is one of the nerve centers of Pauline theol-ogy. In this passage Paul seeks to uphold the truth of the gospel by means of a tight line of argument that encompasses a host of contentious and in-terrelated issues: for example, Jew-Gentile relations, justification, "works of law," faith in/of Jesus Christ, sin, the efficacy of the cross, the resurrec-tion life, and the grace of God. In all of this Paul's understanding of Mes-siah Jesus plays the prominent and pivotal role, and it does so with partic-ular reference to its Israel-specific outworking in the lives of his fellow Jewish converts and the implications of this for the inclusive composition and vocation of the whole people of God.

Paul has just rebuked Peter for bowing to Jewish(-Christian) pres-sure for stricter Torah observance by withdrawing from table fellowship with the mixed (Jew + Gentile) Christian community in Antioch (Gal 2:11-14).[33] Paul's concern is not just that such a move undermines the

---

204; more fully, N. T. Wright, *The Climax of the Covenant: Christ and the Law in Pauline The-ology* (Edinburgh: T&T Clark, 1991) 41-55; cf. 18-40, 157-74.

32. See Blomberg, "Messiah," who lists extensive evidence along similar and related lines.

33. "Jewish(-Christian)" is an awkward but adequate shorthand way of recognizing Paul's interaction with a wide and fluid range of Jews whose understanding of and commit-ment to Messiah Jesus differed in various respects from his own.

inclusivity and unity of the church. Rather, inasmuch as table fellowship is founded and focused upon the Lord's Supper and all that this signifies, it also threatens the community's commensality with their eschatological redeemer as participants in the now inaugurated messianic kingdom of God. Indeed, Peter's failure to remain faithful to the truth of the gospel represents a retrograde step away from his new life "in Christ" and toward his former existence "in Judaism," which Paul now views as bound up with the old evil age (cf. Gal 1:4).[34]

Paul begins his theological reflection on this scenario by ironically appropriating a piece of intra-Jewish polemic espousing Jewish superiority over Gentiles (Gal 2:15), which he immediately relativizes by locating it within his decidedly christological understanding of the messianic people of God (Gal 2:16). He reminds Peter of what he already ought to know: that a person's justification — present standing and ultimate vindication before God — is not a function of adherence to "works of the law" and the way of life they represent, but of "faith in/of Jesus Christ [πίστις Ἰησοῦ Χριστοῦ]."[35] For Paul, the (re)adoption of the "works of the law," and thus of a life "in Judaism," involved putting oneself back "under the law."[36] That is, from Paul's God-in-Messiah-Jesus standpoint, life "under [the curse of] the law" meant that Israel was both bound by and unable to obey an otherwise good Torah, and so incurred its condemnation rather than its blessing. This was due to the fact that Israel (no less than the Gentiles) was bound up with the old age/sphere of Adamic sin. The only solution to this situation is justification "through faith in/of Jesus Christ [διὰ πίστεως Ἰησοῦ Χριστοῦ]."

Given the earlier case for a titular and incorporative understanding of Χριστός, it may be suggested that in making this assertion Paul is claim-

34. For a detailed outworking of this summary estimation, see Cummins, *Paul*, 161-88.

35. Whether πίστις Ἰησοῦ Χριστοῦ is to be interpreted as "faith in Jesus Christ" or "faith(fullness) of Jesus Christ" is much disputed. See the lively exchange between James D. G. Dunn, "Once More, ΠΙΣΤΙΣ ΧΡΙΣΤΟΥ" (arguing for the former), and Richard B. Hays, "ΠΙΣΤΙΣ and Pauline Theology: What Is at Stake?" (preferring the latter), both in *Pauline Theology IV: Looking Back, Pressing On* (ed. E. Elizabeth Johnson and David M. Hay; Atlanta: Scholars Press, 1997), 61-81 and 33-60, respectively.

36. A condition cognate with being "under a curse," "under the elemental spirits of the universe," and "under sin" (cf. Gal 3:10; 4:3; Rom 3:9; 7:14), and in direct contrast to being "under grace" (Rom 6:14, 15).

ing that vindication as a member of God's people is in virtue of the incorporation of one's identity and destiny into *Messiah* Jesus. Moreover, it is likely that "faith [πίστις]" here has in view the exemplary faithfulness of Jesus (not least in respect of the cross), which is both the climactic and definitive demonstration of God's covenant faithfulness (Rom 3:21-26) and that which enables the reciprocal faithfulness of those believers conformed to him.[37] Such is the full scope of divine grace centered upon Christ. And it is "into Messiah Jesus [εἰς Χριστόν]" that Jews such as Peter and Paul believed (Gal 2:16b). On the basis of similar prepositional statements elsewhere (cf. Rom 6:3; 1 Cor 12:13; Gal 3:27; Phil 1:27-30), it is evident that Paul is here reminding Jewish Christians that their belief "into Christ," marked out by baptism, entails dying and rising with him. Vindication is now a function of covenant faithfulness to God-in-Christ, and the eschatological people of God are those Jews and Gentiles demarcated by their common life in the Messiah.

Paul then echoes the objection of those in Antioch (and elsewhere) who hold an antithetical position: "if in seeking to be justified in Messiah Jesus, we [Jewish Christians] are found to be sinners, then is the Messiah a servant of sin?" (Gal 2:17). There is little doubt that the initial premise — that justification is being sought in Christ — is indeed correct. However, commentators are divided as to whether the second premise — that those (Jews like Peter and Paul) seeking justification in Christ are thus found to be sinners — is to be taken as (a) true, followed by a false deduction therefrom (Christ is a servant of sin), or (b) false, followed by an equally false conclusion (Christ is a servant of sin). The answer depends upon the perspective adopted. From the standpoint of those advocating justification via the "works of the law," it is true: Jews seeking to be justified in Christ are indeed sinners, tantamount to Gentiles outside the Torah. And it follows that Christ himself is also a servant of sin, a messianic pretender, duly condemned under the Torah. However, from the standpoint of those advocating justification in Messiah Jesus, it is false: Jews seeking to be justified in Christ are not sinners, for it is precisely in this way that they are found to be faithful to the God of Israel definitively disclosed in this Jesus. Moreover, far from being a servant of sin, the Messiah himself, whose divine equality with God was expressed through becoming a servant unto death, is in fact the startling means whereby God has shown his covenant faith-

---

37. For such a reading, see Cummins, *Paul,* 200-201.

fulness to Israel and thence to the whole world.[38] It is on this basis that Paul immediately and emphatically denies any such claims against Christ and his followers (Gal 2:17).

At this point Paul proceeds to offer both a negative and a more positive explanation for his denial. First, he counterclaims that it is in fact anyone (even Peter in Antioch) who rebuilds his or her dismantled former way of life "in Judaism" by seeking justification in "works of the law" who thereby proves to be a "transgressor [παραβάτης]" (Gal 2:18). This Jewish-specific term carries a certain ambiguity that must be allowed to operate. From a *Jewish* standpoint, were Peter to put himself back under "works of the law," he would show himself to have been a transgressor of Torah during the period in which he had been a follower of Jesus and thus at odds with a life "in Judaism." From Paul's Jewish-*Christian* standpoint, however, the problem is more profound: Peter is in danger of returning to an Israel whose ongoing Torah transgression attests to the fact that it serves, rather than solves, the worldwide problem of sin.

This brings Paul to his second and positive point: the sin of Israel (and the world) has in fact now been dealt with in Messiah Jesus: "For I through the law died to the law, so that I might live to God. I have been crucified with Christ" (Gal 2:19). This highly compressed and much debated statement is to be read both personally and corporately, and it has three interrelated (indeed, superimposed) elements in view. First, there is the individual "I" (Paul-in-Israel-in-Adam), who through his abuse of Torah in service of persecuting the Messiah and his people became confronted with and was transformed by the crucified and risen Messiah (Gal 1:13-16). He thus died to his former way of life in order that "I" (Paul-in-Israel-in-Christ) might live to God. Second, Paul's own experience represents a particular instance of the transformation of the corporate "I" (Israel-in-Adam), which was subject to the outworking of sin's abuse of Torah within Israel (cf. Rom 7:1-25). Yet in virtue of Israel's conformity to its crucified Messiah, and thereby death to that condition it was in, a now transformed "I" (Israel-in-Christ) may live to God.[39] Third, both of these scenarios were made possible because of Messiah Jesus' own experience of sin's abuse of Torah in Israel, a subset of sin operative in the world, which

---

38. See further, Cummins, *Paul*, 206-12.

39. For this reading of Gal 2:19-20 in relation to Rom 7:1–8:11, see Cummins, *Paul*, 219-25.

culminated in his crucifixion at the hands of the Jewish and Roman authorities — thereby paradoxically accomplishing the deliverance of Paul, Israel, and the whole of humanity (e.g., Gal 3:13; 4:4-5; Rom 3:21-26).

Astonishingly, the rejected Jesus was in fact Israel's Messiah who, via his death and resurrection, now has a share in divine glory. Moreover, it is this glorified Messiah who transforms and takes up residence in all of those conformed to his death and resurrection: "I [in Christ] live, but no longer I [in Adam]"; rather "Christ lives in me" (Gal 2:20a).[40] Even now, those in Christ who have Christ in them can, like him, live "to God" (cf. Gal 2:19; Rom 6:10; 14:8-9) as participants in resurrection life, the glory of God's inaugurated reign. Such is the grace of God (Gal 2:21).

The Glorification of the Eschatological Messianic People of God (Romans 5–8)

The divine solution to humanity's sin through a crucified and risen Messiah Jesus, whose indwelling enables those conformed to him to "live to God" (Gal 2:15-21), is played out on an even grander scale in Romans 5–8. The Messiah Jesus focus of Romans is evident from the outset with Paul's announcement that the gospel of God, long promised by the prophets in the holy Scriptures, centers on "his Son, who was descended from David according to the flesh and was declared to be Son of God with power according to the Spirit of holiness by resurrection from the dead, Jesus Christ our Lord" (Rom 1:3-4).[41] In what follows, Paul insists that God's righteousness has been fully manifest in the atoning death and resurrection of Jesus Christ, so that notwithstanding the sin of humanity (Jew and Gentile alike), God can declare even now that all those who believe in this God so revealed in this Messiah Jesus are thereby constituted as his covenant faithful people (Romans 1–4). Then in Romans 5–8 Paul is concerned to unfold the amazing outcome and eschatological outworking of God's righteousness in Jesus. He argues that the complete restoration of humanity and creation has, in principle, been accomplished, and that those con-

---

40. This is further explicated by Paul: "and the life I now live in the flesh, I live in the faithfulness of the Son of God who loved me and gave himself for me" (Gal 2:20b).

41. Thus the interplay between the Davidic Messiah and Son of God, and Jesus' messianic status both before and after the resurrection, both noted earlier, are here also in view.

formed to Christ and the Spirit (who live in the "Spirit of the Messiah," Rom 8:9) are even now participants in the messianic age.[42]

The sheer scope of the transformation is extraordinary: from present justification arising out of Messiah Jesus' redemptive death (Rom 5:1-11) to final justification in the form of glorification (Rom 8:31-39). And the manner in which Paul's argument moves his readers in Rome back and forth across the intervening terrain is spellbinding. Present justification means Jesus-enabled access to divine grace, covenant blessing, and, even in and through suffering, the Spirit's assurance that this will ultimately issue in full glory with God (Rom 5:1-5). Such is the reconciling love of God in the death of Christ (Rom 5:6-11; cf. Gal 2:20). This theme is then immediately recapitulated, with Paul telling the world's story at its widest level: from Adam, to Torah, to Jesus, to glorification with God (Rom 5:12-21). In the Jewish retellings of this story, Israel — or a particular group within Israel — emerges as the people through whom humanity's sin is to be defeated once and for all. But in Paul's retelling it is in Messiah Jesus that Adam's trespass (wherein Israel itself is implicated) is finally undone. The result is "justification leading to eternal life through Jesus Christ our Lord" (Rom 5:21; cf. 6:23).

Moreover, God's covenant people are marked out by their baptism "into Christ Jesus," his death and resurrection, so that "just as Christ was raised from the dead by the glory of the Father, so [they] might walk in the newness of life" (Rom 6:4). Paul does not here elaborate in any detail on the nature of this glorious new resurrection life, but the wider context suggests that even now it includes entrance into that realm within which God is truly worshiped, the Spirit is at work, and the covenant blessings brought about by Jesus are operative (cf. Rom 5:1-2; 12).[43] Now justified rather than enslaved to sin, just as Christ himself "lives to God" so they too are "alive to God in Messiah Jesus" (Rom 6:10-11; cf. Gal 2:19-20), participants in the reign of God, which is yet to be ultimately realized (Rom 6:11-13) — all this attested by their present righteous lives (Rom 6:15-23).

However, at this stage Paul determines that he must say more con-

---

42. Among the many commentaries on Romans 5–8 to which this exposition is variously indebted, cf. James D. G. Dunn, *Romans 1–8* (WBC 38a; Dallas: Word, 1988) 242-513; Douglas J. Moo, *The Epistle to the Romans* (NICNT; Grand Rapids: Eerdmans, 1996) 290-547; and N. T. Wright, "The Letter to the Romans," in *The New Interpreter's Bible*, vol. 10 (ed. Leander E. Keck; Nashville: Abingdon, 2002) 508-619.

43. Cf., for example, Rom 5:1-2; 8:1-17; 12:1-21.

cerning how Israel and the Torah functioned with God's redemptive plans for humanity ultimately achieved in Christ (Rom 7:1–8:11). This passage offers a more extended treatment of the Israel-in-Adam problem so cryptically alluded to in Gal 2:19-20.[44] That is, the subject throughout, the emphatic "I," is Paul the Jew-become-Christian, now viewing retrospectively the problem of the outworking of sin's abuse of Torah within Israel, a Jewish-specific function of the wider problem of Adamic sin.[45] The solution to this problem is Israel's deliverance through Messiah Jesus: "Wretched man that I am! Who will rescue me from this body of death? Thanks be to God through Jesus Christ our Lord!" (Rom 7:24-25; cf. 7:4-6).

Paul therefore concludes that "those who are in Messiah Jesus" are excluded from God's condemnation because they have been set free from the Torah as taken over by sin and are instead the beneficiaries of the Torah's fulfillment in Jesus and the Spirit, who together effect covenant life (Rom 8:1-2).[46] This is further explicated with the claim that what a sin-weakened Torah was unable to do, God did by sending his Son as "a sin offering" (Rom 8:3). God thus condemned sin and enabled the covenant decree (Deut 30:6-20) to be fulfilled by those living according to the Spirit. Hence, Paul can now speak of two antithetical ways of existence, the flesh and the Spirit, with the former hostile to God and leading to death and the latter leading to life and peace (Rom 8:4-7). He then uses a series of interrelated designations to denote the indwelling Spirit: "the Spirit," "the Spirit of God," "the Spirit of Christ," and then simply "Christ." It would appear that the same Spirit is the Spirit of God and of the Messiah. It follows therefore that the Messiah himself lives in believers, providing life-giving power (Rom 8:10; cf. Gal 1:16; 2:20).[47] This, he cryptically adds, is "on ac-

---

44. That this is the case appears *prima facie* likely on the basis of certain common ground: the emphatic "I [ἐγώ]," a concentrated use of the phrases "through the law [διὰ νόμου]" (and "through the commandment [διὰ τῆς ἐντολῆς]"), and shared key issues or themes (Torah, sin, death, deliverance through Jesus Christ/God's Son).

45. The problem, then, lies not with an otherwise holy, just, and good Torah (Rom 7:12), but with sin; see Cummins, *Paul*, 219-25.

46. Christ is thus "the end of the Torah" (Rom 10:4) in the dual sense of cessation and fulfillment: that is, the important but provisional role of the Torah comes to an end as its purposes find their fulfillment in Messiah Jesus, who makes possible covenant faithfulness (righteousness) for all who believe in him.

47. See Wright, "Romans," 583-84. Wright also notes that the difficult parenthetical statement — "though the body is dead because of sin" (Rom 8:10b) — could be an acknowledgment that even believers are still subject to the vicissitudes of mortal life (cf. Phil 3:21,

count of righteousness": that is, a result of God's covenant faithfulness demonstrated in the death and resurrection of the Messiah. Paul then concludes that if the Spirit of that God who raised Jesus from the dead dwells in believers, then that same God will also, by his indwelling Spirit, give them resurrection life (Rom 8:11).[48]

Paul brings Romans 5–8 to its conclusion by reflecting broadly upon the present and future situation of the church within the long outworking of God's covenantal and creation-wide purposes (Rom 8:12-39). He affirms Christ's people as the sons/children of God and "heirs of God and joint heirs with Christ," in both present suffering (in which they are sustained by the Spirit) and ultimate glorification (which they will enjoy "with him [the Messiah]") (Rom 8:12-17). Then, within a Jewish apocalyptic worldview reworked in the light of Jesus and the Spirit, Paul anticipates the ultimate eradication of evil and renewal of all things (Rom 8:18-25). He knows that at present the church finds itself sharing and bearing the birth pains of the new order; they are the embryonic eschatological children of God awaiting the divine glory about to be revealed, in the light of which their identity and destiny will be fully and finally revealed. In the meantime, the Spirit — who, we recall, is also the Messiah — helps the saints, intercedes on their behalf, and enables them to love God (Rom 8:26-28).[49] They are those through whom God has chosen to demonstrate his glory, doing so by having them conform to the image of his Son, the firstborn of a worldwide messianic family (cf. 2 Corinthians 3; Col 1:15-20).

Set within the context of his argument to date, the full content and scope of Paul's very compressed summary remark to the church in Rome can now be unpacked: having chosen them to be his people through whom he rescues the world, God called them through the gospel of Christ; and in obediently responding they show themselves even now to be his covenant people who radiate the glory of God in Christ in the world (Rom 8:30; cf.

---

where Paul speaks of "the body of our humiliation" being transformed by the Lord Jesus Christ into "the body of his glory"); alternatively, it might be a summary referent of the condition just described in Romans 7.

48. The subtle shift from "Jesus" to "Christ" is probably to be explained on the basis of the former referring to the historical human Jesus and the latter to the Messiah who represents and even now is present with his people. On the lack of interchangeability of "Jesus" and "Christ" in this letter, see Leander E. Keck, "'Jesus' in Romans," *JBL* 108 (1989) 443-60.

49. It may be that Rom 8:28 offers an echo of the Jewish Shema (Deut 6:4-5), now made possible in Christ and the Spirit.

2 Cor 3:18). Finally, with a rhetorical flourish at Rom 8:31-39, Paul recapitulates and celebrates the main themes of the entire letter so far: just who is going to bring a charge against the God whose covenant love is demonstrated in the crucifixion, resurrection, and exaltation of his Son, Messiah Jesus; and who has thereby defeated evil and redeemed, justified, and reconciled the messianic people of God; and who thus allows them, as with their Messiah, to have a share in the glory of God?

Conclusion

Jewish messianic expectations envisaged an eschatological redeemer/ruler who would deliver the nation from foreign subjugation and bring about the new age. It was in order to ensure the realization of just such a vision that a zealous Paul opposed the wayward first followers of the crucified messianic pretender Jesus. In the course of this opposition he dramatically and transformatively experienced a divine disclosure, as a result of which he realized that *this* Jesus was indeed the now risen and exalted Messiah, Son of God, and, even more astonishingly, Lord. It was, then, in *this* way that Israel's God had himself acted to fulfill the Abrahamic covenant and rescued, restored, and in principle re-created Israel and all the nations. What was true of Messiah Jesus would now also be true of those who believed in him. In virtue of the Spirit of Christ among them, they were now constituted and empowered as the messianic eschatological people of God. And if they had been chosen, called, and justified by this God-in-Christ-in-the-Spirit, then even in and through their present suffering they would know, reflect, and ultimately enjoy eternally the transfiguring glory of God.

Messianic Themes of Temple, Enthronement, and Victory in Hebrews and the General Epistles

Cynthia Long Westfall

Introduction: The Messiah in Collocation and Scenarios

A point of departure for the study of the Messiah in Hebrews and the General Epistles is the acknowledgment that the term "Messiah" became the central christological concept. At least that holds true historically, and therein lies the rub. "Christ" or χριστός, the Greek term for the Messiah, became the central way of designating the church's understanding of Jesus, with the result that the term "Christology" has become a catch-all term for beliefs about Jesus.[1] Χριστιανοί had become a familiar term for Jesus' followers by the time Luke wrote Acts (Acts 11:26; 26:28; 1 Pet 4:16). At some point "Christ" was incorporated into the name of Jesus of Nazareth so that his default name became "Jesus Christ,"[2] and in time, the religion founded by Jesus and the apostles became known as "Christianity." The challenge is to find where and how the concept of Messiah in Hebrews and the General Epistles fits into this process.

While the title "Messiah" or "Christ" literally means "the anointed

---

1. G. E. Ladd, *A Theology of the New Testament* (rev. ed.; Grand Rapids: Eerdmans, 1993) 133.

2. J. P. Meier asserts, "So current was the name Jesus that some descriptive phrase like 'of Nazareth' or 'the Christ (Messiah)' had to be added to distinguish him from the many other bearers of that name." He adds, "So important was it to use 'Christ' as a distinguishing name for Jesus that, by the time of Paul in the mid-fifties of the 1st century A.D., 'Christ' was well on its way to becoming Jesus' second name" (J. P. Meier, *A Marginal Jew: Rethinking the Historical Jesus*, vol. 1 [New York: Doubleday, 1991] 206).

one," semantically it is used here to refer to God's eschatological divinely appointed and anointed agent whose saving acts would restore or free Israel from oppression and/or inaugurate the Day of the Lord, which is possibly the end of normal time and history.[3] However, it would be a mistake to assume that the Jews shared a common explicit and cohesive picture of the Messiah's identity and function. Furthermore, "Messiah" was not the only title used for this eschatological figure. Various titles were used interchangeably with "Messiah," and certain titles could easily become messianic if used in messianic contexts.[4] As N. T. Wright quips, "Messiahship, it seems, was whatever people made of it." He also states: "Jesus' Jewish world offers . . . a flurry of confused elements, some of which may be present in some messianic movements. . . . The hope of the nation was central, organizing itself as much around symbols, praxis and stories as around prooftexts."[5] Messianic figures and claims creatively exploited terminology, images, and symbols that evoked messianic roles and expectations that were recognized as such even by those who did not possess a messianic hope.

Therefore, Wright and others make a convincing case that Jesus consciously evoked messianic roles and expectations in stories, symbols, and actions that were recognized by the people and the Jewish leaders. Everyone is agreed that the writers of the Gospels and Acts presented Jesus as the Messiah, the Christ. However, it is claimed that "Christ" quickly became a name rather than a title. This raises a number of questions about the concept of the Messiah in the rest of the New Testament. One question is this: As the title "Christ" was becoming a name for Jesus, was it stripped of all messianic se-

---

3. See C. A. Evans, "Messianism," in *Dictionary of New Testament Background* (ed. C. A. Evans and S. E. Porter; Downers Grove, IL: InterVarsity Press, 2000) 698-707. According to Charlesworth, Jewish "messianology" developed out of the Maccabean wars of the second century BC: "Palestinian Jews yearned for salvation from their pagan oppressors. For an undeterminable number of Jews the yearning centered on the future saving acts by a divinely appointed, and anointed supernatural man: the Messiah. This eschatological figure will inaugurate the end of all normal time and history. I, therefore, use the term 'Messiah' in its etymological sense, to denote God's eschatological Anointed One, the Messiah" (J. H. Charlesworth, "From Messianology to Christology: Problems and Prospects," in *The Messiah: Developments in Earliest Judaism and Christianity* [ed. J. H. Charlesworth; Minneapolis: Fortress, 1992] 3-35; see p. 4).

4. Charlesworth observes: "There was considerable fluidity among the various titles that could be or become messianic titles" (Charlesworth, "From Messianology to Christology," 13).

5. N. T. Wright, *Jesus and the Victory of God* (Minneapolis: Fortress, 1996) 482-83.

mantic content and did it become merely a designation rather than a title?[6] A more specific question for our purpose is this: Were references to Christ or Jesus Christ in Hebrews and the General Epistles messianic? Many scholars insist that the answer is an unequivocal No. A further question is this: Is there additional content in Hebrews and the General Epistles that reflects, develops, or reframes the Jewish or early Christian concept of the Messiah? While scholars will discuss the Christology of Hebrews and the General Epistles, they do not often find the Christ, the Messiah, in this corpus.[7]

We will examine three factors to determine the messianic content in Hebrews and the General Epistles. The first factor is the context and partici- pant roles that are relevant in determining whether references to Christ might have semantic content.[8] The second factor is the occurrences of "Christ" in each letter. We will examine the collocation patterns of "Christ" with the name "Jesus" and other lexical items. The third factor is the au- thors' use of messianic scenarios. "Scenario" is a linguistic term that is used to indicate "an extended domain of reference" or associated bundles of in- formation that lie behind a text. A scenario includes setting, situations, spe- cific items, and "role" slots.[9] For example, a restaurant scenario includes a waiter, customers, cooks/chefs, menus, food, tables, and chairs. Mentioning the scenario "restaurant" will activate roles and items in a restaurant, and

6. The belief that χριστός became primarily a name in place of a title is based in large part on the second-century use of the title "Christ" by the pagans Tacitus and Suetonius; in their usage, "Christ" was clearly a designation that lacked messianic semantic content (Suetonius, *Divus Claudius* 25.11; Tacitus, *Annales* 15.44).

7. For those who do look for the Christ, the search is usually limited to a discussion of his divinity or a discussion of the use of "Christ" as a title.

8. The context and the participant roles are two aspects of the register of the dis- course. Registers are "a configuration of meanings that is associated with a particular situa- tion" and also includes subject matter, mode (e.g., persuasive, explanatory, and imperative discourses), and medium (spoken or written). See J. Reed, *A Discourse Analysis of Philippians: Method and Rhetoric in the Debate over Literary Integrity* (Sheffield: Sheffield Academic Press, 1997) 54-55; see also M. A. K. Halliday and R. Hasan, *Language, Context and Text: Aspects of Language in a Social-Semiotic Perspective* (Geelong, Australia: Deakon Uni- versity, 1985) 38-39.

9. A. J. Sanford and S. C. Garrod, *Understanding Written Language* (Chichester: Wiley, 1981) 110. In choosing the term "scenario," I recognize that "frames," "scripts," "sche- mata," and "mental models" are similar concepts that refer to stereotypic representations of default features and are found in psychological and computational approaches to discourse. For a fuller description of these concepts and what differentiates them, see G. Brown and G. Yule, *Discourse Analysis* (Cambridge: Cambridge University Press, 1983) 236-56.

mentioning a partial description of the items or roles in a restaurant, such as a waiter taking an order, will activate a restaurant scenario. Such scenarios are usually shared information between the author and recipients that provide a key to interpreting a text. Messianic terminology, symbols, and images may be roughly categorized into three scenarios that are closely connected with Jewish royal messianic expectation: enthronement, victory, and the temple. References to various aspects of Jesus' enthronement, his victory over enemies or benefits from his victory, and his relationship to the temple would evoke the broader interpretive scenario of Messiah.

If an argument can be made for some messianic consciousness among the authors and recipients, and if there is a significant pattern of occurrences of messianic scenarios both with and without χριστός, we may conclude that Hebrews and the General Epistles refer to Jesus as the Messiah, the Christ. We may then be in a position to understand what was meant by the term beyond a name and to explore what understanding was shared about the Messiah and if the authors added any new information to the concept.

Context and Participants

The participant roles in Hebrews and the General Epistles are important in determining whether the authors and readers possess or share understanding or recognition of messianic terminology and content. Whether the orientation of the author and the text is Jewish or Gentile is particularly significant. Even if a Jewish writer were addressing a church community that was primarily Gentile in orientation, it is not clear that the use of "Christ" or related symbols would be void of messianic semantic content. Whether the recipients were Jewish or Gentile in background is also of importance. It is arguable that χριστός became a name with little semantic content relatively early in the Gentile church.[10] However, it is unlikely that Jewish Christian recipients would have failed to recognize messianic allusions if they had been exposed to Jewish messianic expectations. While Palestinian Jews might have a greater exposure to messianic expectations than Hellenistic

---

10. However, K. H. Rengstorf asserts: "In the Gk. Churches . . . the word *christos,* when linked with Jesus, completed relatively quickly the transition from an adj., which it is essentially, to a proper name. And in the process it retained its traditional reference to Jesus' status." K. H. Rengstorf, "Jesus Christ," in *The New International Dictionary of New Testament Theology,* vol. 2 (ed. C. Brown; Grand Rapids: Zondervan, 1976) 330-48; see p. 338.

Jews, Hellenistic Jews tended to be exposed to apocalyptic and pseudepi-graphic literature that contained messianic content. Furthermore, the circulation of the oral tradition and perhaps one or more Gospels would indicate shared information about Jesus' Messiahship with the authors.

The Occurrence of Χριστός

The collocation of "Christ" with "Jesus" in New Testament and extra-biblical literature is undeniable. One issue is whether Χριστός has semantic value as an honorific title or whether it became virtually automatic as a designation for Jesus by the time Hebrews and the General Epistles were written. The collocation of Χριστός with other lexical items is important. If Χριστός occurs with messianic scenarios that include terminology, symbols, and images, then it is likely that it has more semantic value than merely designation. In addition, if the orientation of any of the corpus is Jewish in background, any name could carry significant semantic weight. When D. A. Hagner describes the naming of Jesus in the nativity narratives, he states, "Names held far more importance in that culture than in ours, being thought of as linked with or pointing to the actual character and destiny of the individual." Furthermore, there was a rabbinic view that the Messiah was named before the creation of the world.[11] According to H. Bietenhard, the demonstrations and teachings of the power of the name of Jesus throughout the New Testament "show that the OT manner of speaking of the name of Yahweh has been transferred to Jesus and his name."[12] Therefore, for a first-century Jewish Christian, the collocation of the name of Jesus with the designation "Christ" could still amount to a direct proclamation of God's salvation through the Messiah.

We must not be anachronistic in our understanding of how the authors and recipients related to names, nor assume that if early Christians did use Ἰησοῦς χριστός as a name it would have equal semantic value to our use of Jesus Christ as a name.

---

11. D. A. Hagner, *Matthew 1–13* (Dallas: Word, 1993) 19. Hagner also adds that the significance of the child and his role "is seen particularly in the importance of the naming in the passage, as well as in the content of the names themselves, Jesus and Emmanuel" (22).

12. H. Bietenhard, "Name," in Brown, ed., *The New International Dictionary of New Testament Theology*, 2:654-55.

Messianic Scenarios

Messianic scenarios that occur apart from χριστός are equally essential in a study of the Messiah in Hebrews and the General Epistles. The three messianic scenarios of enthronement, victory, and temple are overlapping pragmatic categories that correspond to the broad spectrum of Jewish messianic expectations. They are roughly correlated to the anointed kings, prophets, and priests in the Hebrew Bible.[13] It is important to note that references to believers sharing in enthronement, victory, or temple scenarios are also messianic. As C. K. Barrett observes:

> It is a familiar observation that in Daniel 7, the Son of man vision is interpreted as a representation of the people of the saints of the Most High; if he receives a kingdom, that means that the people do. If this means that in any sense or at any stage he is identified with the Messiah, the same interpretation applies, for the king is the representative of the people; in their king the people as a whole experience defeat or victory.[14]

References to believers' salvation evoke the Messiah who saved them, and references to believers' spiritual victory evoke Christ's victory, which is the basis of the believers' victory.

The enthronement scenario is associated with the expectation that the Messiah would be the Davidic king through whom God would rule his people.[15] Enthronement is evoked by royal imagery and themes of lordship and inheritance. Royal imagery is related to thrones, scepters, crowns, and kingdom references. Lordship references relate to the rule of the Messiah. They include patron-client allusions such as the titles "Lord," "Master," and "Shepherd,"[16] as well as references to believers as "slaves" or "servants" and to the obligation of obedience. Inheritance themes are based on Jesus as the primary or firstborn son and heir of God. Jesus' people share

---

13. Evans, "Messianism," 699.

14. C. K. Barrett, "The Christology of Hebrews," in *Who Do You Say That I Am? Essays on Christology* (ed. M. A. Powell and D. R. Bauer; Louisville: Westminster John Knox, 1999) 119-20.

15. Wright, *Jesus and the Victory of God*, 477.

16. Wright states: "Jesus' use of 'shepherd' imagery, therefore, is comprehensible within this Jewish setting as an evocation of messianic roles and expectations" (Wright, *Jesus and the Victory of God*, 534).

his status as heirs and also receive an inheritance by virtue of their royal Messiah who is God's Son. Additional kinship language expresses the believers' relationship to God, Jesus, or each other, relationships that are based on Jesus' messianic identity and work.

The victory scenario is associated with the expectation that "the king was to be the one who would fight Israel's battles" and restore Israel from exile.[17] This expectation was transformed by Jesus and his followers so that messianic victory is evoked through references to the restoration of God's people to himself, salvation and its benefits, and the Parousia. The restoration of God's people includes reconciliation, the believers' approach to God, forgiveness, and fellowship. Salvation and its benefits include eternal life, righteousness, grace and peace, healing, and present and future deliverance. When suffering is viewed as conflict leading to victory, it is related to the victory scenario. The expectation of Christ's Parousia is related to the Day of the Lord, resurrection, and the defeat of Christ's enemies, which includes military associations. The depiction of Jesus as God's final prophet fits best into this eschatological category.

The temple scenario is associated with messianic royal roles and priestly functions. Wright summarizes:

> The temple . . . functioned as the central political, as well as religious, symbol of Judaism. It pointed not only to YHWH's promise to dwell with his people, and to his dealing with their sins, their impurities, and ultimately with their exile, but also to his legitimation of the rulers who built, rebuilt or ran it. It was bound up inextricably with the royal house, and with royal aspirations.[18]

The messianic relationship to the temple is evoked by references that associate Jesus or his people with the building, explanation of sacrifice(s), and the priesthood of Jesus or the believers.

The three scenarios of enthronement, victory, and temple correspond to various expectations that were circulating orally as well as in literature. However, the terminology, symbols, and images that evoke these

---

17. Wright, *Jesus and the Victory of God*, 484, see pp. 126-27, 203-4. See also C. A. Evans, "Jesus and the Continuing Exile of Israel," in *Jesus and the Restoration of Israel* (ed. C. C. Newman; Downers Grove, IL: InterVarsity Press, 1999) 77-100.

18. Wright, *Jesus and the Victory of God*, 411.

scenarios are sometimes "mutations" of the Jewish messianic hope. Nevertheless, even unique associations made by the authors are recognizable as fulfilling Israel's hope in an unexpected way.

Christ in the Book of Hebrews

Hebrews has traditionally been understood as a letter addressed to Jewish Christians. While this view has not gone unchallenged, the author's extensive use of the Septuagint together with the nature of the argument that is based on an emotional connection and understanding of Moses, the law and prophets, covenant, priesthood, and sacrifice would indicate that the author and probably the recipients are Hellenistic Jewish-Christians.[19] The Septuagint was accorded sacred authority for Jewish life and worship in the Hellenistic community.[20] New apocryphal books were added to the Hebrew Bible, and intertextual relationships have been suggested between Hebrews and apocryphal and pseudepigraphical works such as the *Martyrdom of Isaiah, 1* and *2 Enoch,* Sirach, the Wisdom of Solomon, the *Ascension of Isaiah, 4 Ezra,* the *Exagōgē of Ezekiel,* and *11QMelchizedek.*[21] This category of literature offers a variety of messianic expectations that would be "shared information" in the Jewish-Hellenistic community. In other words, the author of Hebrews had a variety of messianic materials in circulation with which he could draw connections and make new associations. Such a literary environment includes rich, if not consistent, messianic associations.

Χριστός occurs thirteen times in the book of Hebrews. It collocates with Jesus only three times (10:10; 13:8, 21). It occurs ten times alone, usually with the article (3:6, 14; 5:5; 6:1; 9:11, 14, 24, 28; 10:12; 11:26). There is a definite pattern of χριστός occurring with messianic scenarios. The partnership and sharing of God's people with Christ is an overarching messi-

---

19. This generalization would not exclude Gentile believers who were first Hellenistic Jewish proselytes or Samaritans.

20. See W. T. Wilson, "Hellenistic Judaism," in Evans and Porter, eds., *Dictionary of New Testament Background,* 477-82, see p. 480.

21. P. J. Hartin, "Apocrypha and Pseudepigraphical Sources in the New Testament," in Evans and Porter, eds., *Dictionary of New Testament Background,* 69-71, see p. 70; H. Anderson, "The Jewish Antecedents of the Christology in Hebrews," in Charlesworth, ed., *The Messiah,* 512-35.

anic theme (3:6, 14; 11:26).[22] Passages that evoke the enthronement scenario depict Christ as seated at the right hand of God after completing the priestly function of sacrifice (10:12), as the son over God's house (3:6), unchanging (13:8), and the means to obedience (13:21). Only two passages evoke the victory scenario. His sacrificial function is contrasted with his salvific second coming (9:28), and Moses is described as sharing Christ's sufferings while he looked ahead to the reward (11:26).[23] However, the passages that evoke the temple scenario dominate with references to Christ's high priesthood (3:14; 9:11), his sacrifice (9:14, 28; 10:5, 10, 12), and his work in the heavenly tabernacle (9:11, 14). One can conclude from these patterns that "Christ" is used with full messianic connotations.[24]

The messianic scenarios apart from the occurrence of χριστός are extensive in Hebrews — we suffer from an abundance of information. All three scenarios are repeatedly woven together. In chs. 1–4, the primary scenario is messianic victory: Jesus is presented as God's ultimate messenger in the last days — a prophet like Moses. We must hear his word to enter the victory or goal of God's rest. Enthronement and temple scenarios are mapped on the dominant victory scenario. Chapter 1 presents the ultimate messenger as the anointed and enthroned Son of God.[25] Jesus' humanity in ch. 2 qualifies him to be a high priest who is able to help people in their time of need. The greatest contribution of Hebrews to our understanding of Jesus as Messiah is the extended argument in 5:1–10:18 that uniquely explains Jesus' high priesthood

22. C. L. Blomberg notes that the believers' partnership with Christ in 3:14 "almost exactly matches Wright's 'incorporative' texts in Paul, in which the messiah is closely bound up with his people." C. L. Blomberg, "Messiah in the New Testament," in *Israel's Messiah in the Bible and the Dead Sea Scrolls* (ed. R. S. Hess and M. D. Carroll R.; Grand Rapids: Baker Academic, 2003) 111-41.

23. The reference to Christ in the OT context of Moses' life in 11:26 leads Blomberg to conclude, "this passage surely is referring to the messiah in the abstract rather than to Jesus personally" (Blomberg, "Messiah in the New Testament," 133).

24. Contra P. Ellingworth, who asserts that in the book of Hebrews, "the traditional title 'Christ' is not developed in any distinctive way." P. Ellingworth, "Jesus and the Universe in Hebrews," *CBQ* 30 (1968) 359-85. N. A. Dahl concludes, "In Hebrews 'Jesus' is a personal name while *Christos* is used with reference to Christ's rank and work as king and high priest." N. A. Dahl, "Messianic Ideas and the Crucifixion of Jesus," in Charlesworth, ed., *The Messiah*, 382-403. However, "Jesus" has similar messianic associations.

25. As B. Lindars claims, "Hebrews here reproduces the apostolic proclamation that Jesus is the Messiah and builds on a well-established tradition of proof-texts in support of it." B. Lindars, *The Theology of the Letter to the Hebrews* (Cambridge: Cambridge University Press, 1991) 35.

and his messianic relationship to central temple institutions: the sanctuary, the covenant, the Law, and the sacrifice. His function as high priest provides the basis of the believers' service in the temple and reconciliation with God so that they can follow Jesus into the Holy of Holies (10:19-22). The last third of Hebrews (10:19–13:25) applies Jesus' roles as messenger and high priest to the believer. The metaphor of running the race with Jesus as the author and finisher of our faith is another victory scenario in which the Messiah leads his people to the goal (12:1-17). The climax of Hebrews depicts the believers' access to God and Jesus in heavenly Jerusalem, which includes messianic restoration (12:18-28), and concludes with going to Jesus outside the earthly "camp" and offering priestly sacrifices of praise and doing good (13:13-16). The climax and conclusion of Hebrews ultimately map messianic enthronement and victory, particularly the victory of restoration and reconciliation, on the temple scenario, which has been developed far beyond Jesus' symbolic actions in the temple.

Barnabas Lindars speaks of how the earliest Christians not only discovered ways in which messianic prophecies were fulfilled in Christ but also "enlarged the scope of what was considered to be prophetic."[26] Wright describes Jesus' claim to Messiahship as one that "redefined itself around Jesus' own kingdom-agenda, picking up several strands available within popular messianic expectation but weaving them into a striking new pattern."[27] These dynamics were at work with the author of Hebrews, who significantly extended the temple scenario. Perhaps the process of inspiration involved the exposure of the author to the Qumran expectations of a priestly messiah and apocalyptic literature about Melchizedek. The author could have looked again at the Scriptures and found that God had made a promise and an oath, declaring that One would be a priest forever according to the order of Melchizedek (Heb 7:17-22; cf. Ps 110:4).

Christ in the Book of James

The Jewish origin of the book of James has been widely accepted.[28] J. H. Charlesworth notes that it is difficult to "judge if a document is essentially

---

26. Lindars, *Theology of the Letter to the Hebrews*, 52.
27. Wright, *Jesus and the Victory of God*, 538.
28. Among other internal evidence, such as the sociological situation characterized

Jewish or Christian. Perhaps it is also time to examine some old problems; for example, have we assessed accurately James, Hebrews and Revelation by labeling them simply 'Christian'?"[29] In fact, the Jewish character of James is so prevalent and the explicit Christology so scarce that some have suggested that the work is not Christian.[30] The author is identified in the letter as James, traditionally linked with James the half-brother of Jesus, and a pillar in the Jewish-Christian church in Jerusalem. This is not inconsistent with the register of the letter, except that the literary quality of the Greek is unexpectedly high. James exhibits intertextuality with the wisdom literature in the Hebrew Bible, other Jewish literature, and the Greek version of the Sermon on the Mount in Q.[31] The recipients are identified as "the twelve tribes dispersed abroad." At most, we can say, "the author looks on the recipients of the epistle as the true Israel," and the word διασπορά would appear to indicate the part of Judaism living outside of Palestine, though some scholars think the word is metaphorical.[32] Given a Jewish Palestinian origin or a Hellenistic Jewish setting, the author would understand messianic scenarios.[33]

There are only two occurrences of χριστός in James (1:1; 2:1), and both occur with the name of Jesus. In 1:1, "Jesus Christ" occurs with "Lord" and possibly "God"[34] and is coupled with James's identity as "slave" or "servant." Some dismiss the phrase "servant/slave of the Lord Jesus Christ" as "formulaic."[35] However, P. Perkins states that in such a context, "the

---

by conflict between the rich and poor, the Palestinian origin is suggested by Jas 5:7, which is characteristic of the Palestinian climate more than other options. P. Davids, *The Epistle of James* (NIGTC; Grand Rapids: Eerdmans, 1982) 14.

29. J. H. Charlesworth, *Jesus within Judaism: New Light from Exciting Archaeological Discoveries* (New York: Doubleday, 1988) 31.

30. See Davids, *James,* 14-15 for arguments against the Christian character of James.

31. For the literary relations of James with Jewish and Greco-Roman literature, see L. T. Johnson, *The Letter of James* (New York: Doubleday, 1995) 26-88.

32. Davids, *James,* 63.

33. However, among some scholars there is a shift away from an early date and Palestinian origin in favor of a later date and diaspora setting. "Scholars most often cite Hellenistic sources, not Semitic ones, to explain details." J. Reumann, "Christology of James," in Powell and Bauer, eds., *Who Do You Say That I Am?* 128-39, see p. 129.

34. Some have suggested 1:1 should be translated as "servant of Jesus Christ, God and Lord" because of the syntactic parallel with 1:27: "before God the Father"

θεοῦ καὶ κυρίου Ἰησοῦ Χριστοῦ δοῦλος (1:1)
παρὰ τῷ θεῷ καὶ πατρί (1:27)

35. Blomberg, "Messiah in the New Testament," 134.

christological titles 'Lord' and 'Master' remind the audience of the disgrace attached to rejecting a divine benefactor,"[36] and Bauckham similarly claims that the phrase suggests that Christians have been bought from captivity or slavery.[37] Similar phrases occur in salutations in Rom 1:1, Phil 1:1, Jude 1, and 2 Pet 1:1. The rate of occurrence in both the New Testament and the Hebrew Bible (servant of God)[38] would classify the phrase as a common collocation rather than formulaic; therefore the collocation of "Lord" and "slave" is best taken as a patron-client reference that evokes a messianic enthronement scenario. The other occurrence of χριστός in 2:1 evokes a clearer enthronement scenario. It is a command not to show favoritism while having faith in "our glorious Lord Jesus Christ." Lordship and obedience are at issue, while "glorious" points toward enthronement and most likely refers to the exalted position of the Messiah.[39]

James activates enthronement and victory scenarios in the rest of the epistle. The poor believer is raised up in status, given a crown of life, and declared to be an heir of the kingdom, while the humble believer will be exalted by God (1:5, 9, 12; 4:10). God gives birth to believers by the word of truth so that they become a kind of first fruits of what has been created (1:18). While lordship and obedience characterize the texture of James, messianic victory scenarios are also evoked. The most natural understanding of the "word of truth" that causes birth and "the implanted word that is able to save your souls" is that it refers to Jesus (1:18, 21), and "the law of liberty" would be his teaching (1:25). A strong eschatological victory sce-

---

36. P. Perkins, "Christ in Jude and 2 Peter," in Powell and Bauer, eds., *Who Do You Say That I Am?* 153-65, see p. 156.

37. Bauckham states: "The more characteristic Christian phrase became 'servant of Jesus Christ,' suggesting the idea that Christians have been bought by Christ from captivity or slavery and now belong to him as his slaves. . . . The phrase could be used of those called to special service, Christian workers, not as an indication of privileged rank, but, as in the case of the term διάκονος ('servant'), indicating that the Christian worker exemplifies the servant role which all God's people are called to play." R. J. Bauckham, *Jude, 2 Peter* (Waco: Word, 1983) 23.

38. Abraham (Ps 105:42), Moses (Neh 9:14), David (Ps 89:3), and Daniel (Dan 6:20) are all called the servant of God.

39. However, this is taking the genitive δόξης in the phrase τὴν πίστιν τοῦ κυρίου ἡμῶν Ἰησοῦ Χριστοῦ τῆς δόξης as either a genitive of quality (Messiah of glory) or apposition (glorious Lord Jesus), because the word order would indicate that it modifies Christ or Jesus rather than faith or favoritism. See Reumann for the other interpretive possibilities (Reumann, "Christology of James," 131).

nario includes judgment (2:12-13; 4:12; 5:9; cf. 5:1) and references to the last days and the coming of the Lord, the Messiah (5:3, 7, 9).

While the Christology is less explicit in James, the lordship and the eschatological coming of the Messiah are pervasive in the epistle. The references to lordship and the parousia would activate a fuller body of messianic information, particularly in a community with a Jewish background.

Christ in 1 Peter

The register of 1 Peter is an interesting conundrum. The traditional authorship of Peter the Apostle through Silvanus that is attested in the discourse (1:1; 5:12) is questioned by the majority of scholarship. Some suggest that it originated with a Petrine "circle" located in Rome,[40] which would associate 1 Peter with Jewish Christianity in any event. Unlike the other General Epistles, the internal evidence suggests that the recipients were largely Gentiles (1:14, 18; 2:9-10, 12, 25; 3:6; 4:3-4). On the other hand, J. R. Michaels observes, "No NT letter is so consistently addressed, directly or indirectly, to 'Israel,' that is (on the face of it) to Jews" (1:17; 2:6, 9, 11).[41] The author chose to address them as if they were Jews, without any language that displaces Judaism.[42] The deliberate use of Hebrew Scripture is one of the distinguishing features of the epistle. Michaels asserts:

> 1 Peter is linked to Judaism not by the law, but by a shared self-understanding. The author sees himself and his readers as a community situated in the world in much the same way the Jews are situated and sharing with the Jews a common past. . . . If they began to see themselves

40. Bauckham insists that there would not be a Petrine "school" because there are no theological resemblances between 1 and 2 Peter to be explained: "The authors cannot both be *disciples* of Peter who share a common debt to Peter's teaching. If both letters derive from a Petrine 'circle,' the circle cannot be a 'school' with a common theology, but simply a circle of colleagues who worked together in the leadership of the Roman church" (Bauckham, *Jude, 2 Peter*, 146).

41. J. R. Michaels, *1 Peter* (Waco: Word, 1988) xlv.

42. Eusebius claimed that Peter wrote to "those of the Hebrews" in the "Dispersion of Pontus and Galatia, Cappadocia, Asia and Bithynia." Michaels sympathizes: "Even though the testimony of Eusebius is not a reliable guide to the audience of 1 Peter, his mistake was a natural one" (Michaels, *1 Peter*, xlvi).

as 'honorary Jews' . . . , they also began to see the heroes and heroines of the Jewish stories they loved as "honorary Christians."[43]

Some scholars find intertextuality with *1 Enoch* in the reference to the preaching to the spirits in prison in 1 Pet 3:19.[44] If so, the reference would assume that the readers know *1 Enoch* so that they would understand the identity of the spirits in prison and the context in which the preaching took place. In that case, the messianic references to the "Son of Man" in the section of the *Similitudes* and the various references to the apocalypse would also be shared information. Furthermore, their repertoire would most likely include additional apocryphal and pseudepigraphical works.[45] The Jewish orientation of the epistle and the author's and recipients' probable familiarity with messianic literature suggest conversance with messianic concepts.

There are twenty-two occurrences of χριστός in 1 Peter. "Jesus Christ" occurs eight times, and "Christ" occurs alone thirteen times. "Jesus" never occurs alone.[46] Every occurrence of "Christ" is linked with a messianic scenario, and all three scenarios occur in 1:2: believers have been chosen and destined by God the Father and sanctified by the Spirit to be obedient to Jesus Christ and to be sprinkled by his blood, and grace and peace are invoked for them. Enthronement is the most dominant scenario that occurs with "Christ." The identification of believers with their Messiah through suffering is the most common theme (2:21; 3:16; 4:1, 14; 5:1).

As in Hebrews, an abundance of signals evokes messianic scenarios throughout the book. In addition to the identification of the believers with their suffering Christ, other messianic themes merit highlighting. The well-

---

43. Michaels, *1 Peter*, 1.

44. C. L. Westfall, "The Relationship between the Resurrection, the Proclamation to the Spirits in Prison and Baptismal Regeneration: 1 Peter 3.19-22," in *Resurrection* (ed. S. E. Porter, M. A. Hayes, and D. Tombs; Sheffield: Sheffield Academic Press, 1999) 106-35, see pp. 124-29. See also W. Dalton, "The Interpretation of 1 Peter 3,19 and 4,6: Light from 2 Peter," *Bib* 60 (1979) 546-55. Dalton argues that the author of 2 Peter used 1 Peter as a source, so that 2 Peter gives a clarification of the identity of the spirits in prison.

45. For a general description of *1 Enoch*, see J. J. Collins, "Enoch, Books of," in Evans and Porter, eds., *Dictionary of New Testament Background*, 313-18.

46. Blomberg suggests that perhaps the fact that "Jesus" never occurs uncompounded indicates that "Christ" really is a substitute name. However, he concurs that "there are no usages of *Christos* in this letter that could not preserve some nuances of its original meaning as 'messiah'" (Blomberg, "Messiah in the New Testament," 135-36).

developed passage on the believers' new birth to an inheritance in heaven and a salvation that is ready to be revealed in the last time evokes messianic enthronement and victory scenarios (1:3-9). The imagery of Jesus the cornerstone and the believers being built together into a temple that houses the presence of God is entwined with the priesthood of the believer (2:4-10). As in Hebrews, the temple scenario is developed beyond other New Testament literature by adding the concept of priesthood. As with Paul and in Hebrews, 1 Peter develops and explains how Jesus' death brought reconciliation, redemption, and restoration (1 Pet 1:18-20; 2:24; 3:18). As R. H. Stein states, "Jesus did not believe that he needed to provide detailed explanations of how his death would bring about forgiveness and seal the new covenant. He would leave to his followers the theological explanation."[47]

The development of the believers' inheritance, the sharing of Christ's suffering, and particularly the temple terminology, including Christ's sacrificial work and the priesthood of the believer, are related to messianic scenarios. The theology of the early church did not develop in a vacuum, but drew on and advanced messianic beliefs that were shared or recognized by Jewish Christians.

Christ in 2 Peter

2 Peter makes a direct claim to Petrine authorship. However, it displays distinct differences in style from 1 Peter that may have been accounted for by the use of an amanuensis other than Silvanus, or even by the direct authorship of Peter. However, the majority of scholars hold that 2 Peter is pseudonymous and probably written by another member of the Petrine circle in Rome. Regardless of the authorship, the occasion for writing the epistle demonstrates a clear engagement with messianic scenarios. The occasion for the letter is a polemic against opponents who denied the Parousia of Jesus Christ.[48] Intertextuality plays a large role in the discussion on 2 Peter.[49] What is most remarkable is its probable dependence on either Jude or a common apocalyptic source and its reference in 3:15-16 to Paul's letters as

47. R. H. Stein, *Jesus the Messiah* (Downers Grove, IL: InterVarsity Press, 1996) 153. See also Rom 3:24-26; 2 Cor 5:21; Titus 2:14; Heb 2:11-18; 1 John 2:2.

48. For further discussion of the opponents to apostolic teaching on the Parousia, see Bauckham, *Jude, 2 Peter*, 154-56.

49. See Bauckham, *Jude, 2 Peter*, 138-51.

Scripture. Besides intertextual ties with the Hebrew Scripture, 1 Peter, Pauline letters, and Gospel traditions, there is an allusion to *1 Enoch* (2:4) and an apocalyptic source such as the *Book of Eldad and Modad.*

Χριστός occurs eight times in 2 Peter, and every time it occurs with "Jesus." However, it also occurs with "savior" four times, which is a messianic reference (1:1, 11; 2:20; 3:18). It is interesting that even though the epistle is particularly concerned about the Parousia, "Christ" occurs with enthronement and victory scenarios that are more concerned with present ethical behavior (1:1, 8; 2:20; 3:18).

The account of the transfiguration of Jesus in 1:16-19 evokes a powerful messianic enthronement scenario. Along with the Father-Son language, the terminology of "power," "majesty," "honor," "glory," and "majestic glory" is royal. However, the transfiguration in context is used to support the apostolic prophetic teachings about the second coming. It more fully confirms the prophetic message (1:19).[50] The author's presentation of the knowledge of the Lord as the basis of piety is developed in ch. 1 (1:2, 4, 5-6, 8), then extensively illustrated by a polemic against false teachers in ch. 2 who bring in destructive opinions and "deny the Master who bought them" (2:1); after they have escaped the defilements of the world through the knowledge of Christ they become ensnared again (2:20). This evokes a victory scenario that is concerned with the present aspects of salvation experienced through the messianic provision of revelation/knowledge. However, it is linked with the acknowledgment or denial of the lordship of Christ, the Messiah and Master. The eschatological victory scenario in 3:3-10 is not only concerned with the denial of the Parousia but is also linked with a concern for ethical behavior (3:11-14). Apostolic eschatological teaching and knowledge about the second coming of the Messiah is viewed as essential and is meant to produce holy behavior in the present.

Therefore, 2 Peter has a very high percentage of messianic content, which maps current victory in righteousness on eschatological victory and utilizes enthronement scenarios for support and confirmation.

---

50. Perkins asserts: "The author's argument has only one point to make: The divine glory conferred on Jesus at the transfiguration is evidence for the truth of apostolic teaching about his second coming in power (Matt. 24:30; Mark 9:1; 13:26; Luke 21:27). Therefore, 2 Peter pursues a new exegetical reading of the story: The divine glory evident at the Parousia was witnessed there" (Pheme Perkins, "Christ in Jude and 2 Peter," in Powell and Bauer, eds., *Who Do You Say That I Am?* 155-65, see p. 161.

Christ in Jude

Jude is often treated after or before 2 Peter because of the parallels between them. The epistle claims to be written by "Jude the brother of James," and the traditional view is that he is the half-brother of Jesus. Among other problems concerning authorship, the Greek is considered too sophisticated for a Galilean Jew. It is difficult to reconstruct the situation of the author or the recipients, except that it addresses the rejection of all moral authority (antinomianism) by appealing to apocalyptic Jewish writings.

There are six occurrences of "Christ" in Jude, which is significant in so short a book. Each occurrence collocates with "Jesus," but four of the six occurrences also include "Lord." In v. 4, Jesus is referred to as "our only Master and Lord Jesus Christ." Jude refers to himself as "a slave of Jesus Christ" in v. 1. These patterns alone demonstrate a concern with Jesus' Lordship, evoking an enthronement scenario. The closing verse is interesting: "to the only God our Savior, through Jesus Christ our Lord, be glory, majesty, power, and authority, before all time and forever." Jesus is a preexistent source or agent who contributes to God's enthronement, and God is called "savior" rather than Jesus. Rather than reflecting a low Christology, Jude is fusing the identities.[51]

Jude's primary concern is expressed in vv. 3-4. He is concerned that the salvation his recipients share may be perverted into licentiousness. In v. 8, he describes the behavior of "intruders": "These dreamers also defile the flesh, reject authority, and slander the glorious ones." This behavior perverts the grace of the Lord and Master Jesus Christ. It is a rejection of the Messiah's lordship and rule. The recipients are told that such behavior is a sign that they are in the "last time," and they are to look forward to the mercy of Jesus Christ that leads to eternal life, which is a messianic expectation of victory.

Christ in the Johannine Epistles

The Johannine epistles are formally anonymous. The traditional view on authorship holds that the epistles, particularly 1 John, were written by the same author as the Gospel of John. Recent scholarship has favored the view that the Gospel and epistles are the product of a Johannine community or school.

51. Perkins, "Jude and 2 Peter," 158.

Another current view that has received wide support claims that the Gospel was written "to undergird a Christian community that had been recently expelled from the Jewish synagogue."[52] If John the apostle is the author of the Johannine corpus, the use of "Messiah" or "Christ" would be consistent with the Gospel. If the Johannine corpus is written by the Johannine community, we may have as a context a community breaking with the parent religion of Judaism. When we see the term "Christ," it would be endowed with Hebrew thought, even though it would now be "a thoroughly Christian community, independent of and distinct from Judaism."[53]

There are six occurrences of "Jesus Christ" in 1 John, and two occurrences where the author states: "Who is the liar but the one who denies Jesus is the Christ? Everyone who believes that Jesus is the Christ has been born of God" (2:22; 5:1).[54] The confession and belief that Jesus is the Christ/Messiah are depicted as essential. In view of the Jewish orientation of the epistle, it is unlikely that "Christ" here is a reference to Jesus' full divinity and humanity rather than his messiahship, as suggested by Stephen Smalley.[55] Six out of eight occurrences have a near reference to Father-Son terminology. Each occurrence of "Christ" evokes the enthronement scenario that involves the relationship between the royal Messiah and his people. There are two interesting references to the believers' anointing in 2:27, which form a cohesive tie with Christ, the anointed one. U. C. von Wahlde states, "Just as Jesus was *christos*, so the believer is also."[56] Anointing and kinship belong to the believer through Jesus. Conversely, those who abandon the community, deny the Father and the Son, and do not confess that Jesus is from God or that he came in the flesh are antichrists, just as the liar and deceiver expected at the last hour is the antichrist (2:18, 22; 4:3; cf. 2 John 1:7). The terms "antichrist" and "antichrists" occur only in the Johannine epistles and are associated with the denial of the kinship between Jesus and the believers and the rejection of the more generic messianic scenario of Jesus being sent.

---

52. L. M. McDonald and S. E. Porter, *Early Christianity and Its Sacred Literature* (Peabody, MA: Hendrickson, 2000) 307.

53. U. C. von Wahlde, *The Johannine Commandments: 1 John and the Struggle for the Johannine Tradition* (New York: Paulist Press, 1990) 1.

54. Blomberg claims, "Clearer evidence emerges in these final texts for an unambiguously titular 'Christ' than in all the previous New Testament Epistles surveyed" (Blomberg, "Messiah in the New Testament," 137).

55. S. S. Smalley, *1, 2, 3 John* (Waco: Word, 1984) 113-14.

56. Von Wahlde, *Johannine Commandments,* 146.

The rest of 1 John is dominated by kinship terminology, which activates an enthronement scenario. The relationship between the Father and the Son is associated inseparably with Messiahship (e.g., 2:22-23). Similarly, the relationship between the believers and the Son and Father is associated inseparably with love for each other (1:10-11; 3:14-18; 4:7-12). There are also references to being born into the family of God, and there is even a reference to God's seed (σπέρμα) abiding in them (3:9; 4:7; 5:4). The believers are called children repeatedly, although the term was used interchangeably for God's children and John's "children." Therefore, a primary concern is family relationship, which is also described as fellowship or abiding in God. The antithesis to being in a family relationship with the Father and Son is the antichrist who denies Jesus' Messiahship or his incarnation (2:18-23; 4:2-3; 5:1). Those who sin also are not in relationship with the Father and Son (1:6; 3:8-10; 5:18). In addition, as in Hebrews and 1 Peter, theological explanations are offered for Jesus' sacrifice for sins that evoke a temple scenario. He was revealed to take away sin, he laid down his life for us, his blood cleanses us from sin, and he is the atoning sacrifice for the sins of the whole world (1:7; 2:2; 3:5, 16; 4:10). Victory scenarios are evoked by conquest terminology and eschatological hope. The believer has shared in Jesus' messianic conquest and conquered the devil, the spirit of the antichrist, and the world (2:13-14; 4:4; 5:4-5). The believer who abides in him will have confidence in the Messiah's second coming (2:28). The one who hopes to be like him when he is revealed purifies himself or herself (3:2-3). The one who has love perfected will have boldness on the day of judgment (4:17). John depicts the believers' reconciliation with God the Father as a symbiotic relationship or network that must include the messianic Son, love for God's people, and ethical behavior.

Second John and particularly 3 John do not add significant new information to the messianic concepts in 1 John. In 2 John, the antichrist is again identified as one who will not confess that Jesus was incarnated (v. 7). The command for the believers to guard themselves so they will receive a full reward is somewhat different (v. 8), but the belief that an eschatological hope in the Messiah's second coming should effect our current righteousness is not unique. "Abiding" is given a slightly different spin, because it involves abiding in the teaching and not going beyond it (v. 9). Whoever abides in Christ's teaching has both the Father and the Son. This letter with thirteen verses evokes messianic victory and enthronement scenarios, and "Christ" occurs in the letter three times. The explanation and development of the concept of the Messiah in Jewish Christianity permeate the literature.

Conclusion

In Hebrews and the General Epistles, we are dealing with churches that are arguably Jewish in orientation if not in unalloyed composition. Furthermore, much of this corpus displays some degree of intertextuality with the Hebrew Bible as well as Jewish apocalyptic and pseudepigraphical literature, which is often characterized by messianic content. In such contexts, the identification of Jesus as the Christ was not void of messianic content. Furthermore, if Wright is correct in his identification of terminology, images, and symbols that Jesus utilized in the Gospels to identify himself as the Messiah, then similar patterns occur in Hebrews and the General Epistles that continue to develop the implications of Jesus' messiahship. Enthronement, victory, and temple scenarios evoked a messianic frame among the early Hellenistic and Palestinian Jewish Christians, in such a way that much of the Christology in Hebrews and the General Epistles should be regarded as messianic.[57] The authors of Hebrews and the General Epistles not only enlarged the scope of what was considered prophetic in the Hebrew Bible, but they were possibly inspired by the variety of messianic expectations and made unique associations with the work of Christ in unexpected ways. Hebrews, 1 Peter, and 1 John provided a theological explanation for how Jesus' death would bring about forgiveness and the new covenant. First John exploited kinship terminology to explain our relationship with God and each other. Hebrews and 1 Peter explained Jesus' relationship to the temple in new ways. Hebrews provided the most detailed and arguably the most original messianic Christology in the New Testament. However, this corpus of literature has often been overlooked in discussions about the Messiah. Part of that may be due to narrow definitions of the concept of Messiah, and part of it may be due to the fact that scholars and theologians have been interested in christological questions that the texts did not answer.

---

57. I do not wish to overstate the presence of messianic themes in this corpus. There is christological information and there are concepts that lie outside of what should be considered as essentially messianic, such as Jesus' divinity.

The Messiah in the Old and New Testaments: A Response

Craig A. Evans

Introductory Comments

The nature and importance of messianism for early Judaism and Christianity continue to be explored and debated. The definition of messianism and how far back it may be traced are among the points that are the most sharply disputed. Simply put, is there messianism in the Old Testament, and, if there is, how does it compare to the messianism expressed in the New Testament? Another important question concerns the extent to which messianism played a role in the shaping of the theologies of various expressions of Judaism and Christianity. What were the messianic ideas with which Jesus and his followers were familiar? Which parts of these ideas were adopted by Jesus and the writers of the New Testament? And finally, does the messianism of the respective New Testament writers cohere and perhaps even form a unity?

The scholars in this volume have wrestled with these difficult questions. To their credit, they have allowed their respective biblical authors to have their say, without foisting upon them a harmonizing synthesis that hopes to smooth away diversity and tension. In my judgment, a great strength in this collection of studies, and the conference out of which they grew, is the freshness of the approaches that are taken. I find no over-trod pathways and predictable conclusions. On the whole, these essays are marked by innovation and insight. It is a pleasure to respond to them.

Tremper Longman III, "The Messiah: Explorations in the Law and Writings"

Tremper Longman has framed the issue well, recognizing that there is nothing in the Torah and Writings that is explicitly messianic, in the sense understood in later times. Yet, later writers did find messianism in the Law and the Writings. By what hermeneutical strategy were they able to do this? Longman's question is right to the point. I found his paper very stimulating.

He rightly begins with the definition of the term *Messiah*. The word tells us little, but other concepts offer some help. The verb *māšaḥ* and the noun (or adjective) *māšîaḥ* usually refer to consecration rituals. In the Law the reference is to priests, consecrated for the Lord's cultic work. In the Writings the reference is mostly to Israel's kings (reflecting custom and usage of the narratives of Samuel-Kings). Longman focuses on the Psalter: Psalm 2, possibly a coronation psalm, perhaps also recited on the eve of holy war. Although it is not explicitly Davidic, the echoes of the Davidic covenant of 2 Samuel 7 encourage understanding Psalm 2 as Davidic (as, indeed, the author of Acts in the New Testament understands it, and as the author of 1QSa also understands it).

Placed at the beginning of the Psalter, Psalm 2 may have set the tone for all that follows, especially those psalms that refer to the Lord's anointed. Longman wonders if perhaps the remarkable claims of this psalm helped to create the hope of a future king who would live up to them, given the fact that Israel's historic kings had not. In my judgment, Longman's critique of Gerald Wilson's theory of the theme underlying the Psalter's organization is devastating.

The "greater king who would derive from the Davidic line [as reflected in Gen 49:10 and Num 24:17] might have captured the imagination of the people."[1] Indeed, it appears that it did just that. These texts are paraphrased explicitly as messianic in the Aramaic paraphrase of Scripture known as the Targum. These texts are also understood in a messianic sense in the New Testament era and earlier, as we see in the Dead Sea Scrolls and in allusions to them in the New Testament, Philo, and Josephus. And for those who object to an appeal to the Targum, which after all postdates the New Testament, I offer the reminder that the edited form of the Hebrew

---

1. Tremper Longman III, "The Messiah," 25.

Bible, the Masoretic Text, is no older. I mention this because of a comment that Longman makes in a footnote,[2] in which he wonders how Gen 49:10 might have been "understood within the context of the original author and audience of Genesis." Very good question. But what is meant by this "original author and audience" is very difficult to say. Genesis 49, edited and contextualized as we now have it in the Hebrew Bible, may well have reflected messianic hope — if not for the original author, probably for many of the earliest readers and hearers.

Professor Longman raises some interesting questions in his discussion of Genesis 14 and Psalm 110. I have little to add, but I might point out that the priest-king of Psalm 110 may well have encouraged the men of Qumran to give priority to the priests in the preparation for and engagement of the great holy war at the end of days, when the sons of light destroy the sons of darkness.[3] One should also recall that monarchs in antiquity often did take on priestly roles. Even the Roman emperor, of a later era, was called *Pontifex Maximus,* "High Priest," as well as *Imperator,* "Commander." Closer to the Jewish context, the Hasmonean rulers were priest-kings, at least some of them (e.g., Aristobolus I, Alexander Jannaeus, and perhaps Antigonus, the last Hasmonean ruler). Therefore, even if elsewhere in Scripture there is expressed resistance to kingly encroachment upon priestly roles, there was a measure of precedent in the twilight of the post-exilic/intertestamental era.

I encourage Professor Longman to give more attention to the mysterious figure described in Daniel 7,[4] especially in light of the fact that it is this figure to whom Jesus refers and probably in light of which he himself defines his messianic task (e.g., Mark 2:10, 28; 8:31; 10:45; 14:62). Longman is right to look at Deuteronomy 18, a passage alluded to in the New Testament (e.g., Mark 6:15; John 1:21; Acts 3:22; 7:37) and greatly emphasized in Samaritan traditions of late antiquity (e.g., *Memar Marqa* 4:12).

The role of Isaiah in the ministry of Jesus and in the exchange between him and the imprisoned John the Baptist is a very interesting area of study. In my view, Jesus' allusion to healing and exorcism is meant to allay John's doubts ("Go and tell John what you hear and see"; Matt 11:2-6; Luke

---

2. Longman, "The Messiah," 25n.22.
3. As seen especially in the War Scroll (1QM, 4QM).
4. I am, of course, classifying Daniel as prophecy, which reflects the Christian view of the canon of Scripture, not the rabbinic view.

7:18-23). These activities of Jesus did not create the doubts. It was John's languishing in prison that created them. After all, according to Isa 61:1-2, on which Jesus bases his Nazareth sermon (Luke 4:16-30), the Anointed One is to set the captives free. Therefore, Jesus alludes to this Isaianic passage in his reply to John. We do not know if this reply satisfied the imprisoned baptizer.

Professor Longman concludes that the "Old Testament did not provide the first century CE with a clear blueprint for the Messiah."[5] This is correct, strictly speaking. But more than one scholar has remarked how texts such as Gen 49:10; Num 24:17; and Isa 11:1 figure significantly in diverse Jewish circles, including Christian teachers and writers of the books that would eventually find their way into the New Testament, writers and collectors of the corpus we call the Dead Sea Scrolls, and various other intertestamental writers, including some of the Old Testament Pseudepigrapha, Josephus, and Philo. These same three Old Testament texts continue to be interpreted in essentially the same sense in later rabbinic and targumic traditions.

I agree that there was diversity in messianic expectation in late antiquity (and have said so myself in various places[6]), but there does seem to be a core of material out of which the diversity could spring. The rub for early Christians — and it was a big rub — was the crucifixion of Jesus. This made it necessary to ponder the Scriptures afresh, as Longman points out in his discussion of Luke 24. I will return to the question of diversity when I respond to Loren Stuckenbruck's paper below.

I greatly appreciate what Longman says under the heading of "Hermeneutical Implications." Those committed to a "single-meaning hermeneutic" struggle to do fair, descriptive exegetical analyses of many New Testament passages that cite and interpret Old Testament passages, often reading New Testament ideas into the Old, or downplaying the innovative element in the New Testament, claiming that it has not really added anything to the Old Testament text.

I would add to Longman's hermeneutical observations by returning to the point I made above. What we call *Bible* may indeed contain very old

---

5. Longman, "The Messiah," 30.
6. For example, see C. A. Evans, "Messianism," in *Dictionary of New Testament Background* (ed. C. A. Evans and S. E. Porter; Downers Grove, IL: InterVarsity Press, 2000) 698-707.

traditions, which in many cases are based on very old sources, but it is the Bible as a whole that is authoritative or canonical. That fact in effect updates its contents. I am not advocating ignoring ancient history or the data of archaeology that address the question of "what really happened"; I am saying that the Bible is in a sense a *contemporary* book, by virtue of its updating by various editors and tradents. The *original* meaning of Gen 49:10 may well have been messianic, in the full sense of the hope of a coming anointed deliverer. Of course, the dying patriarch Jacob very probably was not thinking of any such thing — beyond perhaps a general hope that the God of Abraham is faithful and saving. But the final editor that gave us what became the book of Genesis, in the context of what became the Bible, may well have thought of Genesis 49 as messianic.

I conclude with an example of what I mean, an example that has nothing to do with messianism. What do we make of Deut 26:2? It reads: "You shall take some of the first of all the fruit of the ground, which you harvest from your land that the LORD your God gives you, and you shall put it in a basket, and you shall go to the place which the LORD your God will choose, to make his name to dwell there." Most commentators recognize that the "place" that God will choose "to make his name to dwell" is Jerusalem and the temple. But did Moses know about Jerusalem and the temple? Moses probably did not, but a later editor did. Deuteronomy of the Bible — that is, *canonical* Deuteronomy — knows about Jerusalem and the temple that would eventually be built there. To see the temple in Deuteronomy 26 is not to "read something into the text," but to recognize something that *is* in the text, as it eventually came to be edited and finalized, not in the time of Moses, but in a much later time. Likewise in the case of messianism: it probably is in the Old Testament, the Bible, even if the concept itself does not reach back into the history that parts of the Old Testament narrate.

Mark J. Boda, "Figuring the Future: The Prophets and Messiah"

Mark Boda takes on what I believe is the most complicated area of Old Testament messianism. His learned paper is primarily focused on three of the Minor Prophets: Haggai, Zechariah, and Malachi.

I am delighted that Professor Boda investigates the meaning of the

curious designation "the two sons of oil" (cf. Zech 4:14). Without disputing the question of who were the original referents, I think it is interesting
that this unusual passage appears at Qumran in an eschatological commentary on Gen 49:8-12 (i.e., 4Q254), perhaps suggesting that among some
Jews in late antiquity the two sons of oil were none other than the anointed
king and the anointed high priest who will serve the Lord faithfully side by
side. This diarchic understanding of messianism seems to be an integral
part of Qumran's eschatology.[7] However, here I anticipate an issue that I
shall take up momentarily with Professor Wolters.

I especially appreciate Boda's treatment of Malachi and this book's
interest in the coming Day of the Lord and the messenger that is sent before, a concept that recalls covenant ideas expressed in Exodus 23. Readers
of the New Testament cannot fail to notice the citation of Mal 3:1, combined with Isa 40:3, in the introduction of John the Baptist in Mark 1. But
what often goes unnoticed is how deeply the Baptist is himself baptized in
the themes and images of the messenger prophet.[8]

I found most interesting Boda's observation regarding the *mal'āk
adonai* ("messenger of the Lord") figures, who are no mere mortals. We
may have here an important contribution to the messianic tradition that
created a matrix out of which early Christianity emerged.

As it turns out, the Minor Prophets play major roles in New Testament messianism and eschatology. Jesus, the resurrected son of David, fulfills the prophecy of Amos 9:11 (cf. Acts 15:15-18); the coming of the Spirit,
in the aftermath of the resurrection and ascension of Messiah Jesus, fulfills
the prophecy of Joel 2:28-32 (cf. Acts 2:14-21); while the birth of the Davidic
scion in Bethlehem fulfills the prophecy of Mic 5:2 (cf. Matt 2:1-6). Jesus
himself compares his ministry to that of Jonah, which the church later

---

7. For an investigation of the messianic diarchism of Zechariah and Haggai, see
J. J. M. Roberts, "The Old Testament's Contribution to Messianic Expectations," in *The Messiah: Developments in Earliest Judaism and Christianity* (ed. J. H. Charlesworth; Minneapolis:
Fortress, 1992) 39-51, esp. 40, 49-50. This Princeton conference volume offers a rich collection of studies.

8. See J. A. Trumbower, "The Role of Malachi in the Career of John the Baptist," and
J. D. G. Dunn, "John the Baptist's Use of Scripture," in *The Gospels and the Scriptures of Israel*
(ed. C. A. Evans and W. Richard Stegner; JSNTSup 104; SSEJC 3; Sheffield: Sheffield Aca-
demic Press, 1994) 28-41 and 42-54, respectively; and C. A. Evans, "The Baptism of John in a
Typological Context," in *Dimensions of Baptism: Biblical and Theological Studies* (ed. S. E.
Porter and A. R. Cross; JSNTSup 234; Sheffield: Sheffield Academic Press, 2002) 45-71.

would develop into a typology of death, burial, and resurrection "on the third day" (cf. Matt 12:38-41).

Al Wolters, "The Messiah in the Qumran Documents"

Professor Al Wolters provides us with a succinct distillation of the messianism at Qumran. The questions that he raises in his opening paragraph are indeed the questions that have driven research in this important area, and, sometimes, have actually hindered work — such as confusion over the question of one or two Messiahs at Qumran, a point to which I shall return in a moment.

Professor Wolters focuses his remarks on the recent work of two Scrolls scholars — John Collins and Michael Wise. His assessment of the arguments and contributions of Collins is in my judgment on the whole penetrating and sound. My only reservation concerns what is said about Zech 4:14, the passage that mentions the "two sons of oil," the question of Qumran's binary or diarchic messianism, and the larger question of why Qumran does not seem to be preoccupied with messianism.

Contrary to Professor Wolters, I think there is in fact a measure of evidence that Qumran appealed to Zech 4:14 in support of diarchic messianism. This evidence lies in the discovery of this distinctive phrase, that is, "the two sons of oil" (found nowhere else in Hebrew literature), in 4Q254, among the fragments of commentary on Gen 49:8-12, the oracle pertaining to Jacob's son Judah. Some Qumran scholars, however, wonder if the phrase from Zechariah 4 was part of the commentary on Gen 49:5-7, the oracle concerning Simeon and Levi.[9] In my view, it does not matter, for the "two sons of oil" apply to both Levi the priest and Judah the prince. This interesting fragmentary commentary, when taken in conjunction with the several references to the expected duo called "the anointed of Aaron and of Israel" (CD 2:12; 5:21–6:1; 12:23–13:1; 14:19; 19:10-11; 20:1; 1QS 9:11) — including the blessings on the priest and the prince in 1QSb 4-5 and their seating together in 1QSa 2:10-15, at what is an eschatological ban-

---

9. For further discussion of technical aspects of this line of interpretation, see C. A. Evans, "'The Two Sons of Oil': Early Evidence of Messianic Interpretation of Zechariah 4:14 in 4Q254 4 2," in *The Provo International Conference on the Dead Sea Scrolls: Technological Innovations, New Texts, and Reformulated Issues* (ed. D. W. Parry and E. Ulrich; STDJ 30; Leiden: Brill, 1998) 566-75.

quet of sorts — provides significant evidence for the position that Collins takes. Nevertheless, I find that Professor Wolters's criticism is on the whole on target.

The reason why messianism at Qumran is not clearer, as Wolters rightly observes, is that it is not emphasized. And the reason it is not emphasized is not for lack of interest; it is for lack of controversy. What is at issue with the men of the renewed covenant is the lack of cultic accuracy and the sorry deficiency, in their view, of priestly ethics in Jerusalem. There is no anointed Jewish king to criticize, just the anointed priest and his corrupt colleagues. Because *God* will raise up the Messiah in due course, it is assumed that the anointed prince will be righteous and will follow the guidelines set out by the righteous priests of the renewed covenant, who anticipate restoring true worship and good government in Israel someday. These observations explain why Qumran's priestly and halakic views are distinctive at many points, while their messianism is not. The Messiah for whom they wait is not much different from the Messiah awaited by others.[10]

I appreciate Professor Wolters's critique of Michael Wise's imaginary reconstruction of the founding of the Qumran community and the life of its founder, who is called Judah. Wise does indeed put together a well-informed scenario of what might have been. To quote from my own jacket blurb, "there is much to learn from this engaging and well-written book." What I did not go on to say at that time was that I remain totally unpersuaded. I suspect that Wolters's jacket blurb for this book should be understood in the same spirit. Of it he says, "Simultaneously brilliant, daring, and readable." Professor Wolters and I learned much from this interesting book, to be sure; but at the end of the day, all that Wise gives us is informed fiction. I concur with Professor Wolters's skeptical assessment.

---

10. See C. A. Evans, "Qumran's Messiah: How Important Is He?" in *Religion at Qumran* (ed. J. J. Collins and R. Kugler; Studies in the Dead Sea Scrolls and Related Literature; Grand Rapids: Eerdmans, 2000) 135-49. For an assessment of Qumran's messianism, see L. H. Schiffman, "Messianic Figures and Ideas in the Qumran Scrolls," in Charlesworth (ed.), *The Messiah*, 116-29; and the papers in *Qumran-Messianism: Studies on the Messianic Expectations in the Dead Sea Scrolls* (ed. J. H. Charlesworth, H. Lichtenberger, and G. S. Oegema; Tübingen: Mohr [Siebeck], 1998). All of the messianic texts are listed in M. G. Abegg Jr. and C. A. Evans, "Messianic Passages in the Dead Sea Scrolls," in Charlesworth et al., eds., *Qumran-Messianism*, 191-203.

Loren T. Stuckenbruck, "Messianic Ideas in the Apocalyptic and Related Literature of Early Judaism"

Loren Stuckenbruck begins his paper with a refreshingly clear and precise set of guiding questions, marked by tight controls. He rightly wishes to avoid anachronism and slippery definitions. His selection of *Psalms of Solomon*, *Similitudes of Enoch*, *4 Ezra*, and *2 Baruch* constitutes a well-chosen data base. The potential gains in insight from a work such as the *Testaments of the Twelve Patriarchs* are offset by the uncertainty created by the many Christian interpolations, which often have messianism (or Christology) as their focus. Indeed, it has even been argued that the *Testaments* was originally composed by a Christian. Professor Stuckenbruck rightly omits it.

In *Psalms of Solomon* 17–18 we find a zealous, energetic messianic son of David, who will purge the land of sinners. He is not divine, nor does he have heavenly status. To be sure, he will enjoy divine assistance. In this sense, he is a true descendant of David, through whom the nation of Israel will be restored.

In the *Similitudes of Enoch* (or *1 Enoch* 37–71), which is probably pre-Christian in origin since there is no allusion or response to a specifically Christian idea, we find two passages that mention a Messiah. This Messiah is terrestrial, and he may not be Davidic (at least there is no indication that he is). We are told nothing about the nature of this Messiah. Is he divine? But if he is related to the mysterious Son of Man figure, inspired by Daniel 7, then the Messiah of the *Similitudes* may well be a heavenly figure of some sort. The title "Messiah" does not seem to have shaped the author's messianism as much as the Son of Man figure has.[11]

In *4 Ezra* 7 we have the interesting anticipation that the Messiah and all of humanity will die. There will be a time of silence. The Messiah's death appears to be natural; he is not martyred. His death has no value, atoning or otherwise. The Messiah has no further role.

The Messiah of *4 Ezra* 11–12 plays a different role, taking part in eschatological judgment. In *4 Ezra* 13 the messianic ("my son") figure once again

---

11. The Princeton conference volume (i.e., Charlesworth, ed., *The Messiah*) has several important studies that investigate the messianism of the book of *Enoch*. See F. H. Borsch, "Further Reflections on 'The Son of Man': The Origins and Development of the Title," 130-44; M. Black, "The Messianism of the Parables of Enoch: Their Date and Contributions to Christological Origins," 145-68; J. C. VanderKam, "Righteous One, Messiah, Chosen One, and Son of Man in 1 Enoch 37–71," 169-91.

appears as a judge. I agree with Stuckenbruck's appeal to Ps 2:2, 7, which is also seen in 1QSa: "when God will beget the Messiah among them." Psalm 2, with its metaphorical language of the Lord's Messiah as "begotten," makes important contributions to the messianism of New Testament times.

Professor Stuckenbruck finds a different messianic figure in 2 *Baruch*. The Messiah is revealed and returns "with glory." The righteous are resurrected; the souls of the wicked will rot. This Messiah may be Davidic, perhaps even preexistent. Visions in other chapters foresee a Messiah who will slay Israel's enemies (probably including the Romans) and will sit in judgment on them in court at Jerusalem. A period of messianic bliss will follow.

Professor Stuckenbruck concludes by commenting on the messianic diversity of these Jewish writings of late antiquity. In general I agree with him; the diversity of views in these texts must be acknowledged. Nevertheless, there may be core elements. We find Isaiah 11 echoed in the *Psalms of Solomon* (cf. 17:24, 29, 36, 37) and in *4 Ezra* (cf. 13:10), as Stuckenbruck points out. The "son of man" figure of Daniel 7 is reflected in the *Similitudes of Enoch* and in *4 Ezra*. Three passages in particular — Gen 49:10; Num 24:17; Isa 11:1-10 — frequently appear in contexts that are messianic. But as has been shown in intertestamental writings surveyed here, messianism could be entertained without them.[12]

I. Howard Marshall,
"Jesus as Messiah in Mark and Matthew"

Professor Howard Marshall treats us to thoughtful overviews of the messianic portraits of Jesus as we have them in the Gospels of Mark and Matthew. With regard to Mark, I agree that in referring to himself as the "Son of Man" Jesus was alluding to Daniel 7 and that this passage readily invites a messianic identification. As Professor Marshall notes, the son of man is "given dominion and a kingdom from God."[13] Of whom else can that be said, except the Messiah?

---

12. Another factor to take into account is the date of these documents. Both *4 Ezra* and *2 Baruch* are post–70 CE, so perspectives of messianism may well have been altered in the years immediately following the disastrous rebellion.

13. I. Howard Marshall, "Jesus as Messiah in Mark and Matthew," 132.

There are three points with regard to Mark that I wish to raise. First, I would like to hear more of Professor Marshall's views of the role played by the heavenly voice at the baptism of Jesus (Mark 1:11) and at the later Transfiguration (Mark 9:7), where Jesus is addressed: "You are my son."[14] The allusion to Ps 2:7 seems clear; Psalm 2 is messianic (as seen esp. in v. 2). That it was understood this way in Jewish texts of late antiquity is seen in *4 Ezra* 13, as Loren Stuckenbruck has discussed, and probably in 1QSa 2, in reference to the time "when God will have begotten the Messiah." These two heavenly utterances in Mark's Gospel — the first at the outset of Jesus' public ministry in Galilee; the second shortly after Jesus' announcement to his disciples that he is going to Jerusalem to suffer and die — play a pivotal role. The heavenly voice seems both times to confirm the messianic identity of Jesus.

Second, Professor Marshall treats the "Son of Man" passages judiciously. He rightly comments on the abruptness of the first occurrence of this Danielic epithet in Mark 2 and goes on to explain its meaning in reference to the theme of suffering, which Jesus the Messiah will have to undergo. Daniel makes many other significant contributions to Mark's presentation of Jesus. The announcement of the rule of God in Mark 1:15 ("The time [*kairos*] is fulfilled, and the kingdom of God is at hand"; cf. 10:30; 13:33) probably reflects Daniel's frequent reference to the time of the end (Dan 7:12, 22: "the time [*kairos*] came when the saints received the kingdom"; 8:17-18: "Understand, O son of man, that the vision is for the time [*kairos*] of the end"; 9:26-27: "until the time [*kairos*] of the end"; 11:35: "until the time [*kairos*] of the end, for it is yet for the time [*kairos*] appointed"; 12:4: "shut up the words, and seal the book, until the time [*kairos*] of the end"). According to Dan 7:14, the Son of Man will be "given dominion and glory and kingdom, that all peoples, nations, and languages should serve him." But according to Jesus, the "Son of man also came not to be served but to serve" (Mark 10:45). This is a significant qualification of the Danielic vision, which coheres with the suffering theme that Professor Marshall discusses. Moreover, the very charge brought against Jesus at his hearing before the Jewish council, "We heard him say, 'I will destroy this temple that is made with hands, and in three days I will build another, not

---

14. The heavenly voice speaks in the second person ("You are") in the baptism and in the third person ("This is") in the Transfiguration. The second-person tradition is probably the older tradition and has the strongest claim to authenticity.

made with hands'" (Mark 14:58), surely alludes to Daniel's vision of the
coming stone that will crush the kingdoms that have opposed God and his
people: "a stone was cut out by no human hand, and it smote the image on
its feet of iron and clay, and broke them in pieces" (Dan 2:34; cf. v. 45).
Daniel's visions, especially that of the coming Son of Man, appear to un-
derlie essential components of the Christology and eschatology we find in
Mark.[15]

The third point has to do with the cry of blind Bartimaeus, "Jesus,
Son of David, have mercy on me!" (Mark 10:47; see v. 48 also). Professor
Marshall remarks that the "call for healing . . . does not explain the title."[16]
But perhaps it does, at least in part. I wonder if addressing Jesus as the son
of David has anything to do with Solomonic traditions, in which David's
famous son was well known for healing and exorcism. After all, it was in
his name that Jewish exorcists conducted their ministrations. We have the
example of Eleazar in Josephus, as well as examples in the magical papyri.[17] At least one exorcist, according to Mark 9:38, discovered that the
name of Jesus was effective in casting out demons.[18] It is plausible, then,
that Jesus' ministry of healing and exorcism, evidently consistent with prophetic expectations in Isaiah (such as 35:5-6 and 61:1-2), gave rise to the
hope in the minds of some that he was the awaited eschatological son of
David. Indeed, Qumran's 4Q521 alludes to these very Isaianic passages in
reference to expected healing when the Messiah appears. The blind man's
call for healing may well tell us something about Jesus' messianic status in
Mark.

With regard to the presentation of Jesus as Messiah in the Gospel of
Matthew, Professor Marshall's treatment is again concise and to the point.
The messianism is more explicit, at times almost formal. The royal component comes to the fore. The divine sonship of Jesus is also emphasized; so
is his role as the Lord's Servant. Jesus as teacher of wisdom and even as
Wisdom incarnate constitutes fascinating portraits in Matthew's presentation. Matthew's Messiah Jesus is seen at the end as God's vice regent of

---

15. See D. Wenham, "The Kingdom of God and Daniel," *ExpTim* 98 (1987) 132-34;
C. A. Evans, "Defeating Satan and Liberating Israel: Jesus and Daniel's Visions," *Journal for
the Study of the Historical Jesus* 1 (2003) 161-70.

16. Marshall, "Jesus as Messiah in Mark and Matthew," 127.

17. See Josephus, *Antiquities* 8.2.5 §§46-49; and *Papyri Graecae Magicae* IV.3007-86.

18. Professional exorcists, the seven sons of one Sceva, discovered that the name of Jesus was indeed powerful, but only when invoked by his followers (cf. Acts 19:11-20).

heaven and earth, in contrast to the Roman emperor. Here we have again a theme found in Mark that is then further developed in the Gospel of Matthew. Often what Mark alludes to (such as an Old Testament passage or theme) Matthew develops more fully and explicitly.

I find the portrait of Jesus as master teacher, as almost a new Moses, very interesting. This presentation of the Messiah may well be on the trajectory that will emerge more formally and emphatically in much later rabbinic texts where in the messianic era the Law is studied and obeyed perfectly.[19] Matthew's presentation of Jesus may represent an early stage in this concept. Of course, the presentation of a Torah-observant and Torah-teaching Messiah no doubt was intended to fend off criticism emanating from the synagogue, to the effect that the Jesus movement was antinomian.

Stanley E. Porter, "The Messiah in Luke and Acts: Forgiveness for the Captives"

Professor Stanley Porter argues the thesis that "a consistent and fundamental development of Jesus as the anointed prophet stands at the heart of Luke's depiction of Jesus as Messiah."[20] Porter's thesis is well founded. The prophetic emphasis is seen in the Lukan birth narrative, where one figure after another speaks oracles, sometimes as songs and sometimes specifically noted as due to the prompting of the Holy Spirit. Jesus himself is said to be filled with the Holy Spirit, traveling and ministering in the power of the Spirit. Of course, in his sermon in the Nazareth synagogue, Jesus quotes from Isaiah 61: "The Spirit of the Lord is upon me, because he has anointed me to preach. . . ." The Lukan Gospel ends on a note of prophetic fulfillment, with the risen Jesus instructing his disciples (Luke 24:25-27, 44-49; Acts 1:6-8).

The prophetic orientation of the Lukan infancy narrative is seen at

19. On this topic, see J. Neusner, *Messiah in Context: Israel's History and Destiny in Formative Judaism* (Philadelphia: Fortress, 1984) 189-90. This tradition is based on inferences, largely from the Psalter, that David, the prototype of the Messiah, occupied himself with Torah. On David as a scholar among the rabbis, see *b. Mo'ed Qatan* 16b. However, the rabbis themselves continue in their role as teachers of Torah.

20. Stanley E. Porter, "The Messiah in Luke and Acts: Forgiveness for the Captives," 145.

many points, not least in the points of contact with the story of Samuel, Israel's great priest, prophet, and judge. The births of Samuel and Jesus are brought about by God (1 Sam 1:9-20). Mary's Magnificat (Luke 1:46-55), in which she praises God for what has been done in her, parallels Samuel's mother Hannah's Magnificat (1 Sam 2:1-10), in which she thanks God for her son. The name of the elderly woman in Luke's story, who sings praise, is Anna (Luke 2:36-38), which is from the Hebrew name Hannah. Hannah dedicates Samuel to the temple, which becomes his house (1 Sam 1:21-28). Mary brings the infant Jesus to the temple (Luke 2:22-24), to which he later returns as a lad, calling the temple his Father's house (Luke 2:41-52). In the context of the temple, it is said of Samuel: "Now the boy Samuel continued to grow both in stature and in favor with the LORD and with men" (1 Sam 2:26). In what is clearly an echo of this passage, Luke says of the boy Jesus: "Jesus increased in wisdom and in stature, and in favor with God and man" (Luke 2:52).

Professor Porter also calls our attention to points of contact with the stories of the prophets Elijah and Elisha. The parallels here are not incidental but go straight to the heart of theological issues with which the Lukan evangelist is deeply concerned.[21] Elijah and Elisha provide the examples in Jesus' explication of Isaiah 61 in the Nazareth sermon (Luke 4:16-30, esp. vv. 25-27). The implication is that the ministries of these great prophets of old will shed light on the meaning of Jesus' prophetic ministry. This is indeed the case. The resuscitation of the widow's only son (Luke 7:11-17) offers a half dozen points of contact with the stories of Elijah and Elisha, both of whom raised only sons (cf. 1 Kings 17:17-24; 2 Kings 4:18-37). The incident in which the disciples wonder if Jesus should call fire down from heaven as judgment on the unwelcoming Samaritans (Luke 9:51-56) is a clear allusion to the fire that Elijah called down on the troops of the Samaritan king (2 Kings 1:9-16).[22] The rejection of the would-be follower, who wishes first to return home and bid farewell to his family (Luke 9:61-62), is an unmistakable allusion to Elijah's summons of Elisha (1 Kings 19:19-21). Parallels with other prophets and their various oracles confirm

---

21. Aspects of this interest are explored in C. A. Evans, "Luke's Use of the Elijah/Elisha Narratives and the Ethic of Election," in C. A. Evans and J. A. Sanders, *Luke and Scripture: The Function of Sacred Tradition in Luke-Acts* (Minneapolis: Fortress, 1993) 70-83.

22. The allusion to 2 Kings 1 was obvious to early Christian scribes, who glossed Luke 9:54-55 accordingly (cf. A C D and other authorities).

the inference that the Lukan evangelist has taken pains to highlight the prophetic dimension of Jesus' ministry.

In the book of Acts, Professor Porter rightly recognizes the programmatic function of the Pentecost sermon, on analogy with Jesus' Nazareth sermon in Luke. He also calls our attention to the prophetic role of David. This is no Lukan innovation, for there are pre-Christian Jewish traditions in which David is depicted as a prophet or as one moved by the Spirit of God (e.g., 11QPs^a 27). The parallel between Jesus and David is thus apparent. Prophetic fulfillment finds expression in Paul's later speeches in Acts.

An important concomitant are the hints in Acts that Jesus is the fulfillment of the promise of Moses that God would someday raise up a prophet like him: "I will raise up for them a prophet like you from among their brethren; and I will put my words in his mouth, and he shall speak to them all that I command him" (Deut 18:18). Twice this very passage is cited in reference to Jesus (cf. Acts 3:22-23; 7:37). Thus, the Lukan evangelist has appealed to an interesting diversity of prophetic traditions associated with Old Testament worthies who loomed large in Jewish late antiquity: David, Elijah, and Moses. Such an impressive collocation lends substantial support to the bold claim that in Jesus God has raised up a Messiah who will indeed bring forgiveness to the captives.

Tom Thatcher, "Remembering Jesus: John's Negative Christology"

Tom Thatcher interacts with current Johannine scholarship that has grappled with the complicated history of the development of Johannine literature, particularly the Gospel, and the Christology that it advances.[23] "John's Christology," we are told, "is a formula that makes it possible for Christians to construct memories of Jesus under the guidance of the Holy Spirit."[24]

Dr. Thatcher focuses on two "themes," or what may be better termed strategies: (1) the evangelist's "ability to generate images of Christ that op-

---

23. At many points Thatcher's approach to the Johannine literature is innovative. Readers may wish to consult his *The Riddle of Jesus in John: A Study in Tradition and Folklore* (SBLMS 53; Atlanta: Society of Biblical Literature, 2000); and his contributions to R. T. Fortna and T. Thatcher, *Jesus in Johannine Tradition* (Louisville: Westminster John Knox, 2001).

24. Tom Thatcher, "Remembering Jesus: John's Negative Christology," 175.

pose Jewish claims," particularly with regard to Moses; and (2) the evangelist's "ability to generate memories that oppose the Antichrists' claims."[25]

Concerning the first theme, Thatcher reviews in what ways the fourth evangelist portrays Jesus as superior to Moses. He is so "in every conceivable way, doing everything that Moses did and a great many things that Moses could never hope to do."[26] Thatcher mentions the Jewish teachers' self-designation: "we are disciples of Moses" (cf. John 9:28). This relevant observation opens up some interesting possibilities that Thatcher could pursue further. For example, he could delineate some of the numerous parallels with targumic and midrashic traditions, traditions generated by the "disciples of Moses,"[27] that is, the early rabbis and interpreters of Scripture in the synagogue.[28] These parallels are part of the evangelist's strategy, to find the common ground and, in effect, to prove that he is a better "disciple of Moses" than the unbelieving Jewish teachers of his time.

Concerning the second theme, Thatcher examines in what ways the evangelist counters those whose exalted Christology denies the reality of the humanity and incarnation of Jesus, along with his pre-Easter teaching. They deny Jesus' humanity and earthly ministry, they believe, by warrant of the Holy Spirit. Because they deny the earthly teaching of Jesus, these false teachers, who at one time would have been viewed by the evangelist as Christians, are designated "Antichrists." The elitism and divisiveness of these Antichrists stand in tension with the command to love one another.

Thatcher has again touched on a very interesting and potentially very enlightening theme. One may wonder if the Johannine author's reference to his opponents as "antichrists" *(antichristoi)* in 1 John 2:18 correlates to his assurance in 1 John 2:27 that true believers are to have God's "anointing" *(chrisma)*, which teaches them everything. In essence, the Johannine writer proposes a scenario in which warfare occurs between false christs (i.e., the "antichrists") and the true christs (i.e., the Johannine Christians who have received the divine anointing). The Johannine believers have received the anointing (or spirit) promised them by Jesus (as in the fourth Gospel's upper-room discourse in John 14–16) and therefore know the truth, a truth

25. Thatcher, "Remembering Jesus: John's Negative Christology," 177.

26. Thatcher, "Remembering Jesus: John's Negative Christology," 183.

27. For example, see *b. Yoma* 4a, where in the future, when the temple is rebuilt and sacrifice is restored, two "disciples of Moses" will train the new high priest.

28. See the survey in C. A. Evans, *Word and Glory: On the Exegetical and Theological Background of John's Prologue* (JSNTSup 89; Sheffield: JSOT, 1993) 151-68.

that is now assailed by false christs or falsely anointed ones. Dr. Thatcher does not pursue this line of interpretation, but it seems to me that it could shed light on aspects of his assessment of the Johannine opponents.

S. A. Cummins, "Divine Life and Corporate Christology: God, Messiah Jesus, and the Covenant Community in Paul"

Dr. Cummins divides his paper into three principal parts, each consisting of clearly delineated questions that take us right to the heart of the matter. In the first two parts he investigates Paul's faith before conversion and his faith after conversion. He rightly interprets 2 Cor 5:16 ("even though we once regarded Christ from a human point of view, we regard him thus no longer") as meaning that Paul's understanding of the Messiah has changed, not that the pre-Easter Jesus is of no interest.

It is clear that Paul's understanding of the Messiah changed with his conversion. But how did his understanding of monotheism change (assuming that it did)? That is a question that I would like Dr. Cummins to address more directly. Did God's revealing of his Son to Paul lead Paul to revise his understanding of the Godhead? Did it set him on a path leading to trinitarian theology? These are not easy questions, I realize, but I would like to hear more.[29] I wonder if Judaism's strict monotheism, which excludes hypostases, for example, is a reaction against Christianity? One thinks of the polemical interpretation of Isa 44:6 ("I am the first and I am the last; besides me there is no god"), which is applied against the Christian doctrine of the divinity of Jesus (cf. *Mek.* on Exod 20:2 [*Bahodesh* §5]; *Song Rab.* 1:9 §9). How would Philo have fared, had he spoken of the Logos as the second God *(theos)*[30] in the second or third century, instead of the early, pre-Christian first century?

29. That is, more than what is stated on pp. 197-98 of S. A. Cummins, "Divine Life and Corporate Christology: God, Messiah Jesus, and the Covenant Community in Paul." For a recent attempt to identify trinitarian elements in Paul's letters, see G. D. Fee, "Paul and the Trinity: The Experience of Christ and the Spirit of Paul's Understanding of God," in *The Trinity: An Interdisciplinary Symposium on the Trinity* (ed. S. T. Davis, D. Kendall, and G. F. O'Collins; Oxford: Oxford University Press, 1999) 49-72.

30. "For nothing moral can be made in the likeness of the most high One and Father of the universe, but [only] in that of the Second God, who is his Logos" (*Quaest. in Gen.* 2.62 [on Gen 9:6]; cf. *Fug.* 101; *Migr. Abr.* 174; *Op. Mund.* 20).

The third part of the paper speaks to Paul's ideas of monotheism, Messiah Jesus, and the eschatological people of God. Much of the discussion here focuses on the question of faith, works of the law, and fellowship (involving Jews and Gentiles). In Messiah Jesus the barriers that divided Jews from non-Jews are broken down. Non-Jews today are scarcely able to appreciate the dilemma that Paul and other Jewish believers in Jesus faced. The idea that the Law of Moses no longer had to be scrupulously observed was very difficult. Dr. Cummins explores this complicated problem, suggesting solutions along the way: the fulfillment of the Law in Jesus conveys fulfillment to the believer; believers are therefore excluded from divine condemnation.[31]

Cynthia Long Westfall, "Messianic Themes of Temple, Enthronement, and Victory in Hebrews and the General Epistles"

Cynthia Westfall wraps up our conference with an assessment of the messianic themes in Hebrews and the General Epistles. She examines the respective contexts of these writings and what bearing they may have on their messianic ideas, the occurrences of "Christ" in the respective writings, and the respective "authors' use of messianic scenarios."[32]

She then works her way systematically through Hebrews, James, 1-2 Peter, Jude, and 1-3 John. She finds a variety of approaches and emphases, and she calls attention to the messianic/christological innovations in Hebrews. If nothing else, Westfall's assignment illustrates the diversity of the writings of the New Testament and their respective strategies in formulating Christology, Christology not apparently restricted to what was available in contemporary Jewish messianic ideas and hopes.

The adoption of priestly scenarios in Hebrews is intelligible when it is remembered that most references to the "anointed" one in the Pentateuch are in fact to priests, usually the high priest. Once the identification of Jesus as "anointed" took hold — and indeed, became ubiquitous among his first followers — informing this designation with data under this head-

---

31. See Cummins, "Divine Life and Corporate Christology," 207-8. I would like Dr. Cummins to probe the contribution that Rom 10:4 could make to his insightful thesis: "For Christ is the end [*telos*] of the Law, in righteousness for everyone who has faith."

32. Cynthia Long Westfall, "Messianic Themes of Temple, Enthronement, and Victory in Hebrews and the General Epistles," 212.

ing was a natural consequence. Westfall's suggestions are consistent with this approach.

In 1 Peter, Dr. Westfall underscores enthronement, new birth, and the Christian community as a spiritual building, all of which are evocative images. 2 Peter is distinctive for recalling the story of the Transfiguration (Mark 9:2-8 and parallels). First John is distinctive for describing the believer, and not just Jesus, as "anointed." Thus we have "christs" in the plural, the possible significance of which was probed above in connection with Tom Thatcher's paper. Here it might be added that the Johannine writer has introduced an innovative element into the more familiar eschatological scenario in which the fearful antichrist figure was expected soon to arise. Westfall rightly concludes with the suggestion that the christological contributions of the General Epistles have been underappreciated in much of previous scholarship.

Westfall's perspective coheres with recent, encouraging developments in scholarly investigations into Judaic Christianity, as preserved largely in the General Epistles (James and Hebrews paramount among them) and in the brief quotations of early church fathers. As work in Judaic Christianity continues,[33] the neglect that Westfall decries will, we all hope, be addressed.

In concluding my response, I wish to express my gratitude to Professors Stanley Porter and Mark Boda for convening a superb conference. Thanks also go to the contributors, who enriched participants and audience alike with fresh and insightful studies.

---

33. One should consult the probing studies of Richard Bauckham, Bruce Chilton, Peter Davids, John Painter, Wiard Popkes, and Robert Wall, among others. For recent collaborative efforts, see B. Chilton and C. A. Evans, eds., *James the Just and Christian Origins* (NovTSup 98; Leiden: Brill, 1999); B. Chilton and J. Neusner, eds., *The Brother of Jesus: James the Just and His Mission* (Louisville: Westminster John Knox, 2001); and B. Chilton and C. A. Evans, eds., *The Missions of James, Peter, and Paul: Tensions in Early Christianity* (NovTSup 115; Leiden: Brill, 2004).

Index of Modern Authors

Index of Ancient Sources